Reviews of this book

Excellent navigation for the consultant's journey.
Michael Wright
Institute of Management Consultants

A comprehensive guide to the issues which need to be addressed if you want your consultancy to be effective.
Henry Ratter
ICI Technology

A companion that takes you by the hand and leads you in a simple way through the complexities of consulting.
Doug Odgers
Fellow of the Institute of Professional Sales

This book is a perfect fit to the people that are professionally ready to exercise consultancy and as a handbook for consultants and managers in implementing operational or organisational changes.
Marcio A Barbosa
Royal Phillips Electronics

This is the one book that I wish I had 20 years ago when I became a consultant – it should be required reading for all consultants, regardless of time on the job.
Joe Arnold
ECS, Panama City, Florida

It is a treasure trove of new ideas and wonderful new angles on the tried and true. I look forward to using it with the senior consultants I work with in Washington, DC.
G Matthew Bulley
Bulley-Hewlett & Associates

A tight, practical and thought-provoking guide to the mysteries of the consulting process.
Tony Korycki
BT Consultant

The Seven Cs of
Consulting

FINANCIAL TIMES
Prentice Hall

In an increasingly competitive world, it is quality
of thinking that gives an edge. An idea that opens new
doors, a technique that solves a problem, or an insight that
simply helps make sense of it all.

We work with leading authors in the fields of
management and finance to bring cutting-edge thinking
and best learning practice to a global market.

Under a range of leading imprints, including
Financial Times Prentice Hall, we create world-class
print publications and electronic products giving readers
knowledge and understanding which can then be applied,
whether studying or at work.

To find out more about our business and professional
products, you can visit us at www.business-minds.com

For other Pearson Education publications, visit
www.pearsoned-ema.com

Pearson
Education

The Seven Cs of Consulting

Your complete blueprint for any consultancy assignment

MICK COPE

London · New York · San Francisco · Toronto · Sydney · Tokyo · Singapore
Hong Kong · Cape Town · Madrid · Paris · Milan · Munich · Amsterdam

PEARSON EDUCATION LIMITED

Head Office
Edinburgh Gate
Harlow CM20 2JE
Tel: +44 (0)1279 623623
Fax: +44 (0)1279 431059

London Office:
128 Long Acre, London WC2E 9AN
Tel: +44 (0)207 447 2000
Fax: +44 (0)207 240 5771
Website: www.business-minds.com

First published in Great Britain in 2000

ISBN 0 273 64511 0

British Library Cataloguing in Publication Data
A CIP catalogue record for this book can be obtained from the British Library

Typeset by M Rules
Printed and bound in Great Britain by Biddles Ltd, Guildford & King's Lynn

*The Publishers' policy is to use paper manufactured
from sustainable forests.*

About the author

Mick Cope has been a consultant for 15 years, working in the field of business transformation. He has managed both front and back office activities across in-house and commercial organizational development programmes, including systems integration, strategy development, project management, change management, total quality, ISO 9000, process management, Investors in People, European Quality Award, Stephen Covey Seven Habits and a wide range of personal development programmes. He has published widely in the fields of organizational learning, knowledge management, workshop design, change management and personal development and is a regular speaker at international conferences. He is also the author of *Leading the Organisation to Learn*, published by FT Prentice Hall.

He welcomes feedback on any concepts offered in this book. Contact him at *MickCope@BTInternet.com or on 0973 208617*. His website is at www.wizoz.co.uk

For Paul Oliver

A catalyst and friend

Contents

Part 4 · Seven Cs in action

Preface

Conventional wisdom suggests that an author should focus on the needs of the reader. I confess I took the decision to be selfish. I wanted to write a book *I* would use as a personal guide, memory-jogger and communication tool. However, my belief (and the argument in this book) is that the principles of consulting are sufficiently generic to ensure that what I find of use will also be of interest to colleagues in other companies and industries. The underlying principles are:

- Consulting is fundamentally about change, about helping another person, team or organization make the transformation from one state to another. This might be a physical, cognitive, emotional, structural, technological or organizational change. Unless something changes, then why should any reward be forthcoming from the client?

- Any consulting project will benefit from the application of a change model that makes sense to the client as well as the consultant.

- Consulting is consulting. Scale, context and outcomes may differ, but the basic steps are common to all assignments.

- Since content and context drive a consulting project, no two will be the same. So any consulting framework can only act as an indicative rather than a directive model.

- Successful consulting is about making a difference for the client and consumer – the goal is to deliver the contracted change, not a successful consultancy project.

These guiding principles are used to underpin the Seven Cs, from meeting the client to closing the contract and saying goodbye. However, they are not offered as sacrosanct principles that must be employed in all situations. Such a rigid approach ultimately leads to the desire to implement wholesale replicated change programmes, which in turn lead to only limited success. That approach is often behind the cynicism about the consulting industry. The aim of this book is to offer an outline framework within which each consultant can understand the context of a situation and then develop a solution that is appropriate (Lissack, 1999).

I hope that you accept my ideas in the spirit in which they are offered. Although the intention is always to offer ways and means, not must and should, this is difficult when certain ideals and beliefs are felt with passion. So although parts of the book might appear to be directive in nature, if the reader ever feels that the style or content is offering the 'right solution', then it should be consigned to the waste bin.

> *To prepare yourself for the world that is coming, you must understand why it will be different from what most experts tell you.*
>
> (Rees-Mogg and Davidson, 1997)

About the reader

As I sit at the keyboard trying to visualize what you look like, where you are reading this book and what you plan to do with it, many thoughts come to mind. I see a person who has just left a large company and is about to jump into the white water rapids of consultancy; an internal consultant who is looking for practical ways to improve how they fight their way through the political maze; and an experienced consultant browsing in a bookshop to see if there are any new change tools on the market. I can picture a range of people who might be able to use the ideas in the book. They are not looking for a definitive answer to their problems, just a way to put more structure and consistency into their personal engagement framework.

I believe there is value in this book for anyone who helps others to change. However, it might be useful to indicate the potential reader base and the value they might get from the book.

- **Experienced practitioners:** Although they might already be familiar with some of the ideas in this book, they will find a number of frameworks that they have not encountered before. The underlying idea behind the book is to offer new diagnostic models, not just existing ones.

- **Competent consultants:** They will be competent in a range of roles and might have managed change both as a consultant and practitioner. The book will offer a range of new tools and techniques and, importantly, a valuable structure that will enhance their ability to manage change across various scenarios.

- **Absolute beginners:** They have seen the change consulting process in action but have never taken direct responsibility for a client project. The book will provide a valuable insight into the way that assignments can be managed and in particular how to leverage, rather than control, change.

Treat the book like an airline timetable – not as something you might read every day, but as a guide when you are planning your next round-the-world trip and certainly as something to keep in your briefcase. Although you will have your own experiences and maps, this book will help when you come across new problems or opportunities.

The Seven Cs of Consulting is written on the assumption that you have the capability and knowledge to effect the perfect change consultancy. However, consultants are neither rocket scientists nor miracle workers: they are human beings who want to learn; sometimes forget techniques; and who need the occasional tool in a tight spot. I believe that this book will be an invaluable companion to help you on the odd occasions when *you* are human too.

Acknowledgements

I would like to thank all those people who have helped me in the development of this book. I have found it inspiring that friends and strangers have been prepared to give up their valuable time to help review and comment on the early draft of the book.

In particular, Tony Korycki for his amazingly detailed review of the book; Dave Chitty for helping me through the growing pains; Andy Mcclarnon and Franchesa Cerletti for helping to transform an idea into a living thing.

I would also like to pass on my immense gratitude to the following people who offered their help in reviewing the manuscript: Joe Arnold, Clay Albright, Dr Omar Abu-elbashar, G. Matthew Bulley, L. A. Burke, John Bruce, Angela Barst, Karen Burke, Marcio Barbosa, Phillip Bump, Richard Barron, Scott Bolden, Brougham Baker, Karen Burke, Brian Connoly, Frances Clark, Jane Y. Chin, Jay Curry, Kate Cooper, Peter Cullens, Dr Frances Clark, Marella Cook, Gilli Coutts, Mike and Betty Capuzza, James Cobbett, Mark Conde, Brook Doty, Patrick Damon, John Dickson, David Foster, William Furlow, Cynthia Froggatt, Paul Freeman, Verger Gerad, Art Gelven, William Gregg, Peter Grazier, Paul Glen, Peter Gibb, Ross Gabrick, Pankaj Gupta, Henry Goldman, Bill Haddock, Dutch Holland, Nicholaas Herholdt, Matt Holt, Lynn Hauka, Nicol Dixon, aas Herholdt, Thomas H. Jaekel, Edward Kohl, Wort-Jan Koridon, Brian Kersh, Bryan Kester, Paul Laurence, Raymond Lembong, Pat Leach, Brad Leggett, Jackie Mulrooney, Mike Mister, Ken Miller, Bob Mc Henry, Peter McHugh, Benyamin R. Naba, Pam North, Lars-Ola Nordqvist, Julie O'Mara, Doug Odgers, Steve Ormsby, Graham Parson, Thomas Oswold, David Pickard, Henry Ratter, Dave Simon, Edward Stern, Sylvester Smith, John Self, Jeff Saponja, Lynda Stevens, Stan Stockhill, John Sloan, Dr Roy Thurston, Michel Thirty, Ray Taylor, Andrew Vermes, Carl Vega, Gerad Verger, Martin Wilkins, Michael Wright, Chris Welsh, Stacey Williams, Stephen Wilkinson-Carr, Chris Welsh, Dale Winsor.

Not forgetting the Financial Times Prentice Hall team, especially Amelia Lakin for helping me yet again to wade through the publishing world; George Bickerstaff for untangling and editing my original ideas into a cohesive presentation, and most of all Pradeep Jethi, my publisher, who encouraged me to turn a vague idea into a tangible form. Many thanks to Tony Quinn for editing my final text and Linda Dhondy for the project management.

Finally, without the support of my wife and family none of this would have been possible. Thank you Lin, Michael, Joe (Mathew), Lucy and Susan Caws. Please forgive me for the next six months as I burrow down for the next one.

Part 1

Introduction

Chapter 1

....

The framework background

All consulting assignments share a number of common stages and analytical methodologies. No matter what country, industry, company or field of endeavour, the core actions will be similar: meet the client, help with a problem, confirm that the issue is resolved and close the contract. These common stages form the backbone of the Seven Cs framework and are used to guide the development of the ideas offered in the book.

Consider a company trainer, account manager, car mechanic, hairdresser or even a military advisor on a battlefield. All have a clear role: that of an outsider employed to help solve a problem for someone else. More importantly, they all follow a similar engagement pattern, albeit appropriate to their particular situation. It is these actions that have been synthesized and augmented to construct the Seven Cs model.

My basic proposition is that the use of a structured methodology to drive a consulting project will immediately help to deliver a number of benefits:

- **Control:** Helps to ensure that all your consultancy projects use a structured methodology.

- **Cohesiveness:** Can deliver a greater level of company-wide integration in the way your clients are managed.

- **Competencies:** Helps to define what competencies you and your colleagues need to manage their projects.

- **Performance measurement:** Offers a common framework for comparative performance measures across consulting projects.

- **Knowledge management:** Increases the level of learning and knowledge sharing as you develop a common mental model with associates.

- **Client relationship:** Helps your client understand the stages they will go through as part of the consulting project.

Change consulting examples

It is important to stress that this book is focused on the consulting process, not the consultant. Although many books consider the skills, attributes and experience you need to be an effective consultant, my intention is to put more stress on the life cycle of the whole process. This activity can be found the world over in a variety of situations:

- **Personnel officer:** Over recent years we have seen a dramatic change in the HR sector. No longer are personnel officers expected to act as back office support to the line. They are now being re-badged as HR consultants – with a clear responsibility to provide a consultative service to a range of company departments.

- **IT manager:** Yet again, the IT sector has to understand how it can provide high-quality but cost-effective support to a range of demanding customers. This includes the systems analyst who is planning to upgrade an entire system; the help desk operator who has to manage over 100 diagnostic interviews in a day; and the floor technicians who provide support to people at the front line.

- **Operations:** This might be a process engineering consultant called into a manufacturing company to shave days off the delivery cycle or a quality auditor assessing the level of failure built into an organization's process.

- **Finance:** The plethora of independent financial advisors offers a vivid example of the consulting process in action. These people take someone else's financial situation, create options and (hopefully) take the client through to a position where he or she has a robust financial plan in place.

- **Sports coach:** A tennis coach can take a naïve teenager all the way through to the Wimbledon finals. This is simply one long change process filled with a number of lower-level change projects.

- **Organizational change:** Think about the difficult transformations that so many large companies have gone through in reducing their headcount. Such a massive reduction in size requires extraordinary levels of change management to ensure that the company does not stumble during the transformation.

- **Doctor:** The doctor asked to diagnose a child's illness is a basic consulting engagement, where the parents are the client and the child is the end consumer of the change.

- **War:** You might not envy the army officer directed by a general to take and hold a strategic hill. He probably has just one chance. He must diagnose, plan and execute any action with the utmost precision; otherwise lives will be lost.

- **Customer service:** A client engagement is made every time a waiter deals with a customer, a bartender serves a drink or a railway conductor responds to a customer query. In each case someone has a problem to be resolved (the client), and the recipient of the question (the consultant) has an implied contract to take action.

These examples offer a view of the consulting process in action. They are transitory activities designed to achieve an end goal, where the outcome serves an agreed purpose for the consultant and client. Once the outcome is achieved, then the consultant, coach, doctor, officer and so on will move on to another project, child or campaign. So it is important to emphasize that when talking about the consulting process, this is not just a reference to the business consultant. The Seven Cs can be used in any situation where change is delivered, not just a typical business scenario.

The Seven Cs can be used in any situation where change is delivered, not just a typical business scenario.

Change process – the Seven Cs

The consulting process follows a natural flow of expansion and contraction. A one-year contract to manage the merger between two companies; a three-month contract to install a new piece of hardware; a one-day event to take people through a customer care programme; or ten seconds to intervene in a team meeting: all contain a series of meta-level stages that are found in the Seven Cs framework:

1. Identify and understand the **client's** needs.

2. **Clarify** the root cause or issues to be addressed.

3. **Create** a solution to resolve the problem.

4. Manage the **change** process.

5. **Confirm** that the transition has taken place according to plan.

6. Ensure that the changes will **continue** once the project is complete.

7. **Close** the project and relationship with the client.

The Seven Cs offer a flexible, grounded and cohesive framework that will help you to manage any change. As a trainer, consultant, vet or account manager you will find a clear use for many of the diagnostic models found in this framework. However, the goal is not to suggest that the process offered in this book must be followed explicitly. Although the argument is made that all effective assignments will contain an element of the seven stages contained within the model, ultimately you must follow a path that matches your competencies and the context of the situation.

The one objective that is explicitly enshrined in the model is that all consulting assignments must result in a process of change. Although many consultants might suggest that they 'advise, analyze, counsel, investigate or support', unless something changes then what value have they added? Would you be prepared to pay for a service that didn't result in a change? Although the change might be minimal, if nothing is different once the engagement has been completed, then what was its purpose?

This change can take place on many levels. It might be a physical transformation as in the construction of a new organization, a cognitive shift with the introduction of a new strategic plan, or an emotional change resulting from the resolution of a morale problem. Whatever the level, there must be evidence of some transformation in the client's area. Unless the notion that 'consulting equals change' is accepted, any action you take can fall into the bear pit of 'so what?' – to what extent did your intervention make a long-lasting difference to the client or end consumer?

In conclusion, if asked to define what I mean by a consulting engagement, my response would be that 'it is the delivery of value through sustained change by an objective agent'.

Chapter 2

···

Navigating the waters

Although some people might choose to read this book from cover to cover, the concentration of ideas and tools could make it a long read. The book has been written to help consultants navigate the change process, not to introduce a new structure or discipline. I recommend you use it as a companion or compendium, a guide that can help you to move forward when plans are being developed or problems encountered. As such, it is important to understand how the book is structured and which section will be of most benefit.

The pocket guide

The first point of reference will often be the Pocket Guide, which comes with this book. This is a simple but invaluable tool to keep in your pocket or briefcase. It provides a quick but effective summary of the Seven Cs process and lists all the more pertinent questions that need to be considered in a change situation. You should be able to scan the guide, pick those questions that are relevant to your situation and decide if you have dealt with the topic. If further work is required, turn to that section in this book to consider what specific action might be taken. However, in many cases, it might not be necessary to turn to the book; simply finding the right question can be far more powerful than finding the right answer.

Consulting environment

Although this book presents a framework that helps to manage a consultancy project, it is important to consider the context in which the model will be applied. The world of consulting is driven by dramatic change, uncertainty, short-termism, and demanding and conflicting work. This section considers some of the drivers that make the world of consulting what it is: the commercial nature of the industry; the hidden forces that drive change; the way that energy ripples can distort an assignment; and the effect of erosion on organizational structure.

The Seven Cs process

This chapter offers a simple overview of the framework. It considers each of the seven stages, the timing associated with each stage and sequencing issues. The aim is to suggest that all effective assignments must go through the seven stages and that failure to include any of them will result in limited success for the client, consumer or consultant. Although the vast majority of the book is offered in a non-prescriptive way, this chapter assumes that the seven stages are timeless and universal. Any effective change, be it starting a diet, moving house or managing a global merger, will follow the seven stages.

Any effective change, be it starting a diet, moving house or managing a global merger, will follow the seven stages.

Five steps thinking

This chapter introduces the key aspects that must be considered before you start the consulting process. Success is often dependent on the way a change project is approached. If the needs of the client can be thought through beforehand, then your ability to deliver a successful outcome can be enhanced. The secret is to climb inside the client's head, heart and hands. To understand how they think, feel and behave so that you are able to rapidly develop a sense of close rapport. To help this process, the chapter offers a number of key ideas that you might think about before meeting a client.

The rest of the book

The rest of the book is focused on the diagnostic tools that are used to leverage the seven stages. Each of the seven stages is built upon a further seven tools and ideas that might be used to manage the process. The suggestion is not that all 49 tools need be used. Only you will be able to determine the fit. But it will pay to consider all the components. The tools offered could never hope to offer all the potential diagnostic tools that you might need, but they will increase your ability to draw on a wider range of ideas.

Finally, the book closes by considering some of the issues that need to be considered when the Seven Cs are used in action. Ultimately, the translation of any theoretical model into a practical tool will depend on the person and context. However, this section offers a number of aspects that can have a significant impact on the translation process.

Chapter 3

Consulting environment

Before discussing the Seven Cs model in detail, it might be useful to compare the consultant role to that of a sailor who used to transport goods around the world. Today's commercial drivers are like the trade winds that blow towards the equator from the north-east or south-east. In the days of sailing ships, every sailor's income (and life) would depend on the trade winds to carry the ship from port to port. In the same way, your career or income is derived from the trading activities that blow through your industry.

Consulting is a trade-based operation, where the ability to sell products and services is a core competency. As such, you must be able to tune into the trade winds that blow through your particular organization or industry. Failure to instinctively tap into these winds means that, like sailors in the old days, you will be caught in the doldrums, the calm area where little wind blows. Consequently, even when deep into a client project, you should be looking and listening for future commercial opportunities. The inability to manage this has resulted in total quality consultants who failed to see the rapid emergence of business process reengineering or IT specialists who fell out of step because they ignored the speed at which the Internet would grow. The consultants who survive and prosper are those who have a predator instinct. They constantly search and ride on the emergence of new business theories and schools of thought; they have the old sailor's ability to find and ride on the back of the trade winds.

The consultants who survive and prosper are those who have a predator instinct. They constantly search and ride on the emergence of new business theories.

Another analogy can be seen in the way that it is often difficult to separate the various actions that you undertake in partnership with a client. On a map of the world, the seven seas are marked clearly. They are separate, distinct and can be seen as individual entities. As a result, you can cruise in one particular sea secure that you will not drift into other oceans. However, a map is just a simple representation of the shape of the land masses that border the seas. In reality the water that flows between the seas is one single body and cannot be separated into distinctive units. In the same way, although the Seven Cs model breaks consulting activities into separate chunks, the reality is that you will have to use or be aware of all seven stages at the same time. All of your consulting actions are interrelated and dependent upon each other. Everything is interconnected.

Another analogy can be seen in the tidal pulls that act upon the oceans. The tidal system is one of the most powerful forces on earth, yet the least perceptible to the human eye. Although it is possible to sit on the shore and watch the water wash against the beach, actually seeing a change in the tide is more difficult. The only visible evidence of the tide will be the lapping of the waves and the flotsam left behind as the water recedes. In the same way, although powerful forces operate within the consulting world, the only evidence of the strength and direction of this energy is from the artefacts left in its wake – the files on the shelf from an old training course, software manuals from earlier systems or mugs and badges from the last marketing campaign.

Unless you are aware of the nature and impact of these tidal forces, then it is possible to end up floundering in deep water, often looking like King Canute trying to command the waves to recede only to realize that these organizational forces are beyond the control of any individual. Consider the strategy development specialist who ignores sudden personnel changes on the management board or the executive coach who fails to pick up on a new coaching technique. It is essential to keep attuned to the environment and surf, rather than be submerged by the changing tides of fashion.

Another comparison might be made with waves out at sea. Although waves might appear to move through the water, in reality the water vibrates up and down giving the appearance of movement. All that happens is that the medium acts as a vehicle to transport energy. In the same way, an industry can have waves that ripple through its system. Think of the raw power associated with a rumour on the stock market. This energy can move like a wave, ripping through industry with sufficient power to destroy a company's commercial standing.

Interestingly, it is the wavelength, or pitch, produced by a sound wave that is most significant. Although a high-frequency waveform such as a scream or whistle can hurt, it is often subsonic waves that cause the real damage as they topple buildings or bridges. It is these apparently unobtrusive waves that can in worst cases cause a change programme to be cancelled overnight. As any training manager will know, at the first whisper of a recession it is the training budget that is cut. Even if the rumour of recession proves unfounded, the cut often remains and next year the manager has to fight a major battle just to get back to the original budget.

To survive, you must have the ability to seed the ground with virtual seismometers to give advance warning of high-energy, low-frequency waveforms that might be heading your way. Such advance warnings often arrive through the development of effective relationships, close alliances and strong favour banks within the client organization. The goal is to create a network of people who are prepared to share the whispers and rumours that will precede any organizational upheaval.

The energy contained within waves also builds and shapes beaches using a process known as deposition and erosion. A beach can change in size and shape overnight. One day it will have a particular set of patterns and on the next will have changed beyond all recognition. When working within a client organization you will often face the same problem. As the process of organizational erosion and deposition takes place, the shape, structure and size of a team or organization can change rapidly. Imagine that one day you are working with a team of 15 people responsible for a company's accounting system. The following week the business has been reorganized and the team is now responsible for the accounting system, the audit process and, for some strange reason, the company quality system. You must accept apparently chaotic transition without blinking an eye and, more importantly, be able to factor it seamlessly into the existing change plans. The fact is that as an external agent, you will often have little power to resist a change in this complex process. Like the child whose sandcastle is swept away overnight, you simply have to start again and build on what you have learned.

You must accept apparently chaotic transition without blinking an eye and, more importantly, be able to factor it seamlessly into the existing change plans.

Finally, every sailor needs a chart. Venturing out to sea without any thought for the journey to be taken and the obstacles that might lie ahead is foolish and dangerous. In the same way, any consultant who ventures into a project without a clear map of the proposed journey is being foolhardy and might well cause the client to suffer financially. However, having a chart does not mean that a sailor is locked into taking one particular route. In the same way, a consultant with a plan is not necessarily locked into one set methodology or model. It is possible to deviate from a plan in the knowledge that the path being taken is still safe.

The Seven Cs provide a powerful change framework that allows you to plan a journey, but with the knowledge that a deviation can (and might have to) be taken at any time. The assumptions set out in this opening view are important because they set the tone for the rest of the book. The Seven Cs model does not assume that business transformation is a process that must be controlled and tightly managed at all stages. There are times when this must happen, but there are also times when the system must be left to its own devices. Like the gardener who is trying to grow a garden that will be the envy of friends, he or she must accept that grass cannot be made to stop growing and that it is impossible to eliminate the impact of insects. The garden will grow and manage itself irrespective of whether or not the gardener is around. The gardener's primary role is to make decisions, to understand the points of leverage where he or she can effect the most influence over the garden, persuading it to grow in a way that aligns with the gardener's needs and the goals of nature.

The ideas offered in the book are presented with the same notion that absolute control in a change engagement is not possible. However, it is possible to identify the points where most leverage can be applied to effect a positive and practical outcome. The Seven Cs present the seven key stages that form the backbone of any journey and the components within each stage offer different leverage tools that might help to make the journey easier.

Part 2

The Seven Cs process

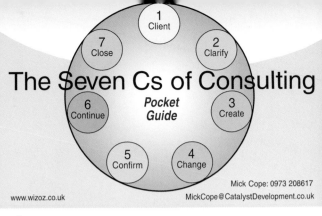

Mick Cope: 0973 208617

MickCope@CatalystDevelopment.co.uk

www.wizoz.co.uk

1 Client *Getting it right from the start*

Orientation: am I able to view the problem as the client sees it?

Desired outcome: have I tested the clarity of the desired outcome?

Change ladder: have I removed the fog from the problem by focusing on where change might be needed?

Situation viability: can the issue be successfully resolved and is the timing right for change?

Decision makers: do I have a clear picture of the decision makers who can influence the initial stages of the contract development?

Ethos: will the change be coercive or participative in nature?

Contract: do I have a contract that sets out a framework for action and measurement?

2 Clarify *Understanding the real issues*

Diagnosis: have I gathered information that will determine the real source of the issue, and not just the symptoms?

Shadow: is there a clear appreciation of the unspoken activities affecting the situation?

Culture: do I understand the deep cultural factors that might affect the change?

System construction: do I understand the structural make-up of the system?

Stakeholders: is there a clear map that indicates who can influence the outcome of the change?

Life-cycle risk: have I determined the extent to which known and unknown factors will have an impact?

Feedback: have I clarified how the client and organization wish to be informed of progress?

3 Create *Developing a deliverable solution*

Managed creativity: have I ensured that any creative solutions can actually be delivered?

Creative blockage: have I understood the potential creative blockages for my client?

Scanning: can solutions be found in the work that others have done?

Storyboard: have I a clear process for deciding on the final solution?

Resources: have I mapped the resource to the potential solutions to ensure the option is viable?

Stream owners: are there clear owners for the solution and do they have the capability and desire to own them?

Positics: have I considered if it is possible to redirect some of the se energy, and turn the negative aspects into worthy ones?

4 Change *Working to make things happen*

Methodology: is there a clear understanding of how the change will be managed?

Energy: is there a clear appreciation of where the change energy will come from, and how it will be dissipated across the different stake-holders?

Engage: do I know how people can be encouraged to be involved in the transformation process?

Entry: am I clear as to the best level of entry to make a long-lasting transformation on the change ladder?

System dynamics: how will the system react to my proposed change?

Uncertainty: is the plan flexible enough to operate in a dynamic and complex world?

Resistance: do I know how people will react to proposed changes?

5 Confirm *Measuring the change*

Responsible: who will own and manage the measurement process?

Timing: have I decided when the measurement will take place?

Design: is the relationship between qualitative and quantitative measures clear to me?

Depth: will extrinsic measurement be used, or will it deal with intrinsic issues such as attitude, motivation and beliefs?

Data map: have measurement activities been controlled to ensure that an integrated approach is taken in the clarification stage?

Consulting performance: do I know if my performance has been up to the standard expected by the client?

Costs: have I a clear view of the impact cost will have on the different measurement processes?

6 Continue *Making sure the solution sticks*

Sustainability: do I have a plan to ensure slippage doesn't occur once the project has been closed?

Language: have I been able to modify the client and consumer language?

Gravity: have I ensured that a bureaucratic system will not strangle the transformation?

Flow: do I know what learning has taken place from the experience?

Knowledge transfer: have I ensured that elements of my competencies will remain in the business?

Knowledge management: will knowledge created as part of the change be embodied as a tangible asset for the business?

Diffusion channels: have I analysed the client's capability to physically diffuse new ideas?

7 Close *Signing off with style*

Client's view: have I encouraged the client to reflect on their view of the world before presenting my view of the outcomes?

Outcome review: have I gauged the success of the programme?

Learning: have I helped the client to consider what has been learned over and above the planned outcomes?

Added value: is there clear indication of a tangible improvement to the operational or commercial viability of the organization?

Build: have I identified what opportunities exist for further work?

Re-engage: is there a plan to leave the relationship in a controlled way?

Exit: have I ensured that unnecessary levels of dependence have gone from all sides of the relationship?

Chapter 4

Defining the Seven Cs

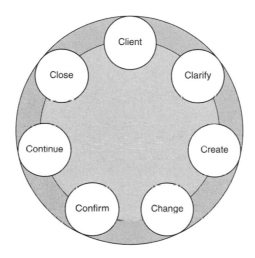

The Seven Cs framework is constructed around a number of dynamic stages, each of which emphasizes a different aspect within the consultancy life cycle. Each stage represents a particular phase that a consultancy process will follow. Within each stage is a set of sub-elements and diagnostic tools that are used to ease the engagement process. These all come together to form a total framework that will act as a guide to any engagement. Each of the stages can be undertaken independently, jointly or in parallel with each other. The seven stages are:

1. **Client:** Define the client's orientation of the world, their perception of the situation, what goals they have regarding the final outcome and who has power to influence the outcome. Once this stage is concluded, you will have a clear agreement as to what value you will deliver to the client and what value they will offer in return.

2. **Clarify:** Determine the nature and detail of the problem to be addressed. Map the construction of the system under consideration, identify what and who is to be included and excluded from the change and determine what areas pose a risk for the assignment.

3. **Create:** Use creative techniques to develop a detailed plan that specifies what action will be included in the change process, the appropriate resources, stream owners and potential change problems.

4. **Change:** Understand the fundamental aspects that drive and underpin the change process, such as the energy sources, change points, entry levels, emergent factors and evidence of success.

5. **Confirm:** Ensure that change has taken place, taking into account the issues of data focus, ownership, depth, timing and design of the measurement process.

6. **Continue:** Ensure that the change will be sustained, using learning that emerges from the transition, the skills of the change agents and the sharing of new knowledge and skills.

7. **Close:** Close the engagement process with the client, emphasizing the need to understand the final outcomes, the added value, new learning and what further action you might undertake.

Contained within each of these seven stages are a further seven elements that include a series of tools and diagnostic models that are applied during the consulting process (Fig. 4.1).

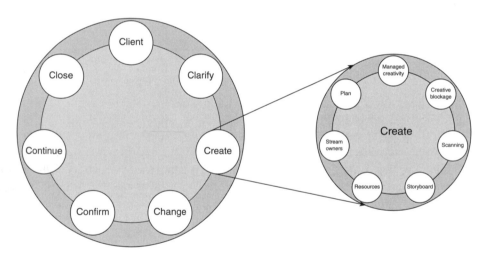

Fig. 4.1   Stage–element relationship

The framework is meant as a guide for action, not a rigid process that needs to be followed slavishly.

These tools are not meant to be exclusive to the stage and can be used at any time within the life of the project. This reinforces the notion that the framework is meant as a guide for action, not a rigid process that needs to be followed slavishly.

Timing

You will be able to use this model in any situation where a change is being managed, irrespective of the time-scale. The following are examples of possible time-scales associated with each of the stages in the Seven Cs model:

Market strategy presentation: In this assignment, a consultancy team has spent most of its time in data gathering, data analysis and solution development. Once conclusions have been reached, the team has one hour to present to the board and gain agreement on the new market strategy. If this is successful, the end of the presentation will be focused on confirming that the board has understood the implications of the proposition and agreeing any closing actions.

Systems integration: A consulting team is consolidating a group of different billing and sales systems to bring them together on a common platform. The first three months are focused on the data flow analysis and system design, with two months for the switch over and training. The last two months are used to validate the billing process and ensure that no inter-system links have been corrupted.

Facilitator group engagement: in this situation, a group facilitator is aware of a problem within the team she is supporting. She signals to the chair that an engagement needs to be made, undertakes a rapid analysis of the situation, diagnoses what is happening, and develops an engagement strategy. The engagement takes a few seconds, with another 45 seconds observing the group to check that the engagement has been effective.

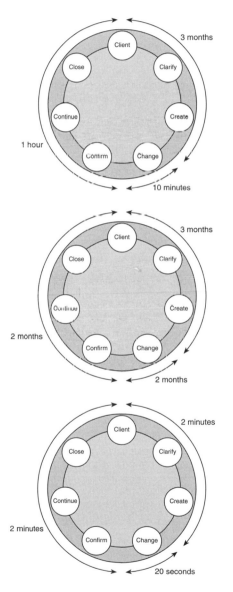

Fig. 4.2   Time-scales for various tasks

All Seven Cs will be used, even if the consultancy cycle takes seconds as opposed to days, weeks or months. The change process can be physical, such as installing a new telephone system; behavioural, as in shifting how people deal with customers; or cognitive, helping to change how someone thinks about a topic; or emotional, as the marriage guidance councillor helps a couple transform their relationship.

Sequence

It is important to emphasize that although the stages in the Seven Cs model are shown in a linear fashion, it is a rare consultancy project that would follow such a structured path. Consulting projects are like life – they are unpredictable and will throw up new and different surprises around every bend. The stages are symbolic rather than prescriptive, offering different actions and viewpoints to be applied depending on the needs of the client, consumer and consultant.

For example, your first meeting with the client might take place when the company is in a dire situation and needs urgent action to be taken the following day. So although the pressure will be on to jump directly into the Create and Change phases, at some point you might need to backtrack to clarify a few things, such as forming a more structured contract with the client and identifying what caused the problem in the first place. Without this knowledge, a sense of imbalance might occur. The client might feel that you have failed to get to the bottom of the issue while you believe that the client has little real interest in the engagement.

Alternatively, you are asked to take on a sub-contract for a specific part of a programme from another consulting firm. For example, your project is to manage the Change stage within the model, specifically to deliver a known and prescribed output. As a project manager you will still need to consider the before and after factors. In undertaking any project, it is important to understand who the client is, how the project is designed and what options there are to develop the project plan. Finally, when completed, you will have to measure and confirm that the change has been delivered according to plan. So even where the sequence is broken up to offer other people discrete packages, all of the elements in the Seven Cs have a clear role.

Lastly, even when focused on one particular stage of the model, you still need to be aware of, and draw on, elements from the other stages. In the Create stage you will need to be aware of the issues that help to maintain Continuity; how the Change will be Confirmed or measured; what research data within the Clarify stage might have been slightly suspect; or if the contract with the client needs to be modified as a result of changes in the implementation plan. So although at any time there will always be a dominant stage, you might need to run a number of other stages in parallel.

Chapter 5

....

An effective client relationship in five steps

The client–consultant relationship is the foundation stone that supports the entire assignment. Consulting is driven by the extent to which you can get close to the client. To professionally and sensitively arrive at a position where you become more of a confidant or trusted advisor than a supplier of services. How far you can build a sense of rapport with a client before the consulting process begins will to a large degree affect your ability to deliver change.

Rapport isn't something that occurs when you first meet the client. It is something that you must think through *before* the first contact. Your goal is to ensure that when you walk through the client's door for the first time you are totally tuned and focused on their mindset and needs. By the time you take the last five steps into the client office, you must be clear and confident on the following five issues:

- **(Balanced) Stool:** Who is the client, who are the end consumers of any change I might make and what is my primary role within the relationship?

- **Trust index:** To what extent do they trust me and how can I make it more likely they will before the first contact?

- **Engage:** What is the likely level of engagement? Will it be a highly interactive relationship where both parties play an active role, or is one of us likely to be more passive than the other?

- **Push/Pull:** Have I been invited in to meet the client because of my skills or is this a promotional bid where I need to convince them of my added value?

- **Shadow diamond:** What surface and 'shadow' issues will drive how the relationship might be managed? What are the unspoken or suppressed issues that need to be brought to the surface before we can build a sense of rapport?

The effective consultant can operate on three levels: understanding how the client thinks; what they feel; and why they behave in a certain way. If each of these levels is understood, then the extent to which you can develop rapport with the client will be enhanced. By thinking through these simple ideas, you will be five steps closer to understanding your client and your shared relationship.

19

Consider one of the most common engagements that we all experience – the double glazing salesperson. Although the job is primarily viewed as a sales process, a successful sale will actually go through all seven stages in the framework. Now, the secret of a good sale is not in the techniques that the sales person uses, it is in the mental framework that is in place before the client meeting take place. A good sales person is not thinking about their products or what products the client might want. As they walk up the driveway they will be reflecting on the deeper emotional issues that will come into play: how does the customer feel about the visit?; have they any preconceptions about me or my company?; do I have any way to build an emotional connection with them early in the relationship?; who is the real decision maker in the family? Although the sales person might not have the answer to these questions, they will be mentally focused on getting an answer to them in the first few minutes of the engagement.

In many cases the emotional decisions that people form in the first five minutes of a meeting will drive how they think and behave towards someone for the next five months. As a consultant you must be able to manage this window of opportunity to ensure that the client as a minimum warms to you as a person, and ideally starts to respect your professional capability. To achieve this you must quite deliberately think through your opening approach and how you can influence their perception of you.

This approach must be used whatever your situation. It might be that you are about to make the first telephone call to the client to arrange for a meeting; the time you are about to meet for coffee and a bagel; the conference where you are about to present to 300 people; or simply making eye contact with an old client at a party. Before you utter the first word it is essential that you have thought through and appraised your relationship against the five steps listed below.

Step one: Stool

Consulting projects often fail because all the needs of the various stakeholders are not taken into consideration. This puts the whole project out of alignment because one group's needs are given priority over another's. Like a three-legged stool, the consultancy process must always be in balance, and the needs of the client, consultant and consumer (end user) understood and maintained.

All three have deep motivational needs and if one is left partially dissatisfied, the project is likely to hit problems. In any project that has failed this lack of alignment is likely to be a source of the problem:

Like a three-legged stool, the consultancy process must always be in balance, and the needs of the client, consultant and consumer (end user) understood and maintained.

- You have developed a good sense of rapport with the client, agreed a contract and are ready to start the implementation phase. However, you discover that in reality the client has instigated the assignment for personal or political ambitions and has not taken the needs of the consumer into account. Therefore, the project will possibly fail because of resistance from the end user. (Consumer mis-alignment)

- You contract with the regional director to implement a new customer service technique. However, as you start to role the programme out, the client takes on a new set of operational responsibilities. Therefore he offers figurehead support to the change but little else. (Client mis-alignment)

- You meet a client who has gained significant support for a change process. Although you agree to manage the change, the client has beaten you down on price and you are running at a loss on the project. This is because you have only taken it on as a stopgap until a more lucrative contract comes along. Although you deliver the project to the letter of the contract, your heart is not in it, so valuable opportunities to improve the outcomes are missed. (Consultant mis-alignment)

In these three examples the imbalance shows as a lack of energy on the part of the client, consumer or consultant. This mis-alignment arises because each of the three agents has a different perception of the purpose of the project. In a change programme, all three agents may think they have a clear and shared understanding of the change. But, when viewed collectively, it turns out that they are all thinking in different ways. This results in one of two situations In the first, the different parties go into fight mode, each battling to assert their model over the other group. In the second, the weaker party decides to take an apathetic stance and let the others win (though often only in the short term, their vengeance may come eventually in more subtle ways).

Imagine a traditional personnel project where you have contracted to install and develop a new appraisal system. The client's view is that the line managers have been ineffective in appraising their teams because they do not have the necessary feedback and counselling skills. The client views this as primarily a capability issue and has contracted you to improve the organization's ability to manage its people. However, although you are building a whole system for the company, you believe that the need for a new appraisal system is merely a symptom. You feel the key issue is the poor morale created by the fact that managers have little desire to follow the procedural guidelines laid down by the personnel department. For their part, the line managers, or end consumers, think you have been employed simply to install another bureaucratic system, effectively changing the procedures that direct how the senior managers want the business to operate.

The problem is that the operational managers will ignore the new procedure because they prefer their own local methods. They are convinced that managers should be allowed to manage their teams as they think fit and that it is unlikely that any top-down mechanistic system will help them to deal with the problems they face at the operational end of the business.

Unless any imbalance is brought out and resolved early on, it will fester away behind the scenes only to explode later. It is essential that you take time out at all stages of the consulting cycle to review constantly and check with the client and consumer that a shared appreciation of the issue is being addressed. Unless this happens then problems will eventually arise, typically in the guise of political wrangling, deferred milestones, communication problems and even industrial action.

> **Back pocket questions**
>
> Who are the client and consumer? What is my relationship with them, and are our needs aligned?

Step two: Trust index

Trust is the cement that builds and sustains any client relationship. It provides the underlying bond to ensure that promises are kept, work is completed on time and knowledge shared. Even before this, it is what gives the client the confidence to seek your services in the first place. O'Shea and Madigan (1997) ably make this point:

> *The decision to bring in management consultants is one that can place at stake the careers of the very people who hire them, the jobs of thousands of employees, millions upon millions of dollars invested by shareholders, and long-term relationships with customers. Indeed, the most valuable asset a corporation has, its reputation, can be put on the line. And all these risks are connected to the motivation of outsiders whose primary interest is in fattening the treasuries of their consulting partnerships.*

Whenever a potential client thinks about employing you as a consultant, they are betting on the future. They need to make a rational decision based on the premise that you will deliver an outcome. However this decision is often taken on little more than a guess or gut feel and much of this intuitive process depends on the extent to which they trust you.

The choices you make about the baby-sitter, frozen food or new car are all influenced by the trust you have that the product or service will deliver an agreed conclusion. So when you purchase these products, what is it that gives you this sense of trust? While you are thinking about this, you might ask yourself: 'how do I engender this same confidence in a potential client? What do I need to do that will help them to choose my products and services over a competitor?'

But before you can start to manage the client's perception, you must first define what trust is and then identify how to measure its impact. This is difficult because trust is such a subjective topic. However, certain core indicators can be used to develop a basic appreciation of the level of trust in a relationship:

- **Truthful:** The extent to which integrity, honesty and truthfulness are developed and maintained.

- **Responsive:** The openness, mental accessibility or willingness to share ideas and information freely.

- **Uniform:** The degree of consistency, reliability and predictability contained within the relationship.

- **Safe:** The loyalty, benevolence or willingness to protect, support and encourage each other.

- **Trained:** The competence, technical knowledge and capability of both parties.

There is often a link between the level of trust and the entry method used with a client. There are a wide variety of ways that you can first come into contact. They might include follow-on work, referrals, seminar presentation, journal articles or cold calls. For all of these, the trust factor will vary in intensity: from high, where trust is given without question, down to low, where the trust has yet to be earned.

A matrix can offer a picture of the potential level of trust and the entry channel. In Table 5.1, the status of high indicates that the trust factor has developed between the parties; medium suggests that some opportunity to build trust may have taken place; and low means that it has not had a chance to be established. I am not suggesting that entry methods with low against them are bad or less effective, just that you might need to focus more energy on these areas to develop a closer sense of rapport.

One example is the provisional meeting that takes place after a client reads one of your articles in a trade journal. While the article might help to indicate your reliability, capability and responsiveness, the client will have little direct evidence of your truthfulness or capability to be loyal. At the initial meeting, it might pay to spend a percentage of your time talking about previous assignments. In particular, offer stories, case examples or references that indicate your ability to develop and maintain a relationship that is grounded in truthfulness and loyalty.

Table 5.1   Trust entry matrix

	Follow-on	Referral	Seminar	Article	Cold call
Truthful	High	Med	Med	*Low*	*Low*
Responsive	High	Med	High	High	Med
Uniform	High	Med	Med	Med	*Low*
Safe	High	Med	*Low*	*Low*	*Low*
Trained	High	Med	Med	Med	Med

In business, as in private life, trust is something that has to be earned and is rarely given freely. Even worse, it can be lost with a slip of the tongue or a mis-directed memo. As such, it is important to ensure that the appropriate energy is applied in the right area and not squandered. There is little point in trying to convince the client of your professional capability if they are actually looking for a demonstration of your ability to keep secrets. Before entering into any client relationship, you should take some time out to map and understand your trust index. You should be able to step into your client's shoes and from their point of view see how much confidence they will have in you and your ability to deliver the required outcomes.

This idea of trust is not focused just on the relationship with the client. Within any project there is likely to be a third person involved – the individual, team or organization that is going to be the recipient of the change. Although in many cases this might also be the client, there will be times where it will be someone different. If this is the case, you will also need to build a similar matrix to understand how the end consumer of the change feels about you. Developing a trusting relationship with the client doesn't mean that corresponding levels of trust will exist with the consumer. In many cases, you will be employed by the client to deliver a forced change into another area. In this case, you will need even more effort to develop a trusting relationship with the end consumer.

Back pocket questions

To what extent do the client and consumer trust me? How can I increase this trust?

Step three: Engage

Anyone who has shared a house with another person can testify that a relationship is not just a relationship. It can be many things and can operate at a range of different levels, from warm and cuddly to passive and distant. Your aim is to manage the shift along this continuum and get as close as possible to the client. The objective is to develop a relationship that is highly interactive and grounded at a personal rather than contractual level.

This continuum can be mapped against a 'relationship bridge', an indicator of how effectively the client-consultant relationship is being managed. In the worst case, it might be inactive, with little real energy in the relationship and little attention paid to the potential value contained within the partnership. Although the capability exists to deliver a value-added change in the individual, team or organization, there is little desire to make it happen. This is often seen in corporate organizations where the client has been directed to use a consultant by the board and therefore has little personal motivation to become involved. In this situation, you might naturally feel a sense of animosity and choose to focus your attention elsewhere, either in other parts of the business or with different clients. This results in a low-level passive relationship, one that makes it difficult for you and the client to put any energy into the engagement.

At the other end of the spectrum, the relationship might be classed as interactive, where both the capability and the desire exist to derive real value from it. This is characterized by the type of relationship where you and the client give plenty of diary time to meet, are happy to expose your dreams and fears about the change and view the relationship as an opportunity for collaborative success rather than competitive aggression.

Between these two extremes there are a further three stages on which the client-consultant relationship can operate:

- **Inactive:** Relationship is used to manage the cold contractual elements of the project.

- **Reactive:** Relationship is important to both parties but is essentially still used to manage the consulting process.

- **Active:** Both parties use relationship to stretch the boundaries but still within the domain of the project.

- **Proactive:** Relationship is seen as important to the assignment, with both sides prepared to take the initiative in a wide range of areas.

- **Interactive:** Client relationship is seen as an integral part of the change process, not just a medium for managing the change.

Unless you are able to move the client relationship across this bridge then the chances of a successful outcome will be impaired and the opportunity to gain further contracts minimized. Ashford (1998) emphasizes this point when he suggests that human relationships are the bedrock of business. He suggests that no matter how good you might be in delivering a product or presentation, if the client doesn't like you or your tie then you will be in trouble. No matter what other issues you might have in your life, the client wants to feel special and important. The more they feel that you value them and their time the closer you will be able to get to them and their problem. Only once the relationship is operating at the interactive level will you be able to ask the awkward questions without seeming unruly or unprofessional. By achieving this level of intimacy, you will be able to get to the heart of the problem and not spend all your time messing about with the symptoms.

> **Back pocket questions**
>
> What is the nature of my relationship with the client and consumer? Is it positive and interactive or is it passive and with little value?

Step four: Push/Pull

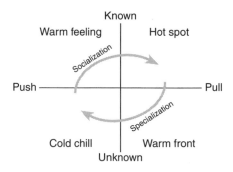

Fig. 5.1 Contact model

Two key factors affect the nature of the opening relationship (Fig. 5.1). The vertical axis measures how close you are to your client, be it through personal acquaintance, previous work or past friendship. This can range from a continuum of 'known' to 'unknown'. The second factor, on the horizontal axis, is the extent to which your marketing is based on a push or pull model. Push is where you target potential clients and then undertake a cold sale. Pull is where the client has identified that you have the particular competency to help resolve a problem.

In the 'warm front' or 'warm feelings' quadrants, you clearly have a market edge over those in the 'cold chill' quadrant. The question is, how can a consultant in the 'cold chill' quadrant start to build a relationship with a prospective client or market segment? The first option is the common approach of socialization. Successful consultants often spend a large degree of their time in 'getting to know you' situations, through business conferences, trade fairs or other social introductions. This ability to get on a personal level with a potential client makes it much easier to form a working and lucrative relationship.

The second option is to take the specialization route – to build a known brand in the market such that people value the skills or knowledge that you can offer. This is the 'guru' path, where the likes of Hammer and Champey, Porter, Peters and Kanter have trod. Their access to market is often based on the fact that people have heard them speak, seen them on television or read their books. As a result, the client becomes convinced that this person will be able to offer a solution to a problem. This process is clearly seen in the big league where the gurus reign supreme and to a lesser degree at the lower end of the market, where consultants offer their wares as presenters at conferences or business fairs.

However, getting into the 'hot spot' does not guarantee a contract. Just knowing and liking someone does not mean that a working partnership can be developed. Once in the 'hot spot' you must be able to develop a credible, convincing and close relationship with the client – one that helps them feel confident that you will be able to resolve their problem.

> ### Back pocket question
> Is this a cold sale, or have I been invited in on the client's wish?

Step five: Shadow diamond

Whenever people come together, there are two sides to the association. The surface issues, which relate to those things that people are happy to share with others, and the 'shadow' issues, which are the hidden behaviours, thoughts and feelings that people are less comfortable about sharing. The shadow issues are important because they often drive the force and direction of any change. You probably know people who are scared of spiders or have a particular aversion to a type of food. Although these fears are seemingly silly, they can significantly influence the decisions people take and how they manage their lives.

Although you might be fortunate enough to know your client well, in the vast majority of cases you will not be emotionally connected with the client. This can be like the first fumbling teenage date, where both kids are trying to second guess and satisfy the goals of the other person without compromising their personal values and integrity. In the same way, the early meetings with a client can end up as a series of fumbling encounters, where both people are trying to understand the needs and goals of the other. Part of the reason why this dilemma occurs is because we all operate on two levels of interaction, the surface and the shadow.

The surface issues are considered on an open and level playing field and the shadow issues are the factors that both sides choose to hide from each other. This linkage is shown as a diamond in Fig. 5.2. The left and right sides of the shape indicate the client's and consultant's position and the upper and lower sections indicate the surface and shadow issues.

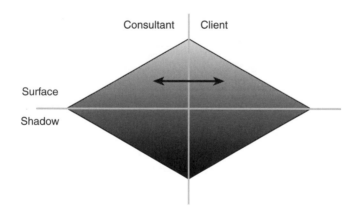

Fig. 5.2 Shadow diamond

In a typical consulting project, you might offer what appears to be a practical and sensible change proposition, which the client may rebuff with arguments and concerns about its feasibility. But are these rebuttals coming from the reasoned head of the client or are shadow concerns forcing unrelated and often irrelevant issues to the surface? For example, let's suppose a reengineering proposal has been turned down because it involves head office relocation. On the surface the proposal offers a number of financial and operational improvements for the client. However, the unseen shadow implication is that the client's children's education will be interrupted and his or her partner's work and social life hampered. This type of personal prejudice can swing the balance against a rational solution, thus destroying (for an unknown, or at least unstated, reason) your proposal.

One way round this problem is to make the undiscussible discussible and create an environment where the client feels comfortable talking about shadow issues. Although this is not an easy process, you can develop personal strategies that make disclosure easier. These strategies are a set of words and behaviours that you can draw upon when faced with a client who doesn't want to open up their shadow side.

First, you can use the shadow 'hook'. Try to understand and influence your client's world by entering their shadow domain through the back door. Your strategy is to bring out private and personal issues that are so often subsumed or pushed to one side in the business world.

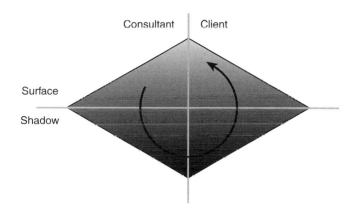

Fig. 5.3 Shadow diamond: shadow hook

As seen in Fig. 5.3, and taking the example of head office relocation, you might talk about your own personal experiences, possibly by discussing how difficult it is to get a balance between the pressure of a consultant's life style and the demands of a growing family. Whatever words are used, you are effectively using *your* shadow side to pace and lead the client's language and thoughts. You are making it possible for the client to release the intangible and hidden issues. Once the two shadow parts are in harmony, then you can encourage the client to slowly bring their issues to the surface and deal with them in a non-threatening way.

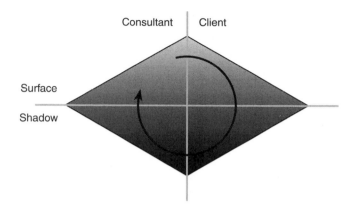

Fig. 5.4 Shadow diamond: open link

An alternative version is seen in Fig. 5.4. In this example, you enter through the surface level and challenge the client to look inward and think about some of the deeper issues associated with the contract proposal. This might entail asking questions such as: 'How would this affect your family?' 'What difference will the proposal make to your lifestyle?' or 'How would you feel if the proposal is not accepted by the board?' In this approach, the engagement is reversed and the client is encouraged to look inside at their hidden issues and share these on an open level. This is a much more high-risk strategy because the client might feel that you are stepping outside the acceptable work boundaries. You must always be ready to pull back if you feel that the client is unsettled or agitated.

Crucially, when developing a relationship with the client, you must listen to what they say and, more importantly, watch what they do.

Crucially, when developing a relationship with the client, you must listen to what they say and, more importantly, watch what they do. The pained facial expression as your client talks about the business goals or the involuntary eye movement as the topic of relocation emerges are valuable indicators that highlight a shadow problem. They will not automatically tell you about the deeper issues at play but they certainly offer signals that the topic could be explored further to pull out any shadow factors. However, before you start to delve into the client's shadow areas, you need to understand the extent to which the client trusts you. Clearly the thought of some stranger trying to understand some of deep personal concerns and issues is off-putting and you might end up alienating the client.

Back pocket question

What are the client's unspoken issues and how can I understand them?

Application of these five steps will not guarantee a successful first client contact, but it will guarantee that you have at least prepared professionally. This professionalism will show through immediately with the client because you will be seen to care about them and their needs.

Clearly the business world is driven by a macho sense of bravado, backbone and bull. However, the reality is that in the vast majority of cases, a client will take a decision based upon an emotional feeling, and then post-rationalize the decision by careful 'reasoned' internal debate. This is not to suggest that the client is wrong, just that we are all human and not machines. As such emotions play a large role in any decision that we might take. Therefore, it does matter if the client feels cared for; it does make a difference if you understand what personal fears they might have; and clients will cancel a large contract if they feel that the consultant does not understand their personal needs.

By thinking through and preparing around the ideas in the five steps model you will enter the client stage of the process with some degree of confidence. If you attempt to move into the first part of the life cycle without this mental preparation, then you will be winging it, and in the majority of cases the client will immediately sense this. Just imagine you are about to spend a large sum of money on a set of replacement windows for the house. Who would get the larger chunk of your time, someone that walked in the door and launched into how great their products are, or the person that took time out to understand you and your needs before talking about their products?

Part 3

The Seven Cs toolkit

Chapter 6

Stage one: Client

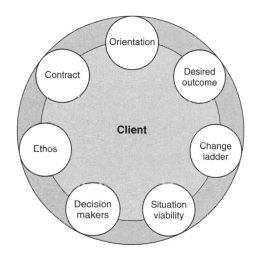

Trade is a social act
John Stuart Mill

The whole consulting process begins and ends with the client. And it is imperative you apply sufficient time and energy to understanding the person as well as the problem. The client is the voice of the organization, the paymaster and the confidant in times of trouble. It is important to establish a solid relationship that will hold together when unforeseen problems occur.

One reason why so many consulting projects fail or get a bad name is because the commercial need subsumes the drive to manage an effective relationship. As a result, the client is treated as a thing, rather than a real person. Just think of the Tom and Jerry cartoon films where Tom will look at Jerry and see the next meal rather than a mouse. In the same way, the client can feel like a large dollar sign, as a revenue stream rather than a valued individual. It is important that you never treat the client as a means to an end, where the end is a contract or money.

Whether you are already close to the client or the contact arose from a cold call, the one goal you have at this stage is to engage the individual emotionally.

You must develop and agree a clear, concise and collaborative contract that sets out what action each party will take and what benefit will emerge from the collaboration. However, the journey from the first meeting through to the agreement of the contract is fraught with potential land mines and hidden traps. These traps are often so submerged that even the most experienced consultant can fail to spot the warning signs:

- The IT specialist who finds that the new personnel system doesn't solve the client's problems because the real issue was the management team's inability to control a diverse and downhearted workforce.

- The project manager who has signed a contract to lead a new product launch but suddenly realizes that what the client has asked for cannot be delivered because a new competitor is about to launch a more advanced product.

- The process reengineering company that fails to secure a bid because the proposal is based upon a centralized control methodology whereas the client is looking for a style that allows freedom at a lower level.

If these types of problems are to be avoided, you must ensure that discipline and rigour are built into the early stages of the client relationship. Although this seems obvious, in reality this stage is often dealt with superficially, causing problems to emerge later. The seven steps outlined in the Client stage help to address many of these issues by offering a simple but effective framework to ensure that all of the key elements are dealt with at the start of the life cycle. They include:

- **Orientation:** From the very beginning, seek to view the problem as the client sees it, not how *you* see it.

- **Desired outcome:** Through the use of questions, draw out the client's real wished-for outcome.

- **Change ladder:** Remove fog from the initial situation problem by focusing on the dominant area where the process might need to take place.

- **Situation viability:** Question if you can deliver a successful outcome by asking 'can this issue be successfully resolved?' and 'is the timing right for a change?'.

- **Decision makers:** Root out and map the genuine decision makers so that a true and effective contract can be established.

- **Ethos:** At the heart of any change is the underlying ethos being used to drive the change – will it be participate or coercive in nature?

- **Contract:** Agree a contract that will set out a framework for action, define the roles and responsibilities of each party and offer a tool by which the success or failure of the change process can be measured.

Orientation

Before you can start to understand the client's problem, it is imperative to appreciate how they make sense of the world. Unless you are able to develop a real appreciation of the client's view of the world, problems will inevitably occur at a later date.

Imagine two people, one an avid vegetarian and the other a passionate meat eater, cooking a meal together. If their personal viewpoints are understood, then it will be possible to cook a meal that satisfies both their needs. However, if their views remain unspoken, then at best the meal will turn into a fiasco. At worst there will be a fight as they both strive to assert their frame of reference.

Before you can start to understand the client's problem, it is imperative to appreciate how they make sense of the world.

This mis alignment happens because people often do not understand how they map the world, let alone how other people build their maps. All people filter the world according to their experiences, values and beliefs. These perceptual filters are invisible to the owner and are only made visible by a process of comparison, feedback or reflection.

You must do two things to ensure that perceptual filters do not create a problem during the early stage of the change. First, understand and calibrate your own perceptual filters. Second, develop the capacity to quickly diagnose other people's filters. This diagnosis and calibration often has to take place over a coffee or game of golf, since the socialization phase of a new relationship is relatively short. You must become adept at listening to verbal clues, spotting visual indicators and monitoring your client's close environment so as to take initial stabs at their perceptual filters. This data is then used in the ongoing relationship to verify your judgements.

Although there are many perceptual filters, some of the more common ones include:

- **Time:** People talk about the future, about the past or are grounded in the present. The client who is 'past-based' will refer to the successes and the deep-rooted values that helped the company to survive. The future-orientated client will talk about the five-year plan, the next acquisition or expansion into new markets. The present-based client will focus on the here and now, will not be interested in past successes and will have little desire to discuss long-term plans.

- **Information:** Another filtration process is seen in the way that people 'chunk up' information. One client may take a conceptual view of the world, looking at global markets, total system changes or the entire customer base. Another considers the small detail in a proposal. They might leave the large chunks of information to the specialists but need to understand issues such as workshop design, IT specifications or market segmentation.

- **Relationship:** This is concerned with people who look for similarities in the world and those that map it by looking for differences. So if the client operates on a similarity model, it can make sense to relate a new proposal to previous corporate programmes or case examples of best practice in the same industry. For clients that operate through a difference filter, you will need to think about how to present an idea so that it is essentially matched against other change programmes. For example, you can accentuate how certain aspects have been modified or improved over other programmes that have been used within the company.

- **Direction:** Some people view change and disruption as a problem, seeing life as an obstacle course that has to be tackled every day. Others see life as a basket of opportunities, a rich world that throws up chances for people to grow and develop. The latter will see the consulting situation as an opportunity and talk about 'walking towards' it. The problem-centred person might view it as a negative issue, something they are trying to 'move away' from.

- **Referencing:** This is the way a client measures the business success. Are they externally referenced, such that they feel that the customer service results, market share or stock price indicates the level of success? Or are they internally referenced, so that their focus will be on internal measures, feeling good when morale surveys or process measures indicate that the company is performing well?

- **Association:** In the consultancy world, the associated client might well talk about a problem in terms that indicate their personal pain or concerns about how it affects the business. The disassociated client will take a distanced view, talking about the issue as an objective commentator, not positioning it as something in which they are personally involved.

The relationship may be sufficiently relaxed at the start for you to ask the client how they view the world. Do they prefer to work at a concept or detail level, are they focused on the future or the here and now, or do they have a preference for the way performance is measured? However, this is probably rare and in most cases a high level of deductive and inductive reasoning will be needed to understand what filters the client uses. The end result should be that you see the world as the client sees it – to understand the assumptions, biases and values they use to filter the world.

In making use of the filters as a relationship tool, you will have four key steps to consider:

- Understand *your* filter system.
- Identify your client's filter system.
- Match your filters to the client's.
- Lead (where necessary) the client into a different filter system.

The first two steps are the most difficult. To understand your own filters, you need to be able to take a cold and dispassionate look at yourself and often this is difficult, if not impossible. It is easier to ask a colleague or friend to offer some constructive feedback on their perception of the filters you use. If this feedback is taken from a range of sources then you should eventually be able to draw a clear map of your filters.

The second stage requires that you map the client's profile. This is a skill that becomes easier with use but in the early days it can help to do some research. Talk to people that know or have worked with the client and get their views on how the client orientates the world. Then, at the first meeting, use some of the socialization time to listen out for clues. Listen for specific words and try to match them against the filter profile. For example:

- I think this problem is quite like the one that caused the production down-time during the shift changeover last March. (Past, Detail, Similar)
- The senior team's view is that there have been some production problems occurring regularly for the past three years. (Past, Disassociated, Concept)
- Although I am really fed up with the continuous breakdown in the bypass flange, let's look at ways in which we can lose that part of the process and reduce the production costs. (Future, Detail, Associated)

This type of analysis is more of an art than a science and as such is dangerous if used without thought and sensitivity. It is important to appreciate that any inter pretation drawn about the client's language or behaviour is corrupted as it is filtered through your mental models. So any conclusion must be treated with the utmost care, as it can only ever be conjecture.

Once your client's filter profile is mapped, the next stage is to modify your language and behaviour to align with that of the client. Imagine a consultant who has the filter profile of Future, Concept, Differences, Internal and Associated. She is trying to build a relationship with a client with a profile of Past, Detail, Differences, External and Disassociated. Apart from the similarity in the way they look for differences in a situation, the client might consider the consultant to be a spaced-out tree-hugging hippie with little to offer the business. The language they use will be different and the way that they manage tasks and projects are likely to be different as well. For each of the profile factors the consultant must be prepared to (initially) modify her language, behaviour and possibly physiological actions. Only by matching the client will a sense of rapport be developed and the relationship moved to a level where an open relationship is established.

> **Back pocket question**
> Am I able to view the problem as the client sees it?

Desired outcome

Your role in this stage is to help the client achieve two things. First, to be clear on what they believe to be the source of the problem and, second, to be clear on how they think it might be resolved. Although there is every chance that both ideas will be modified as the project matures, it is important to help the client gain clarity in the early stage of the change. To achieve this, you need to take them through two ways of thinking. The first is to funnel down and understand what they believe to be the real source of the issue, and the second is to help them focus on what they believe to be a valid and productive outcome.

In clarifying the course of the problem, you need to be clear about the symptoms; then understand the setting, i.e. where specifically is it happening; and, lastly, to drag from this the source of the issue under consideration.

Take as an example, your young daughter arrives home from school and complains that no one likes her. At this level she might be seen to be talking about the symptoms of the problem but with little clarity as to what is really happening. Your role as a parent is to get below this to understand what is causing the problem. Your first step might be to ask her to describe the problem as she sees is, to mentally list all of the symptoms that are causing her to be upset. At this stage it is important not to argue or criticize the symptoms, as she will probably believe that they are the source of the problem rather than just the symptoms. Next, it can help to understand the setting where the problem has occurred. This will be based on the typical, who, where, what and when type questions. By the end of this stage you should have a good view of what is happening. Lastly, your role is to act as a mirror and play back what she has told you. By doing this she will start to take a more objective view of the situation and can start to question some of her earlier assumptions. In doing this, you can work through the problem to understand the core source of the issue, which in the vast majority of cases will be attributable to one root cause. So for the daughter, the source of the problem is probably that she has had an argument with one of her friends and believes the whole world is against her.

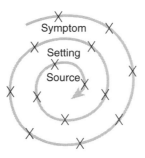

Fig. 6.1   Barbed-wire funnel

Taking someone through this process can be like climbing down a funnel of barbed wire (Fig. 6.1). At every step of the journey you can hit a potential prickly spot, one that triggers a negative response, often aimed back at you. Clearly, there is no simple solution to managing this tenuous process. It is generally down to you to make decisions based upon your experience, the client's problem and the context in which the funnelling is taking place. However, it is important to emphasize the importance of this step in the process. Unless the client is challenged to explore the root source of the problem, you can end up wasting everybody's time, including your own.

Once the source of the problem has been unearthed, you can start to consider how the problem might be resolved. At this point, it can be easy to offer a potential solution based on your expertise in other areas. Unless you have been explicitly called in to offer such knowledge and service, this will be a disastrous idea. If the client is not able to build a solution that they own, love and cherish, then the engagement is likely to have the rug pulled out at any stage from that point on.

The goal is for the client to develop an outcome or solution that they feel will 'really' resolve the source problem. Forcing them to consider both sides of the equation can be a powerful and catalytic process. Often the client will have a good idea of what is wrong but be unable to describe clearly how the situation should be resolved. Alternatively, they might come to you with a great idea but not really understand what it is they are trying to resolve. Even where they have an idea of what the end goal is, in many cases it is vague and blurred, almost a 'just make things better' statement. Your role is to act as an investigator and catalyst, to help draw out a realistic, tangible and measurable solution for the client, consumer and consultancy team. You can help achieve this by asking seven simple questions in the OUTCOME framework:

- **Owns:** Who owns the outcome and is it self-maintained? Ultimately, at the end of the project, you will move on and the client will be expected to maintain the change. The question is, do they have the desire and capability to hold the gains or will other external forces be able to erode any movement forward?

- **Unease:** What triggered the need for change? Ask why the issue is really important at a deep, rather than superficial, level. Why has the issue surfaced now and what priority does it hold over other issues?

- **Trade-off:** What will you have to give up to achieve it? One oft-forgotten fact is that people or organizations adopt certain policies or behaviours because there is a payback. Effecting a change within an organization means that something will have to change and something will have to be lost. The client must think through and appreciate the potential loss before they can confirm what outcome is required.

- **Changed:** How will life be different when the change is made? At this point the client has clarified the desired outcome and you can help to solidify the changes. One way of doing this is by asking the client to take a mental step forward in time, to consider how life will be different at the end of the project. To imagine what language will be used, what the environment will look like, what the productivity figures will be; anything that helps the client to actually 'be' in the future.

- **Others:** What impact will it have on others (losers, winners and neutral)? In effecting a change, one of the dangers is that short-term and urgent forces are being responded to and little attention is paid to the impact that any change will have on other parties or groups. It is important to consider 'all' people that are affected by any change and to possibly consider them in terms of winners, loser or neutral. From this the client should be able to offer a realistic picture of who will be affected by the proposed change and, more importantly, what reaction can be anticipated.

- **Measure:** How will outcome be measured? How will the client know if the change has been successful? To be sure that the outcome is one that the client really wants and can achieve they should be able to describe in simple terms how they will 'know' that a successful change has been delivered.

- **Engage:** What value can this engagement add? You must always ask 'Why me?' Why has the client chosen to use an external resource as opposed to drawing upon his or her own resources? Building on this question, the next step is to understand what is stopping them from rectifying the issue at present and what are the restraining forces that any engagement must overcome.

Once the outcomes are clearly defined from the client's perspective, you need to focus on what the change will be and your role within it. You need to develop a much firmer picture of the type of change that you will be asked to make. More importantly, ensure the client has the necessary resolve and stamina to manage the transition through to its completion and not be waylaid by diversionary forces.

> **Back pocket question**
>
> Have I tested the clarity of the desired outcome?

Change ladder

Before finalizing what the problem really is, it will help if you determine what type of change is needed. Often, when you are first asked to help with a problem there will be a great deal of uncertainty. Since the client is often influenced by subjective needs, the views of other political players and the vagaries of history, the issue offered to you might well consist of a hotch potch of different stories and concerns. Consequently, when the relationship first begins, the client will implicitly be looking for you to help take away some of the surrounding fog. As Schein (1994) suggests:

> *In reality the manager often does not know what he is looking for and indeed should not be expected to know. All he knows is that something is not working right and he needs some kind of help. An important part of any consultation process, then, must be to help the manager or organization to figure out what the problem is, and only then decide what further kind of help is needed.*

The problem is that getting to the core of the issue is difficult when it is surrounded by other factors. However, when dealing with any problem, it is better to focus on one area at a time rather than trying to impose multiple solutions. Trying to take actions in two areas at once can often lead to confusion and, more importantly, make it difficult to measure the success of any change. If a mechanic tries to tune a misfiring car engine by changing the spark plugs and coil at the same time, then it will be difficult to prove which modification resolved the problem. Only by dealing with each change separately can he or she be sure that the cause of the problem is identified and resolved.

Picture a large multinational firm that has a problem with its computer system. Because of the historical changes in organizational structure and IT policy, the system consists of a complex mix of hardware and software. The result is that the IT system is unable to provide adequate support to the customer service teams. Hence, the company commissions a large systems integration contract to upgrade the system.

While developing the project plan, you suggest that it might be appropriate to rebuild the company mission and vision. This will help place greater emphasis on customer service as a core company purpose. However, this changed emphasis means that along with the strategic review, your client now needs to review and upgrade the in-house training procedures in order to enhance customer-influencing skills. Finally, it makes sense to run a series of value development workshops, so that people buy into the need for a greater emphasis on customer service.

In this example, the initial change has been corrupted: now the client is trying to effect a significant change across a broad range of hard and soft systems. This escalation to a range of multiple changes can make it difficult for the client, consultant and end consumer to really focus on delivering an effective change. Although change can take place across different systems, it is important to ensure that attention is paid to each core issue separately.

The vast majority of change actions will fall into one of these categories.

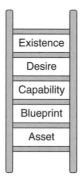

Fig. 6.2   Change ladder

- **Asset:** The tools, plant or equipment used to deliver a product or service. For the company this is land, building and production equipment; for the racing driver it is the Formula One car; and for the pop musician it is an electric guitar. In the case of a professional services firm or the Rolling Stones, people are the primary asset as they deliver the final product and services.

- **Blueprint:** This is the method by which a system is managed. For the large organization it is the strategic and tactical plans, processes, quality systems and personnel procedures. For a theatre company it is the script, lighting schedule and backstage directions. For the financial trading group it is the standard internal procedures and the external regulations that control the trading operations.

44

- **Capability:** These are the ways and means by which an output is delivered. For an organization they are contained in its people's skills and competencies and its relationship with customers and suppliers. With a football team, the capability is contained within the players' tacit ability, the manager's knowledge and experience, and the capability of the ground staff to maintain a quality pitch. For the racing driver, it is the driver's ability to outperform competitors on the racetrack and the team's ability to maintain the car at top performance.

- **Desire:** This is the deep-seated motivation that drives people to take action. Within an organization, it is a hierarchical process, from the mission that drives the business goals, down to the personal motivation that stimulates each individual. For the neighbourhood watch organization, it is the need for people to fight against burglary. For the racing driver, it is the single-minded determination to win.

- **Existence:** This is the core reason why a person, team or organization exists. For the organization it is the real (as opposed to the stated) values and culture. At an international level it is the way that countries will go to war over what might be seen as minor issues. At a micro level, it is the charity that an individual will give to or where they decide to allocate their time.

The five factors are shown in Fig. 6.2 as the change ladder. Change can be delivered in any one of the areas, though the optimum approach is to focus on a single rung. This does not preclude the idea of multiple change activities but it does suggest that where more than one system is being acted upon, it should be treated as a separate change.

However, this does not mean that each action is managed in isolation. Where multiple changes are undertaken, a holistic approach is essential. The impact of one change must be understood in relation to any other action. The end result will be a mapped order of engagements, where each change will contain a further sub-set of engagements. The total map will clearly indicate the level and nature of the relationship and interdependency between each one.

The potential danger, as seen in the systems integration example above, is the tendency to grow and 'explode' the initial change. In a commercial environment, it is natural to expand any revenue stream when the opportunity presents itself. The danger is that this can soon go into overkill, where the change becomes messy for you, draining for the client and confusing for the consumer. It is practical and entirely ethical to encourage further system change where appropriate, as long as it is kept within the boundary of commercial and operational sensibility.

This idea of the change ladder is considered in more detail in Chapter 11. It is important to appreciate the complex relationship between the five steps of the ladder. In particular, accept that a change in one area will, in the majority of cases, result in a counter action from one of the other four areas. You will need to be aware of the potential response to any action that you choose to make.

Back pocket question

Have I removed all the fog from the initial problem by focusing on the area where the change might need to take place?

Situation viability

One of your goals at this stage of the life-cycle model will be to focus on the viability of the situation. You need to ask if you really can deliver a successful outcome within the given limitations. In many cases, the viability of the change may only be determined if the forces that surround the problem are understood. So rather than worrying about the content of the problem, you might need to understand some of the meta-processes that surround it. Two of the specific factors addressed in this section are the driving force matrix and phase mapping.

Driving force

In any change situation, you must ask two questions:

● From where is the drive for the change coming (forced or chosen)?

● What is the dominant type of change (hard or soft)?

You need to understand where the decision to go for change originated. Did your client decide on it (chosen) or was it the result of external pressure (forced)?

And what about the type of change? 'Hard' change is where the client requires a tangible and visible output such as a new computer system, global strategy or quality system. These are structural elements that are independent of the people that drive and operate the business. When people go home at night, the effect of the change will stay with the business. For 'soft' change, the primary focus in on dealing with people issues – culture change, empowerment, leadership, facilitating a team's development, etc. With this type of change, when the people go home at night, so will the impact of the change.

In talking about the types of change, I have used the terms hard and soft with some trepidation. Clearly, hard change projects are implicitly dependent upon the soft issues and soft change must deliver a tangible benefit. Unless people are motivated to use a new computer system, then the business benefits will be slowly eroded. Conversely, simply making people more motivated and empowered will be of little use unless there is a clear improvement in business performance, i.e. a hard and tangible outcome. However, I have used the classification because the type of change that the client is looking for will significantly affect the approach you take in later stages of the engagement. These parameters are combined in a simple matrix in Fig. 6.3.

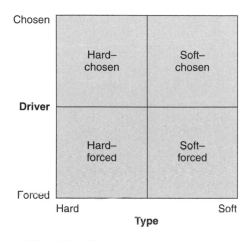

Fig. 6.3 Driving force matrix

Examples of projects in the Chosen–Hard quadrant are a software upgrade, process modification or office relocation scheme. Your client has taken the decision to make a change and already has a clear and tangible outcome in mind. Your role is as a delivery agent, taking the situation in hand and managing it through to a successful conclusion. Although soft issues will be encountered along the way, the client's primary goal is the delivery of a hard and tangible outcome. Any people factors that emerge along the way will be of secondary interest, only to be considered if they affect the end goal.

On the Chosen–Soft path, your client has decided that some of the softer issues need to be addressed. This might involve dealing with morale, introducing a new competency development programme or improving the senior team's ability to take critical feedback from line managers. One interesting question you might choose to ask is, why has the client chosen to address soft issues? Do they have prior experience, which proves that a soft change can work or have they read an article that suggests that the proposed outcome will offer certain benefits? If the client's need emerges from a deep belief about such ideas, then you are in the role of delivery agent. If the client's motivation for adopting such an approach is driven by hearsay or fad following, then it is critical that you check out and challenge what the client really wants to achieve. The key here is to manage the client's expectation as well as the consultancy process. Many change initiatives promise fantastic benefits but in reality deliver only limited improvement.

47

With the Forced–Hard option, the client has been pushed into a position where a change must be made. This might be a team manager who has to implement new quality procedures; a plant director who has to re-locate a division; or a marketing manager under pressure to adopt a new segmentation strategy. In this case, you will possibly be dealing with a client who has little personal motivation to deliver a success. This is a potential minefield since the client often has a hidden agenda to ensure that the change process fails and blame is apportioned to you. It will pay to think carefully about accepting this type of contract. Only if you are certain that you will be able to muster sufficient leverage (political, financial, etc.) should you accept the contract. The forces that will act against you are likely to come primarily from the client and this is an insidious position to be in.

The Forced–Soft quadrant is one of the most difficult and frustrating. Imagine a manager who has been told she is not performing and must attend a motivation course; a team manager who has been told that his team should attend a values definition workshop; or an engineering director who has been forced to allocate scarce funds to a new corporate culture change project. All of these projects will be difficult because you are trying to impose a transition at a deep and personal level, something that the majority of people will fiercely resist. This is like trying to enforce a no-smoking regime in a company where cigarettes have been commonly used. It is imposing a change at habit level, something that takes time, energy and desire to achieve. It cannot simply be mandated. This is possibly the biggest minefield of all the situations that you will face since people have the choice to either make a real change or just deliver a pseudo-transformation.

To ensure that change in this quadrant is effective, you need to spend energy on developing a close sense of rapport with your client rather than focusing on the content. Only when you have a decent level of trust and rapport will you be able to gauge the chances of success. Unless you are able to get a deep level of intimacy with your client then you will be undertaking a potentially fruitless assignment – one that proves frustrating for your client and yourself.

The message is quite apparent: unless you are very clear about where the drive is coming from and what type of change is being used, costly mistakes are likely to be made.

Phase mapping

The second point to consider is how the different components within the system relate to each other. Most engagements act on sub-systems of other systems, such as teams within a unit, a unit with a division, a division within a business and so on. As such there will always be external factors that can suddenly affect the engagement. These might include inward investment, changing personnel policies, corporate expansion schemes, downsizing, etc.

Imagine a product development team that needs to recruit new people to complete a market review. Unfortunately, the division that it sits in has budget constraints from head office resulting in headcount restrictions. Additionally, at a group level, there may be plans for downsizing. The decisions taken at each level make sense in isolation but when taken as a whole, result in discontinuities across the organization.

It can help to view these variations at each level as waveforms with differing amplitudes and frequency. There will be times when the waves complement each other and times when they are in conflict. You need to be able to map these energy waves and determine if the change is timely, taking into account any wave conflicts.

For example, at times investment will be green-flagged and capital will be readily available. At other times capital might be rationed and teams will struggle to fund their projects. Given the complex structures that exist within many organizations, this change in state will not always be common or clear to everyone. Thus different levels of the organization will have opposite views as to the availability of capital.

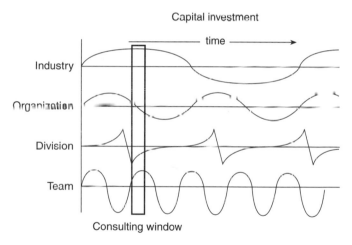

Fig. 6.4   Wave alignment

In Fig. 6.4 the consulting window suggests that the team is about to progress with a capital investment programme that is tacitly supported at divisional level. However, once the business case reaches organization level it is likely to be rescinded as they are on a downward cycle. Although the organization has advance knowledge of the impending scarcity of capital at an industry level, this is invisible to the team.

The danger is that if that if you are unaware of this phase mis-alignment, then time and money can be spent developing a proposal that is rejected once it reaches another part of the system. Although the investment project might make sense to the team based on its local view of the world, if it is unable to appreciate how the world looks to the other systems then it will be frustrated in its change process.

One way to avoid this trap is by networking. If you consider the client system in isolation there is a risk that phase problems will occur. Obviously you must focus on your project area but it is also important to cultivate relationships across other systems within the organization, both vertically and laterally. Only by creating a network of 'informants' will you be able to understand the total picture. For example, a police detective will not focus on the criminal in isolation. The shrewd one will draw upon his or her entire network of informants and contacts to understand what is happening in other parts of the criminal world. By doing this, they are able to manage both the immediate crime investigation and the bigger picture.

Once you have a clear view of the problem, the nature of the change and the viability for success, you must identify those people with power over any proposed changes. Although your client is often the person that has the power to take decisions on the progress of the project, in the majority of cases many of the real decision makers only come out of the woodwork once the project has progressed beyond the contracting stage.

> **Back pocket question**
>
> Can the issue be successfully resolved and is the timing right for a change?

Decision makers

The person that you meet, greet and contract with is often not the true decision maker. He or she may hold the title, reserved parking space and corner office but in reality may just be a puppet the organization presents to the world. Sitting behind this person will be a range of hidden power brokers. These are the people who can green light your proposal with the blink of an eye. Alternatively, they can consign it to the bottom of an in-tray to collect dust for months. Unless you are able to root out and map the genuine decision makers it is likely that your effort will be frustrated before the change starts.

This mapping process is akin to playing a game of poker with a group of strangers in a strange town with a strange pack of cards. You have to develop intuition and blind sight, the ability to look beyond the words and external factors and understand the interplay that takes place between people. The person dealing the cards may be the perceived leader at the table but in reality there are subtle messages that indicate who really wields the power to take decisions.

As an example, consider the following decision-making types that are found in most organizations:

- **Kingmaker:** This is the person who prefers to hold and wield control through another individual. Just as Rasputin influenced the Russian monarchy in its last years, the kingmaker will find people who are pliable and can be presented to the public as a passable face for the organization. The best way to tackle this person is by offering yourself as an ally rather than an aggressor. There is every chance that they might perceive you are entering their kingdom to do damage. Take the time to understand their power base and their rationale for sitting as kingmaker rather than king and how you might be able to help them in their goals.

- **Queen of hearts:** One individual might have the formal power to agree a contract with you but another 'queen of hearts' may hold a greater degree of influence over people in the organization. There is every chance that this person is operating from a value-based rather than a logical standpoint as their power is likely to be at the desire level on the change ladder. You need to understand why this person appeals to the consumers. Once you have done that you can appreciate how best to gain their confidence. The one danger with this type of power broker is that they can go quickly from being in favour to being ostracized by the crowd. You must always watch which way the wind is blowing to ensure that you don't fall from grace with the queen.

- **Knave:** The knave is the common individual that sits at the bottom of the organization pile – deemed to be of little consequence by the senior people within it. However, it can often be the 'little people' that have the greatest influence over a business. Think of the gatekeepers that can make your life hell in a client organization – the car park attendant or the director's PA. Although these people might not block the high-level processes within a change, they can cause significant problems once the project is rolling if they are not brought into alignment.

- **Joker:** This is the unexpected wildcard – the person who appears to be invisible most of the time, only to pop up with a solution or problem that completely throws the whole change proposition. Although by their very nature these people are difficult to spot, one ruse is to talk to people in the organization to find out what problems beset earlier change initiatives. It might well be that one person's name starts to crop up.

- **Ace:** In working with the ace in the pack you will be dealing with the person that has the true power to agree and effect a decision. Like an ace up the sleeve, you might need to pull this person out when facing real problems, when blockages occur at a certain layer in the organization or funds start to run dry part-way through a training session, for example. However, the danger may be in exposing the person too soon in a conflict and effectively giving the game away.

It is a rare and privileged person that has the right and ability to take one single all-embracing decision and see it completed in full. People have to lobby, cajole, bribe and influence others to initiate and complete a decision. Presidents, prime ministers, CEOs, dentists and doctors all have paymasters who can influence the decisions they take. You must take the time to consider any organization critically and really understand who hold the reigns of power before signing a contract. Failure to do this can result in wasted time and resources being expended on a project that has little chance of being delivered.

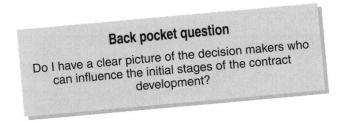

Back pocket question

Do I have a clear picture of the decision makers who can influence the initial stages of the contract development?

Ethos

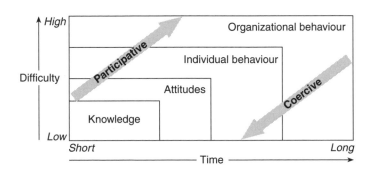

Fig. 6.5

Before setting out on any change, you have to consider the strategy that will be used to underpin the transition (Hersey and Blanchard, 1972). When push comes to shove, what rules will govern the decisions to be taken? This ethos will essentially be driven by two questions that the client will ask at some stage during the change:

- How difficult will the change be?
- How long will it take?

In responding, you need to agree what ethos will underpin the assignment. Will it be participative so that people have the freedom to decide their personal rate of adaptation? Or will it be coercive, where an authoritative source brings pressure to bear by attempting to modify the behaviour of the whole group? Although there are degrees between the two extremes, any change is likely to have a bias in one direction (Fig. 6.5).

Participation is based on the idea that giving people a new knowledge base modifies individuals' behaviour. This is like the government campaign that tries to stop people smoking or to avoid drinking and driving. The objective is to offer people information about the destructive impact of cigarettes or drink. In the same way, an organization might try to modify behaviour by offering people knowledge about a new quality system, ideas scheme or advanced competitor product. The problem with this approach is that it can take time and often requires a high level of back-up. The benefit is that the change will last over a period of time and is not dependent on a directive transformation process.

In the coercive model, the client or consultant decides that urgent change is necessary and stimulates rapid behavioural change across the organization in the expectation that everyone will quickly adopt a new range of behaviours. This is seen in the way that the UK government introduced car seat belt and motorbike helmet laws to curb the high death rate on the roads. For an organization, this type of action is seen in the introduction of new process measures, quality audits or enhanced personal objectives. Each action will be reinforced by the idea that failure to reach the prescribed target will result in some form of disciplinary action. However, although behaviours will have been modified, people are doing it under duress. In many cases, deep-set attitudes and beliefs will not have been modified. Only over time might they start to embrace the new ways of working and accept that the new knowledge is valid as part of their normal working style.

Such a change process is dependent on the people or system that originated the change. If the support mechanism is taken away, there is every chance that the transformation will collapse and there will be a shift back to the original behaviours. Imagine a school that has been beset with problems of ill discipline, drugs and violence. A new head teacher might be able to ride in to save the day by enforcing a code of discipline. However, until the change has worked its way deep into the culture, there will be a high level of dependency on the new head. If for any reason he or she leaves there is a chance that the old problems will return. This approach is suitable in a school environment, where the churn rate is relatively low, but in fast-moving industries such as electronics, communications or marketing, such an approach is risky. The problem is that as people move on to new positions, so the initiatives they introduced fade away with their replacement introducing a new set of changes.

The net result is that when a client asks about the difficulty and length of time associated with a consultancy project, they might need to be educated about the trade-offs that must be made. You might be able to deliver speed and ease of implementation but add the caveat that it might not include true and deep gain in the short term. For example, a company that wants to improve its level of quality has a decision to make. Does it look for a quick implementation, on the premise that it will be owned and driven by one of the senior managers? Or does it take a longer view and allow people to absorb and adapt to the new ideas at their own rate of change? Although you can help facilitate the decision, the ultimate responsibility for the judgement must be down to the client.

> **Back pocket question**
> Will the change be coercive or participative in nature?

Contract

The initial contract that you form with your client will set out a framework for action and offers a tool by which the success or failure of the engagement can be measured. There are many models that outline a basic structural framework that the document and process can follow and it would be foolish for me to try to offer a definitive answer. The danger is that in offering a potential structure of the contract process, 99 per cent of practising consultants will say 'yes, but you missed this item'. Hence the content offered in this contract model is meant to be indicative and is not offered as a definitive model (Table 6.1). For example, it does not include any of the financial and legal aspects that will be found in many contracts.

Remember that the contract should never include anything that will surprise the client. If the client observes a new clause, proposition or assumption, trust will be eroded. If you or the client cannot be trusted at the opening stages of the relationship, what chance is there that integrity will be maintained once the project gets into turbulent waters?

Table 6.1   Indicative content for a contract

Heading	Sub-heading
Background	• Outline description of client area • Situation under consideration • Business context
Outcome	• High level goals • Specific objectives • Measurement content • Measurement process
Engagement plan	• Timeframe • Methodology • Resource allocation • Key milestones and breakpoints • Initial known data requirements
Responsibilities	• Client • Client representative • Stakeholders • Consultancy team • Sub-contractors
Boundaries and scope	• Areas for inclusion • Areas for exclusion • Potential risks
Specifics	• Payment • Terms and conditions • Termination process • Liability
Confidentiality	• Confidentiality ring • Disclosure policy
Review process	• Review process • Review goals • Deviation management
Closure	• Closure reviews dates • Closure process

In developing the contract, it is important to remember that it is a framework for the delivery of a service or product. It is not being written as a stick for either party to beat the other. If the contract reads like a 'screw-down' document then there is every chance that the relationship will operate according to those principles. If it is written with the intention that it will not see the light of day until the process is complete, there will be a greater chance that the relationship will operate with a collaborative spirit. However, before the contract is written, many of the details contained within the document must be negotiated, and this is where problems can surface.

As the old adage goes: 'measure twice, cut once'. The goal at the contract stage must be to take extra care in the specification of the desired outcomes. This must be in the criteria specified in the document and more especially in the allocation of roles and responsibilities between you, the client and the consumer. One of the biggest causes of downstream problems can be disagreement over who owns what action or who is responsible for a particular aspect of the change. Simply by locking in clarity at this stage it is possible to minimize any problems that might occur at a later date.

Contract negotiation

The negotiation phase is difficult because it is often the point when the undiscussable has to be discussed. When you first meet with a new client much of the emphasis is on the pleasant aspects of the business – the future benefits, change methodology or who will be involved at various stages. However, as you get closer to signing the contract, the more difficult issues need to be brought up and resolved. This is where you must move your client out of the comfort zone and into the reality zone, discussing issues such as remuneration, risks and results. However, in dealing with such difficult issues, there can often be a tendency to go for fight or flight. Fight means that you go into battle with the client, battling to leverage every bean out of the situation. Flight means avoiding dealing with the difficult issues and sticking with a basic contract that does not offer any tight agreements.

Always go for a balanced outcome – one where both parties are genuinely happy with the result and where, even better, there is a sense of collaboration rather than compromise. In this type of agreement, you and the client are not people staring at a problem from different sides of the street. You are standing together trying to reach an equitable, aligned and mutually beneficial solution. If this happens then there is less chance that either side will see itself as a winner or loser. The moment one person agrees to a contract with a voice in their head telling them that they have lost the negotiating game then the relationship is doomed. In driving for an aligned negotiation process the goal is to avoid the fight/flight syndrome and to come to a position where the outcome is win/win.

One final point to mention is that although the model suggests that the negotiation phase is at the *end* of the client phase, in reality it starts from the point when you first meet the client. Negotiation is a fact of life. Children negotiate for sweets, partners negotiate for wardrobe space in the bedroom and you will negotiate throughout the life cycle of the change.

Back pocket question

Have I agreed a contract that sets out a framework for action, defines the various roles and responsibilities and offers a tool by which the success or failure of the change can be measured?

Chapter 7

Stage two: Clarify

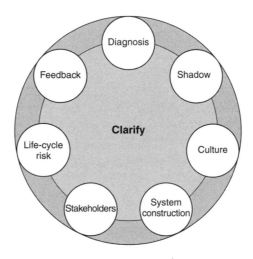

The wise man doesn't give the right answers;
he poses the right questions.

Claude Lévi-Strauss

Once your client has been emotionally and contractually engaged you need to move beyond what is a relatively narrow field of vision. The goal is to take away some of the haze, to understand the real source of the problem. Only then can you make a firm proposal as to how the situation can be resolved.

It is at this stage that the first dilemma can occur. Often a client will employ you because they have a problem which is urgent and pressing. The trouble is that when the wolves are at the door, it is difficult to suggest that your client should set aside time for detailed diagnostics. With a client in panic mode you may be expected to be in the same frame of mind. The expectation is that you will be able to walk in, fix the problem, take the 50 pieces of silver and then let the organization carry on with its affairs.

If you are being paid on a daily rate and employed solely to deliver a focused outcome your client may well regard activities such as investigation, research and diagnosis as wasteful (and unnecessarily expensive). This is because they (often) think they know what the cause of the problem is already; you are just expected to fix it. But while there are occasions when time is of the essence, the same underlying disciplines and rigour need to be applied so that errors are not made. Rushing in and attempting a quick fix is as dangerous as a doctor prescribing an operation based on the patient's own diagnosis.

You have a legal responsibility to deliver an agreed outcome and you also have an ethical responsibility to deliver the 'appropriate' one. Prescribing a solution without correctly diagnosing the cause of the problem may offer short-term income but leads to long-term erosion in your market credibility. If clients realize that a consultant's solutions do not result in a true resolution of their problem, so the jokes become perpetuated (a consultant is someone who borrows your watch and sends a bill to tell you the time).

Failure to really clarify the symptoms and source of a problem leads to a range of common problems:

- The strategy consultant who fails to gain a contract because she is a strong advocate of the Porter Five Forces model. The problem is that the client wants to find out what is unique about the company rather than use a pre-existing framework.

- The training consultant, employed to implement an empowerment programme, who suddenly realizes that the culture is based on autocratic dominance and centralized decision making. Simply dropping a new empowerment model into the culture will have little impact and is unlikely to be successful.

- The HR expert who fails to deliver the desired outcome because the regional managers block any changes out in the field.

- The activity-based costing expert who works slavishly for six months analyzing the business costs drivers only to find that the board rejects the final recommendations because she has failed to keep them in touch with her findings.

Effective clarification is the fuel that provides the energy, wisdom and guidance for the rest of the consultancy process. Unless this part of the cycle is managed with care and rigour, then it is possible to waste a lot of time, money and goodwill.

The process offered in this stage of the Seven Cs model follows this pattern:

- **Diagnosis:** Gather information that will help determine the real source of the issue and not just tackle the symptoms.

- **Shadow:** Determine the extent to which unspoken activities and arrangements affect the situation.

- **Culture:** Understand the cultural factors that affect the change process.

- **System construction:** Understand the structure of the organizational system and how it is likely to react to any changes.

- **Stakeholders:** Develop a map that indicates who can influence the outcome of the change and to what extent they have the capability and desire to wield their power.

- **Life cycle risk:** Determine the extent to which known and unknown factors within the change process will affect its potential for success.

- **Feedback:** Clarify how the client and organization wish to be informed of progress, both in terms of content and process.

If we follow the seven components of the Clarify stage, it becomes possible to ensure that the Create and Change stages actually resolve the source of the problems rather than simply eradicate the evidence.

Diagnosis

At this stage our primary objective is to discover timely, robust and accurate data. However, before you can start to collect data you must make a methodological decision on the approach you are going to use. There are many schools of thought behind the process of data gathering and research but the two common models are the outside-in and inside-out models.

Outside-in model

The outside-in model is based on the idea of prior hypotheses. Data is collected against a pre-determined model or mental framework. You will be trying to prove or disprove a specific argument or develop a test bed for future expansion. A strategist might use Porter's Five Forces model as a tool to understand a company's strengths in the market; an organizational development consultant will use Lewin's force field tool to map and understand what negative and positive forces are operating in the organization; the marketing consultant might analyze the company's product positioning against the Boston matrix. You are working on the assumption that a pre-defined model or paradigm can help to identify a clear solution to a problem. This type of research is driven by the following assumptions:

- **Hypothesis:** A pre-defined model is used as a guiding framework to drive the data-gathering process.

- **Independence:** There is no subjective bias. The data sits on the table and is manipulated without being clouded by your personal views.

- **Value-freedom:** Objective criteria rather than human beliefs and interests determine the choice of what to study and how to study it.

- **Operationalism:** Concepts need to be operationalized in a way that enables facts to be measured quantitatively.

- **Reductionism:** Problems are better understood if they are reduced to their simplest elements.

- **Generalism:** In order to generalize about regularities it is necessary to select sizeable samples. Once a statistically sound sample is used then any conclusion drawn from the process is applied across the entire population.

Inside-out model

The alternative approach is built around an inside-out, or grounded, model. With this model the research process is open-ended and uncluttered by the mental framework of the consultant. Any output will be guided purely by the content of the data. This model uses a set of principles that are quite different to the outside-in model:

- *Natural setting:* Realities cannot be understood in isolation from the context in which the study is undertaken. So although Porter's Five Forces model is suitable for the areas he studied, it might not be applicable in all contexts.

- *Human instrument:* Only humans are capable of grasping the variety of realities that will be encountered. Rigid and structured data-gathering processes will be unable to pick up the minor nuances of inflection that can indicate so much during, for example, an interview.

- *Use of tacit knowledge:* Intuitive/felt knowledge is used to appreciate the existence of multiple realities and because it mirrors the value patterns of the investigator.

- *Qualitative methods:* The use of words rather than numbers makes the data more adaptable when dealing with multiple realities and patterns and influences.

- *Emergent design:* It is impracticable to assume you know enough ahead of time to build a research design that could capture all the necessary data – the research process must emerge with the findings from the data.

This approach operates on the basis that discovery and diagnosis is not a black and white process. Since most data gathering will involve people, there is a good chance that the process will be full of uncertainty, emotion and confusion. The gathering process needs to be built around an emergent rather than fixed design.

Diagnostic process

When you visit the doctor, take a car to the mechanic or attend counselling, it involves some form of diagnostic exercise. Does the doctor warm the stethoscope before applying it to your chest? did the mechanic clean his or her hands before touching the upholstery? and did the counsellor find a comfortable seat for you? These issues might seem minor but they are significant in that they indicate a person's process capability – their ability to appreciate all of the factors that will affect an effective diagnostic process.

In the same way, your diagnostic process is likely to be the client's first experience of your professional capability. You need to ensure that you have a clear map of the process. Even more important will be your capability to explain the process to the client. If your client likes to take an interest in the process then you must have a clear and concise model that will explain how you will define, gather and analyze the data.

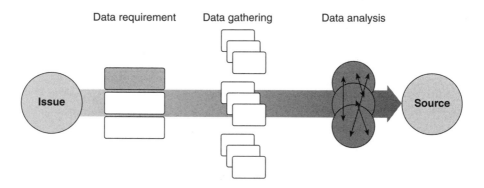

Fig. 7.1   Diagnostic process

Although there are many diagnostic styles and frameworks used in the consulting cycle, they all fall within three basic actions (Fig. 7.1).

- Define what data is required.

- Gather the data.

- Analyze the data and draw conclusions about the source of the problem.

A range of different tools and techniques has augmented these three steps but in essence they form the backbone of a typical diagnostic project. Two additional factors I would stress are the need to ensure clarity about the actual issues being researched and that you should undertake a reality check to ensure that the diagnosis has not drifted off track.

Issues

As you start on the data-gathering process, it really does pay to stop, sit down and think about the issues being addressed. Once the data collection phase begins you often find out that the world has moved on since the contract was signed. People leave, new team members join, organizations merge or split. In many cases the client who initiated the contract might no longer be around to clarify what is required. So, while the contract process within the Client stage does focus on outcomes and deliverables, it pays to spend time at this stage to confirm that the issue is still current and active.

One of the best ways to frame and clarify the issue is to ensure that it is built around a statement of 'we can't', 'we are unable to', or 'X isn't doing Y'. Once this is defined then it becomes quite easy to map what data is required. We need a negative focus because a positive one can lead to misdirected outcomes. For example, saying 'we want new sales bonus scheme' can lead to a range of outcomes, many of which do not address the real issue causing the problem. What we should say is 'the present bonus scheme does not encourage a collective style of working between the account managers'. Then the options for resolution are not linked into the provision of a new bonus scheme. The statement offers the problem and goal without presenting a prescriptive outcome.

Using a negative issue statement challenges the client to question what area of the concern is being dealt with and what value will be added by any change. For example, as a consultant you will often be employed simply as an excuse to delay or defer action. The introduction of an external agent can offer convenient breathing space for the client if they are in battle with others in the company. In forcing the research issue to be framed in this way, both you and the client will have a clear understanding of what *isn't* happening and what information you will need to retrieve.

> *The introduction of an external agent can offer convenient breathing space for the client if they are in battle with others in the company.*

Data requirements

Once the issue has been clarified and a shared model is held by each member of the data-gathering team, the next step is to make sure you know what data is required. One way to do this is by breaking down the total data load into sets that define a unique package of information to be discovered. The set description will indicate the data type, source, owner, purpose, etc. Only by taking this type of structured approach can you ensure that you do not spend valuable time and money gathering redundant information. But though this helps to clarify how the data gathering is managed, it does not resolve the issue of how to identify what data *needs* to be gathered.

Gathering framework

The content and context of whatever problem you are dealing with will drive the actual data sets. But in many cases it can be difficult to take the first step. Modern organizations hold millions and millions of units of data they use to run their business. Once you start to delve into the archives the amount of data will explode. Financial reports, customer complaints, supplier receipts, memos, staff surveys, etc, all come together to form this mountain of information. So in deciding where to start, the framework set out in Fig. 7.2 will help to focus on what data needs to be gathered.

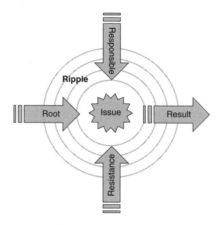

Fig. 7.2   Data set drivers

In any situation where a change has to be made, there are five sets of data that need to be understood:

- *Root:* Is it possible to carry out an audit to identify the original source of the problem? In the case of industrial action in a small manufacturing company, it might be changes in pay rates, poor industrial relations or a change in government policy.

- *Result:* What is the true impact of the issue? Is it something that affects the whole organization, one particular group or is it something that causes a problem for one product area? Whatever the breakdown, you have to get firm and valid data that describes the impact the issue is having. The key point is the need for data that indicates what is really happening rather than what the client or consumer believes is happening.

- *Responsible:* Whatever the problem, someone somewhere must have allowed it to happen. This 'permission' might have been given explicitly – the managing director deciding to reduce the organization's cost base by running a reengineering programme. Alternatively, it may have been given implicitly – a parent leaving too many sweets around the house, thus tempting a child.

- *Resistance:* There is often a temptation to ignore an issue in the hope that it will disappear once the problem has been resolved. However, there can be data elements within this area that might be of interest to you. Consider the resistance that might arise if a company announces plans to change its policy on using company phones for private calls. The level of any opposition to such a change can indicate a number of important factors such as the strength of the culture, the extent to which people are prepared to accept centralized decisions or the capability of the people to form co-ordinated counter-attacks to any imposed change.

- *Ripple effect:* The first four data areas are visible and can readily be measured and mapped. But with any issue there will be an intangible radiation, or energy, emitted as change 'ripples' through the organization. This is the anger and emotion that surrounds a downsizing exercise or the excitement released by an impending global merger. This radiated energy must be understood as it will often contain the power to amplify or attenuate the change process associated with any consultancy project.

The ease with which these five factors can be translated into data sets is shown in Fig. 7.3. The example shows a consultancy project looking at the issue of falling product sales. For each of the five data drivers, a range of hard, focused and relevant data sets are shown. Each of these data sets has a purpose within the analytical framework and is seen to add value to the total picture. Although the ripple factors are perceived as 'vague', they can add valuable qualitative data that will help to make sense of the quantitative data emerging in the other four areas.

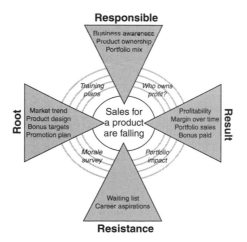

Fig. 7.3 Data map example

Although the data you capture in these five areas might not offer the total picture, it does help to build a robust and rigorous data map that is less clouded by an intuitive and emotional decision-making process. It also offers a simple but effective tool that will help your client and the consumer to understand your data-gathering strategy. As such they will be able to quickly look at the map and point out data sets that are obsolete and other areas where data sets are needed to highlight a certain issue.

Data richness

When planning how to gather data, it can help to take a slightly different approach in setting the boundaries. Data gathering often pushes for hard, tangible and actionable facts whereas the actual problem may lie in the soft, intangible areas of the business. If you take a clinical view of the problem, the resulting data will offer a robust story about the situation but will have little heart. If, however, it is possible to get data sets that reflect some of the softer issues, it becomes possible to enrich the picture so that it tells the real story of what is happening.

In using the model offered in Fig. 7.3, far greater value could be mined by using the full depth and breadth of our capability to gather data. I like to categorize this as gathering information at the cognitive (head), behavioural (hand) and emotional (heart) level. Just consider the examples below and see if you have had a similar experience:

- Your son starts to keep his bedroom tidy after receiving the fifth warning that it must never happen again. Although there is a short term change in behaviour, he soon drifts back again because he does not understand the reason why a bedroom must be kept tidy and feels that it is not as important as playing with his friends. (High Hand, but low Head and Heart)

- A manager listens to a passionate call from the chairman for a reduction in costs and goes back to the office fired up to deliver an improvement. However, although he believes in the need for change, he doesn't really understand what can be done and what he can deliver personally. It ends up as something that other people will have to deliver. (High Heart, low Head and Hand)

- An organization decides to put its people through customer care training. The goal is to help people to understand why customer service is important and what they can do to make a difference. People leave the course knowing the process they have to follow when dealing with a customer, but the change is short-lived and the old routines soon return because they are unable to translate what they know into what they do. (High Head, but low Heart and Hand)

Table 7.1   Identifying data needs

	Head	Hand	Heart
Root cause What caused the problem?	How did people perceive their remuneration in comparison to other companies in the region?	What training did people receive?	Is there a system that tracks morale within the call centre?
Responsible Who allowed it to happen?	What level of churn did the senior team want to aim for?	How has the company been seen to respond when people leave?	Do the senior team really care about the churn, or is short-term profit the real driver?
Resulting impact What has happened as a result?	Do people think that the competition will offer a better career alternative?	How has the churn affected business performance?	Do the call operators believe that this is a problem and are they thinking about leaving?
Resistance What forces are trying to stop the problem from happening?	What plans do local managers have in place to stop the problem from getting worse?	What action have the team managers taken to stem the flow?	Who are the leaders that really want to fix the problem as opposed to those that see it as a minor issue?
Ripple What are the side issues?		Is this affecting how people behave in other parts of the company?	

For each of the five factors identified in the model shown in the data map (Fig. 7.3) always try to gather data that represents the head, hand and heart factors. For example, if you are trying to get information about high staff churn in a call centre, Table 7.1 identifies questions which might help to determine what data is required.

Data gathering

Once the data sets are clearly mapped, the next stage is to start the gathering process. You must determine where the data is held and how it can be accessed. This stage of the diagnostic process is well documented and I do not intend to go into much detail. Instead, a simple overview highlights some of the more common forms of data gathering.

Questionnaire survey

This is one of the more common methods used to elicit data from a large population. It offers a quick and dirty way to gather information about the views of your customers, staff, suppliers, etc., in a comparatively cost-effective manner. The basic steps are:

● decide what you need to know;

● code it into a series of questions;

● send the questionnaires to the target population;

● draw general conclusions from the questionnaires once they are returned.

The major problem with this method is the typically low rate of return. A good result will be a 50 per cent return but in many cases it can fall as low as 10 per cent. In this case it is important to ensure that a good statistical model is used to ensure that any conclusion can be generalized as representative of the entire population.

Sampling people at random is relatively simple, but it is difficult to ensure that an accurate representation is drawn from the total population. Although a true random selection might offer a fair selection, it might be that your population does not have an even distribution and there may be heavy clusters of responses from a particular area. You deal with this possible bias by stratifying your sample. This resolves a problem where a particular tendency exists in the population, such as a localized ethnic group, focused skill set or age profile. For the sample to be representative, random samples should be taken from these particular sub groups or strata. Another alternative is the quota sample, where the sample is based on a prescribed quota criterion. There is no pre-set make up of the sample; the criterion is simply to gather sufficient information to meet the sample requirements. For example, the target may be to interview the first 30 people that walk into a shop.

Face-to-face interview

This has the advantage that it is flexible, probing and sensitive to changing moods in the population. It allows you to get a first-hand feel for the intangible problems associated with the project. Furthermore, meeting people reduces some of the anxiety caused by your presence. The downside is that it can be prone to bias by the interviewer and it can be difficult to compile the information into a meaningful form. These problems can be partially eliminated by carefully structuring the interview. The options are a pre-defined question structure, limited questions and prompted responses. However, in doing this you start to eliminate some of the richness associated with this approach.

Focus group

This takes the idea of the single interview and expands it to a wider group of participants. A focus group might consist of between five and 20 people and in some cases even more. The initial benefit of this approach is that it brings disparate people together and so saves time. One important benefit is that it offers the opportunity to extract a sense of synergistic spontaneity from the group. As people interact and share knowledge, so a vein of new knowledge can be elicited that might not have been uncovered by other methods. This data can be used as information to feed into the analysis stage or as foundation data to help construct a questionnaire.

Observing people

In some cases you might want to find out what people do rather than what they say they do. In this case is can be useful to gather data by observing people in their normal setting. This process is sometimes used in process reengineering. Although you might gather data as to the effectiveness of a particular process, you might also choose to watch how people operate over a longer period. Often this will highlight valuable data that would have been unavailable by other means. The short cuts that people take to save time or the way that a team interacts can only be identified by observation at close quarters.

Personal logs

Another method is to ask people to observe themselves and to record what actions they take, to whom they talk and what they think about certain issues in a personal log or diary. Although diaries are often used for social science research, they are less used in consultancy. However, this is a wonderful tool for gathering specific information at local and specific levels within an organization. Diaries record both qualitative and quantitative information and can be constructed to include some pre-analysis coding. The advantage is that they offer the employees', rather than the consultant's, perspective of what is happening. They also allow the use of comparative analysis, possibly to compare how different people feel about the same issue. One final advantage is that diaries operate in the background, freeing the researcher to do other activities.

Customer database

However, not all data analysis is concerned with understanding what people think, feel or do. One of the most important assets of any business is the database of financial, operational and customer information. It is also one of the most under-used assets in many consultancy projects, partly because it is an erratic process fraught with bias and error. However, there are tools on the market that might help to extract some of the necessary data from company archives. These are divided into two types. Predictive modelling is used to determine the relationship between data and the desired outcomes. The most common statistical tools used in this type of analysis include stepwise multiple regression, logistic regression, discriminant analysis and neural network modelling. These models all share the same basic idea – to predict the future; for example how customers will respond to a direct mail campaign. The alternative is descriptive statistics. These are used to describe and summarize what the existing data sets are indicating and what is in the database and how it is organized. Some common types of descriptive tools are frequency distributions, cross tabulations, employee age profile, customer profiles, penetration analysis, factor analysis and cluster analysis. While this type of analysis does not predict a future event, it does describe past events very accurately.

Data validity

Although data-gathering methods differ, there are common rules that ensure that the data is of value.

- Be relevant. The process must really gather knowledge about the subject area and not just cloud the issue.

- Always take the process for a test run. Use a sample population from the targeted areas or use a group of volunteers. Ask them to test drive the process and take it to breaking point so that it will be robust when applied in the field.

- Trying to save money at this stage can severely limit the whole process. As the adage goes, 'garbage in – garbage out'. If the gathering process fails to deliver data of any real value then the rest of the consultancy process will suffer.

- Market yourself in the data gathering process. If people receive a dirty envelope with a questionnaire full of typing mistakes, they will form an immediate (poor) opinion about you and the whole process.

- Above all else, ethics are crucial. Unless people believe that their information will be held in confidence then the process and content will end up being corrupted. If the process cannot be trusted then people will only put down what they think the researchers want to hear.

- In gathering the data, ensure that people are told why it is wanted and how it will be used. Just because people are performing mundane jobs, it does not mean that they have mundane thoughts. Treat the data donors with the same respect accorded the client.

- Be aware of timing. The classic mistake is to come up with wonderful project plans only to find that the data research phase falls smack in the middle of August when everyone is on holiday.

The construction of the survey will often be driven by practical constraints. Although you must take an idealistic stance when you define the methodology for gathering data, at the end of the day the client's hand is on the tiller. They will have to bear the cost of the process so you must ensure that they are fully aware of the process being used, the associated costs and the potential benefits of each methodology. Be able to defend each strand in your diagnostic phase. Otherwise your client might start arguing for cuts, with the risk that the whole assignment is put in jeopardy because of insufficient or inaccurate data.

Data analysis

Towards the end of the diagnostic phase you will start to find yourself awash with data. This increases the chance that critical aspects may be missed through data overload. The data analysis phase needs to ensure that:

- The data has been reduced to a manageable size.
- It has been synthesized to provide an indication of the root issue to be addressed.
- The data is prepared in a form that will help to develop a compelling argument for action.

The two views that drive the analysis phases, the outside-in (pre-determined analytical model) or the inside-out (emergent analytical model), were mentioned earlier. In the first, you use a degree of scientific rigour to analyze the data and understand how it matches the initial proposition. In the second approach, an inductive framework is used, where you will draw upon some form of emergent cognitive framework to tease out patterns and themes in the data.

Outside-in

With this method, your task is to take the data and find out if it proves or disproves the hypothesis offered at the outset of the diagnostic phase. This is a relatively simple process and can be facilitated by the use of a comparative matrix.

Table 7.2   Data matrix

Hypothesis test	Data set 1 Morale survey	Data set 2 Focus groups	Data set 3 Readiness survey	Data set 4 Previous projects
Proposition 1 Change needs support of the top managers	Indicates that senior managers are only partially trusted, pocket of good and bad	Suggests that support is fragmented	Certain key managers are sending out the right signals	Have had problems due to stalling once into the areas of difficult change
Proposition 2 People must be able to express their concerns about the change	Good sense of openness across total population	People concerned about impact of change on their personal lives	In general, but some project groups have concerns	Some have failed due to industrial relation problems
Proposition 3 The new order must be appealing to the population	No data	People do not understand what is expected of them	Willing to change, but don't know what they have to do	No data

Table 7.2 offers an example of such a process. For example, you might have identified three core propositions that you believe are true. These propositions are then tested against the data collected during the research phase. The result is a number of summary statements, each indicating how the data stands up against the core propositions. Your first proposition may be that senior managers must actively support the change for the transition to be effective. However, data from the morale survey suggests there are doubts about trusting the senior team. The implication is that even if the senior team offers support for the transition, staff might not believe it. This offers both evidence that a problem might exist and a completing argument that the senior team needs to take immediate action.

As an analytical tool, this method is powerful, simple and cost-effective. However, the downside is that it limits your level of flexibility. Since the whole emphasis is on the original hypothesis, this limits the opportunity to pick up on some of the more spurious or complex indicators. At the end of the day, you are simply getting an answer to the question posed at the outset of the diagnosis phase. However, you are unable to say confidently that the questions were correct.

Inside-out

Rather than using a fixed argument at the outset, this approach uses an emergent model where the continuous analysis of the data will drive the questions and processes used. This is often driven by a desire to discover how things 'are' within an organization or to come up with an innovative solution that has not been tried before. This search for innovative and creative solutions means that you will be breaking new ground every time the process is used.

The outside-in model is like building a house according to a prescribed architect's design; the inside-out approach, on the other hand, is like building a house according to the materials available (Fig. 7.4).

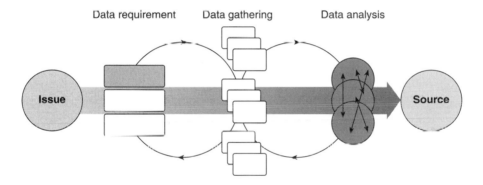

Fig. 7.4 Inside-out data analysis model

Source check

One of the biggest mistakes people make in data collection is to draw conclusions regarding the source or root of the problem, only to forget the original issue under investigation. The danger is that after weeks or months of frantic data gathering, followed by torturous days of data reduction, the consulting team finally let out a *eureka*, and brings forth their view of the source issue that needs to be addressed. However, in this euphoric moment, no one thinks to go back to the source problem, undertake a reality check and ensure that resolution of the problem identified by the data analysis would actually address the issue first raised by the client.

For example, a consultancy team is investigating why sales are falling on a particular product line. After weeks of data gathering, they come to the conclusion that the problem lies in the method used to manage the sales team's bonuses. Although this diagnosis is sound on a superficial level, before the team progress to the Create stage of the consultancy model, it would pay to undertake a quick and dirty reality check. Only when they check with the original problem raised by the client do they realize that the bonus scheme operates across *all* product lines but the problem only exists in one area. This indicates that the problem cannot lie solely with the bonus and that a more local problem must be at work.

The tendency to drift in the diagnosis stage is a common occurrence. After labouring away at the data definition, gathering and analysis, it is easy to lose sight of your goal and slowly slip into another frame of reference.

> **Back pocket question**
>
> Have I gathered information that will determine the real source of the issue, and not just to tackle the symptoms that surround the issue?

Shadow

We have already discussed the surface and shadow aspects of personal and corporate life and all diagnostic processes will fail unless they unearth some of the deeper, shadow organizational issues. This opens up four separate areas for consideration: the open and hidden individual; and the open and hidden organization. Table 7.3 offers examples of the behaviours associated with each category.

The shadow routines are driven by the operation of an unspoken understanding between the individual and the organization. This agreement is a tacit and unspoken contract to avoid those issues that might prove potentially damaging to their well being. This phenomenon is referred to as 'defensive routines' and has been extensively covered by Argyris. They might be defined as routines used by both people and the organization to keep themselves deliberately in the dark so as to avoid unpleasant surprises, threats or anything that might be construed as uncomfortable (Egan, 1994). Defence routines exist but they are undiscussable.

Table 7.3 Shadow factors

	Organization	Individual
Surface factors	Published reports and accounts Espoused ethos and ideals Company values Mission statement Personnel systems Formal communication channels Planned strategy	Personal objectives Team goals Personal plans Team briefs Monthly reports Casual conversations Yearly appraisal
Shadow factors	Internal politics Untapped potential Failed projects Local custom and practice Knee jerk reactions Race, gender or religious prejudice Decision making Informal networks Emergent business strategies/plans Shadow structure	True personal goals Personal fears Unexplored potential Family problems Personal relationships Mistakes made Desire to change roles or company Feelings about manager or team Historic problems with company

Argyris (1992) suggests that there is a fundamental set of behavioural rules that crosses all nations and cultures. People keep these rules in their heads to help them deal with embarrassment or threat:

- Bypass embarrassment or threat whenever possible.
- Act as if you are not bypassing them.
- Do not discuss this bypassing while it is happening.
- Do not discuss the undiscussability of the undiscussable.

In tacitly following these four rules, people will inherently lock themselves into a 'I know it's true because I say so' style of behaviour. The problem surfaces when you attempt to tackle any of these four rules head-on – asking people to clarify what the problem is and trying to discuss some of the deeper issues as part of the diagnosis process. All of these are likely to trigger some form of defensive reaction.

Suspicion often surrounds the diagnostic stage. People are likely to ignore anyone who tries to delve deeply. You must be able to mentally climb inside the person under investigation, to take on board their beliefs and goals and feel what they are feeling, no matter how alien or bizarre it might seem. In doing this, it becomes possible to understand what their personal needs are and why they are operating from the shadow side of their personality.

In carrying out the diagnostic element within the Clarify stage, there is a danger that depth and quality can be sacrificed for speed and urgency. It is important to avoid this and ensure that the diagnostic process really gets to the problem under consideration. This type of deep diagnosis can be likened to the 'double loop' style of learning advocated by Argyris (1992).

With adaptive, or single loop, diagnostics, the process or system is perceived at a superficial level (Fig. 7.5). The underlying norms, values and assumptions are not questioned or reflected on. For example, if sales of a product are falling, the response might be to alter the promotional discount, increase the number of outlets or in extreme cases sack the product manager. Where a team member is failing to meet expected goals, the response might be to increase the level of monitoring, reduce their pay rating or in many cases take steps to discipline the individual. In neither of these cases has any of the deep, underlying issues been considered.

In taking the double loop, or generative, approach, deeper questions can be asked regarding the falling sales of a product. To what extent is there conflict in

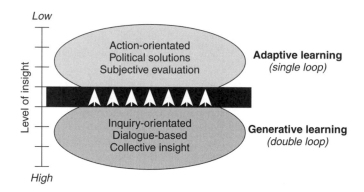

Fig. 7.5 Double loop learning

the market place with other products that the company sells? Are cross portfolio problems emerging? Has research and development lagged so that the product is becoming dated? Are the sales performance targets at odds with the needs of product turnover levels? For the individual who is under-performing, is there a problem at home causing concern? Does the individual need a change in roles to make the work more interesting? Is there any conflict in the relationship with the manager?

The key to double loop inquiry is in the art of turning the question back on the questioner, to ask what underlying assumptions are being made and what are the values of the questioner in suggesting that a problem exists in the first place? For example, instead of a manager asking why the performance of a team member has fallen, he or she might ask why it took so long to notice or what steps have been taken to develop the individuals in their team.

Generative diagnosis is often used when a range of different solutions have been implemented but failed to deliver a result. For example, where a product promotion or re-design failed to increase sales or sending a team member on a number of courses failed to result in a change in performance. The enlightenment that can occur as a result of these diagnoses can be both rewarding and daunting. The rewarding parts are clear in that a deeper level of inquiry can be of benefit to the organization. The daunting part starts when one considers some of the discomfort that will surface as the shadow issues are highlighted.

In triple loop learning (Fig. 7.6), the embedded customs, ethos and behaviours

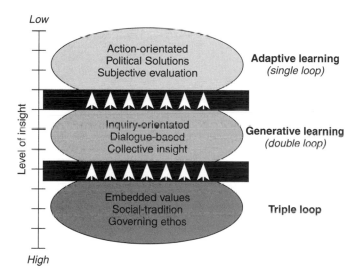

Fig. 7.6   Triple loop learning

are held up for scrutiny. The organization looks at the bedrock that it has been built on and its appropriateness. This approach forces the organization to ask, 'what type of company do we want to be, do we wish to exist in this market and who are the key stakeholders for the business?' This questions why they behave in certain ways, what has happened to make them develop certain views and beliefs, and how might they change their lives to a greater degree of alignment and balance. However, taking the Clarify stage to this level of analysis means that people and the organization must be prepared to be challenged and confronted about all of their beliefs, values and business goals.

> **Back pocket question**
>
> Do I have a clear appreciation of the extent to which unspoken activities and arrangements might affect the situation?

Culture

In clarifying how change is undertaken, the culture of an organization needs to be understood. Culture can stall and kill a project with hardly the blink of an eye. All of the professional and passionate planning initiated by a consultant will be ruined if the change and outcomes do not align with the culture. You must clarify three things: what is the cultural make-up of the target audience?; what personal cultural bias do you have?; and what is the degree of cultural diversity within the group?

Cultural audit

A cultural audit is designed to offer a clearer view of the culture you are dealing with. This knowledge is used to aid the diagnostics process, ensure that an appropriate change methodology is applied and test the viability of any solutions. This is clearly an art as opposed to a science. An organization's culture is simply an approximate description of the preferred style that the people choose to use. As you deconstruct the organization, so the approximation becomes less accurate because individual personalities and tendencies will emerge. At best, the outcome of any audit must be treated with some scepticism and at worse treated on a par with a horoscope. However, it is fair to say that, in general, it is possible to get a feel for a culture even if it cannot be specifically calibrated. A simple test is to walk into the foyer of three different hotels. There is every chance that within a few minutes, you will have an intuitive grasp of the culture of the organization. You will be able to guess

At best, the outcome of any audit must be treated with some scepticism and at worse treated on a par with a horoscope.

what is acceptable to the staff, who wields the power and the extent to which the hotel has verve and energy. Although you would not invest your money on the strength of this, it can offer enough data on which to make a number of broad suppositions about an organization's operating style.

It can help to think of an organization as an empty canvass that has been painted with a varied mix of different attributes. Like the artist who slowly builds up a picture, often not knowing quite how it will end up, as an organization grows it adopts a range of different cultural attributes. When investigating the make-up of the picture, the consultant's role is to deconstruct the colour base and understand how the way they have been mixed contributes to the end picture. Just consider what a varied mix of pictures an artist can create from a simple range of colours. In the same way, although each organization will be unique, it is essentially made up from the same set of cultural attributes:

- **Artefacts:** Physical evidence left in the wake of human interaction that can help to indicate a particular cultural bias. This can include rituals, behavioural norms, shared language, reward systems, logos and office design.

- **Beliefs:** What does the organization value and regard as being important? This is seen in the moral and ethical codes offered by the business. The difficulty is that beliefs are deeply personal things, so in trying to define them at a global level, averaging or levelling will occur and some degree of compromise can take place.

- **Control:** Is power based around the structure of the organization or capability of the individual? To what extent does this leverage negative or positive political action?

- **Discourse:** What is the balance between the open and hidden elements within the business? To what extent will people open up and talk about issues in a shared environment and to what extent are issues held for debate in private, closed and secure groups? This gap between the open and hidden levels of discourse can be used to understand the difference between the espoused and actual cultural factors.

- **Energy:** Where is the energy expended? Is it on issues that are concerned with internal processes or is it externally-orientated, where the primary focus is on the customers, suppliers and stakeholders?

- **Flow:** How do people move in, out and within the organization? What is the accepted churn rate, what is the balance between formal and informal recruitment processes and why do people leave the business?

- **Generative:** To what extent does the organization understand and drive its capability to innovate and learn? Do individuals feel that they are empowered to develop themselves? To what extent is knowledge shared between individuals and what infrastructure exists to facilitate the sharing of knowledge?

One danger in this type of culture model is that it might be viewed as a prescriptive paradigm. This in itself runs counter to the underlying idea of cultural definition and analysis. Culture is dynamic and unpredictable, hence dissecting an organization at any time, region or level will produce a range of varying ideas and themes, some of which align while others conflict. Any cultural analysis can only offer a subjective snapshot and should never be treated as the definitive model of an organization's style of interaction.

However, the purpose of the analysis is not just to understand the culture but to develop a multi-perspective map and to understand how the culture is perceived by the various elements within a business.

Table 7.4   Culture audit matrix

Cultural factor	Directors	Senior managers	Line managers	Process operators
Artefacts				
Beliefs				
Control				
Discourse				
Energy				
Flow				
Generative				

Table 7.4 shows the cultural model mapped against the hierarchical levels within an organization. In this case, the matrix might highlight potential issues:

- To what extent is there culture blindness between the various layers within the business? Does one layer believe that certain behaviours are natural while another group feels that an alternative set of norms is in place? One example might be that the directors and seniors managers believe that learning is encouraged at all levels while line managers and process operators feel they do not get the opportunity to develop their competencies.

- The extent to which there is a cultural paradox. For example, directors advocate cross-team migration to encourage knowledge flow across the business. However, from a control perspective, they operate a highly centralized system where all internal transfer must be signed off at senior management level. This creates a 'gate' that inhibits internal movement because people are wary of requesting a transfer in case their current manager sees it as a reflection on their ability to retain staff.

Trying to gather information on culture is difficult because it is intangible and subjective. If the goal is to gather descriptive information then that is relatively easy. All the respondent needs to do is outline the world as they see it. You can then undertake a comparative analysis to identify potential mismatches or inconsistencies.

However, it becomes harder if you are trying to encourage participants to offer an evaluative comment on the culture. It will be difficult for people to say if anything is good or bad because the response will be biased by the culture in which they exist. And they will often be least able to diagnose the culture in which they operate. However, it is possible to draw objective data from a subjective position through comparative measures. It is difficult to ask someone to describe a sound or picture. However, asking them to describe it in relation to another sound or colour will make life easier.

Personal bias

As part of any diagnosis process, it is important to map your own cultural bias. All people have schema, or maps, that drive both the thoughts they have and the actions they take. In understanding this, you must try to calibrate your own cultural schema. You do this by calibrating your schematic view against a range of alternative views. For example, you might ask yourself the question: When are organizations most effective? When financial control is: (1) held at the most senior level; (2) devolved to the lowest level.

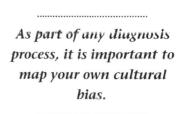

As part of any diagnosis process, it is important to map your own cultural bias.

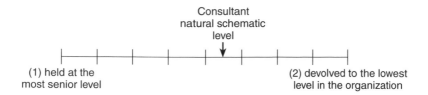

Fig. 7.7   **Personal bias indicator**

Once your cultural bias has been mapped (Fig. 7.7), then you can take it into account when developing the client's map. For example, if you naturally orientated towards the individualistic style of control then some organizations might appear to be excessively autocratic and vice versa. This can never be calibrated in a truly scientific way as it is built upon a subjective precept. However, if you have a clear view of your schematic map, then it can help to temper how your opinions are formed about the client organization.

Cultural diversity

In any change, the level of cultural diversity within an organization will be significant. What seems natural to a white Anglo-Saxon male might appear as rude to an Asian female; what might appear to be a natural action for a Japanese businessman might feel uncomfortable to an American. Cultural diversity is an everyday issue as cultural differences are found in coffee rooms around the world. Whereas culture was once broken simply into blue- or white-collar, now no two cultures will be the same since all organizations are made up from a complex mix of people from different backgrounds. This can emerge as a significant problem when companies try to effect large-scale change. Consider the following example of problems associated with a global merger:

> *A potentially damaging clash of cultures is brewing among executives at the newly merged oil giant BP Amoco just a month after the deal was approved. British executives fear their new US counterparts do not share their concern about corporate expenses, according to a senior source at the conglomerate. Attention has focused on the retention of a corporate jet by the American chairman, the costs of last month's board meeting in London, and the use of Concorde by US executives. There is increasing irritation at every level in the company and a feeling that this is totally inconsistent with the culture of BP.*
> (Cracknell, 1999)

Cultural diversity can cause major problems within a company that has an inherent and embedded dislike for change and variety. However, an organization that welcomes the richness of diversity can build on this variety to enhance its ability to sell and operate in diverse global markets.

Your challenge is first of all to understand the make-up of the cultural mix within the client organization and second to manage the engagement within this bias. In trying to understand these issues, there are two main areas to consider, the 'intra' and 'inter' cultural factors.

An intra-cultural mix is where an organization is constructed using people from different geographical, religious or ethnic backgrounds. As this internal mix changes so the overt and covert rules that drive and underpin the organization are constantly being challenged, sometimes in horrific ways. Consider the case of the US oil company that set up a drilling operation on an island in the Pacific using local labour. Within a week all the foremen were found lined up on the floor with their throats cut. It turned out that hiring younger people as foremen to supervise older workers was not acceptable in a society where age indicated status (*Economist*, 1984). The absorption of people from different cultural backgrounds is fraught with problems and you must be alert to two things: the mix ratio and the extent to which the diversity is openly accepted. If the mix ratio is one where there is a predominance of one cultural group and the others are in the minority then there are issues held in check by the majority group. This leads to the second point, the extent to which the diversity of cultural drivers is discussible within the business. Is it OK to talk about the different cultural beliefs and ideas or are they repressed by the dominant cultural force? Unless you are able to map and manage the intra-cultural dynamics, there is a risk that they will be wasting both your and your client's time and money.

The inter-cultural mix is considered at the point of inter-connection between the business units. This may be at the level of a long-term international relationship, the development of a joint venture or teams within the same company operating from different continents. When two culturally diverse groups meet and work together, the shear difference in values, beliefs and accepted work practices can cause chaos and in some cases result in the cancellation of a multimillion pound contract. Consider the case of the American firm that purchased a textile machinery company in the UK as a bridgehead into Europe. The American management team was unhappy with the idea that tea breaks in the UK could take up to half an hour as each worker brewed his or her own tea. To cut down the waste time, the American team installed a tea machine. As a result, the local workers boycotted the company and it finally went out of business (Stessin, 1979). This highlights the problem of one group attempting to work with another. Although the ideal approach is always focused on a collaborative model, often the relationship becomes embedded in competitive game playing as each side tries to assert its own cultural schema over the other.

The inter and intra cultural mix and degree of openness must be mapped before attempting any type of change. If the idea that all change involves people is accepted and all people are critically influenced by their cultural upbringing then clearly, the 'total' cultural source of the target audience must be understood in relation to the desired outcome and the delivery process. So in using the cultural model outlined above it might make sense to undertake the same diagnostic process but using the cultural groups as the comparitor. The first step will be to identify the major cultural groups that make up the organization. This might be by gender, religion, race, etc. Once understood, each of these groups is mapped against the six cultural factors (artefacts, beliefs, control, discourse, flow and generative). The result will start to indicate what cultural disruption might occur as a result of the change and where any barriers might surface.

Only the foolish consultant ignores the impact of culture. Just consider the spate of corporate mergers that go through trauma or indeed fail simply because their different cultures are deemed to be incompatible; the way that an entrenched culture will resist any form of action by people from outside the organization; and the significant differences that exist between profit and not-for-profit sectors. As the consultant managing any type of change, you must ensure that you take sufficient time and space to understand your client's culture.

> **Back pocket question**
>
> Do I understand the deep cultural factors that might affect the engagement?

System construction

Whether you are trying to implement a culture change programme, build a new marketing strategy, or implement a financial management system, you must be able to develop a real feel for the system under consideration. You must be able to predict with a fair degree of accuracy how the system will react to changes. Will it take the hedgehog approach and curl up into a ball at the first sign of danger? or does it become like a Labrador dog and actively welcome strangers?

In the same way that an architect will diagnose and map the stresses and strains that hold a building together before knocking down a wall. You must be intimately aware of the corresponding factors that bind an organization and allow it to be effective. Taking this analogy, you might consider the client organization in terms of its structure: what holds it together?; where are the stresses in the system?; and what prevents it from collapsing at the first sign of subsidence? In using this analogy, it can help to ask questions around the following areas:

- **Stress:** the extent to which the organization feels pressured by external forces.
- **Strain:** the tension that exists within the organization, pulling people between different choices.
- **Strength:** the capacity of the organization to resist external force.
- **Surface tension:** the ability of the organization's skin to prevent intruders from entering.
- **Stretch:** how far the organization can expand when an external force is applied.

By understanding and mapping these factors, you will gain better clarity and start to develop a feel for the way that the organization might respond when the change is made.

Stress

Stress is a measure of how hard the atoms within a material are being pushed together as a result of external forces. The stress at any given point is the force in a given direction divided by the area over which the force acts.

(Gordon, 1978)

With a little effort you will be able to see how external forces can create stress for a person, team or organization. The individual being pressured by an excessive workload; the team that feels pressured by an unremitting manager; or the company that has to operate in a shrinking market. Alternatively, working with an organization that doesn't feel stressed can also be quite apparent. The simple fact that equipment is readily available; first class travel is accepted as standard; or that there is time and space in which to be creative, all indicate that time or money is not in short supply.

Neither situation is advocated as good or bad. It is simply that internal pressure of any type will affect your ability to manage change. Imagine trying to implement a new empowerment model in a company that has recently introduced a cost-reduction programme. The stress caused by this type of action will have a significant impact on the engagement, perhaps so much so that you might decide to withdraw until the issue has been removed from the system. Alternatively, consider a stress-free company operating is an expanding market. Senior management recognizes that their fortunes are likely to change in the near future so they employ you to deliver a new productivity programme. What chance of success will you have in convincing people of the need to cut costs and focus on raising quality?

In clarifying the system construction, you must develop the capability to instinctively tune into stress points. A builder adding an extension to a house will walk the job and test out different stress points in the infrastructure before taking any action. The builder needs to separate the supporting walls from those that can be modified without disrupting the stability of the building. In the same way, you must be able to walk the job and determine the areas that are highly stressed. Once understood, then you can decide how best to ensure that problems don't occur as a result of the change. Unless you develop the capability to calibrate stress levels, then there is a chance that your project will trigger problems that disrupt any benefit associated with the change.

Strain

Strain indicates how 'hard' and far the atoms at any point are being pulled apart – that is, by what proportion the bonds between the atoms are being stretched. It is measured at a particular point in the cross section of a piece of material.

Strain differs from stress because it looks at the extent to which people are being pulled in different directions. So whereas stress might be having to deal with too much work, strain might be the problem associated with managing a home and work life. Unless the level and location of the strain is fully appreciated, any change will potentially exacerbate the tension that people are experiencing.

Within an organization, strain can be seen in a number of ways:

- The tension that surfaces as people are pressured to follow top-level procedures while being compelled by line manager to deliver increased customer service by breaking the rules.

- The anxiety that emerges from internal company politics as people are forced to choose between two different powerbrokers.

- The frustration that people can feel when asked to attend a workshop when they believe that it is better to stay at their post to deal with their in-tray.

The issue of strain is important because it helps determine how far you can push your client's organization before it becomes damaged. This might be at a senior level where the general manager is forced to adopt new business principles or methods that he or she believes are inappropriate. Alternatively, it might be at a line level, where the cleaner is unhappy with the imposed reduction in time he or she can spend in certain areas. Any action that pulls people away from their normal work pattern will cause some form of strain, your role is to understand the risks associated with this pull.

When a change proposition is offered to a client, you need to ask two questions:

- How hard am I pushing the client or consumer with this change proposition? Will it be too much for the system to sustain and will it spring back on my departure?

- How far am I pulling them from their natural operating position and will it take them too far from the natural point of equilibrium and cause them to lose balance?

You must recognize that pushing people into a change strategy that is not appropriate will result in tears or reversion at a later date. Your role is to understand this and be able to diagnose what type of change is appropriate for the system.

Strength

The strength of any structure is measured in terms of the burden that will break the structure. This is known as the breaking load.

Some people can give up cigarettes easily while others fight a frustrating battle for years. This internal capability might be likened to their personal strength or power to combat problems. This level of strength can be seen in organizations. Some companies have the potency to shrug off misfortune or overcome market downturn by reinventing themselves. Others seem to lose the will to live the moment they have a crisis.

Unless you are convinced that your client organization has the necessary stamina to see change through to its conclusion, then problems will occur at some stage. It might start with a flurry of flags and banging drums, but unless they have the willpower to see it through then both you and your client will be left with egg on your face.

It is important to recognize that strength is both a positive and negative factor. The positive side is an organization's ability to deal with and resolve problems that might cause other businesses to stumble and fall. The negative is the business's ability to shrug off change processes. Clearly, some major programmes might fail because the organization does not have the strength to maintain momentum. However, they might also fail because the inherent power within the organization's culture has the ability to resist external invaders. Simply diagnosing strength is not sufficient. You must be able to determine if the strength will be used to aid or oppose any change you are trying to deliver.

Ultimately, you must make a decision as to where the strength lies. More importantly you need to determine if it will be an amplifying or attenuating force. If an amplifying one, then effort should be made to map the dominant areas and use this energy to enhance the change. If the strength is deemed to be lacking or an attenuating one, then urgent action must be taken to raise the profile of the problem and make the client aware of the possible consequences of the situation.

Surface tension

Surface tension: creating a force to resist external energy requires energy to be drained from inside the structure.

Surface tension, too, is both positive and negative. On the positive side, it is shown by an organization's ability to fight hostile take-overs or resist external agents. Just consider the flurry of activity that takes place once a company realizes that it is a target for possible acquisition and break-up. With the barbarians at the gates, it is amazing how quickly a management team becomes energized. Old mission and visions are dusted off; the five-year profit forecasts look increasingly rosy and the PR agent actively campaigns to sell the idea that a break-up would not be in anyone's best interest. All of the energy and time that has previously been focused on internal issues is used to build a response to the alien invasion. The extent to which the organization can muster and co-ordinate such resources often determines the level of surface tension they can create. This in turn determines their ability to ward off the corporate raiders.

One example of this was the BTR bid for Pilkington Glass. When a bid for £1.2bn was made, few gave the glassmaker much of a chance of escaping. Though Pilkington had gone public in the 1970s, it retained the dull air of a family concern. But Pilkington mounted one of the most extraordinary defences ever seen. In addition to working institutional shareholders with a blockbusting profit forecast, it gathered local support from staff, company pensioners and councillors. Raising fear about job losses, Pilkington even had trade union leaders demanding that BTR be stopped. The campaign worked brilliantly. BTE decided to withdraw its offer rather than overpay for the pleasure of taking on so much political pain (Randall, 1999).

The downside is the ability to resist new ideas as they surface in the market. An organization is often able to build such a thick skin that it is unaware of significant changes. Companies have often disappeared because they were unable to adapt to a changing environment. In the same way that musicians, actors and authors need to be aware of changing trends and fashion, so company directors and product managers need to stay tuned to the changing business market. In the current climate where product life cycle is shortening all the time, the development of a thick corporate skin can be disastrous.

Clearly if you are about to start work with a client, then surface tension will be key. If you are able to break through the outer membrane, there is a chance that the change will be delivered. However, if the surface tension is such that you are unable to break through then there is less chance that the transformation will be accepted. As a consultant you can see this in your first presentation to the board – do they welcome you and value what you present, or is there a tacitly held view that consultants are parasites and offer little value?

Two issues will affect your ability to break the skin – the level of trust with the client and consumer and your ability to manage the marketing process. Trust is significant because it oils the hinges that open the door to the client. In cases where the surface tension is solid, there it little chance that you will penetrate the corporate skin unless people believe you are truthful, responsive, uniform, safe and trained. Second, unless you are able to position yourself and your services in an attractive way then the surface tension will doggedly resist any advances that you might attempt to make.

The first step is to determine the extent to which the surface tension will inhibit the change. Once understood, you need to create a strategy to help break through the membrane. In factoring this into the Clarify stage, it is useful to align the level of surface tension with the strength within the system. If you are faced with a high-strength system with impenetrable surface structure then change will face significant problems.

Stretch

Stretch is the extent to which something can stretch and contract in relation to its length and so store energy without causing permanent damage. This is seen in ropes, masts and trees, any structure that is capable of being flexed elastically.

This aspect is used to consider the extent to which you can encourage an individual or organization to move beyond their natural state of equilibrium. You might decide to offer ideas and suggestion that take the company into more exciting and emergent markets, thus adopting a potentially high-risk change strategy. Alternatively, you might feel that the organization is at heart conservative and hence would not be able to take on the associated problems that emerge with a radical strategic shift.

You must calibrate the extent to which the individual, team or organization is able and willing to stretch. The effective consultant will start this calibration from the very first contact with the client by talking about past change actions or problems that emerged in previous transformation projects. In doing this you are gathering both tacit and explicit knowledge about your client's ability and desire to change.

You must be wary of the gap between perceived and actual stretch. Imagine you have been engaged to introduce a statistical quality management process in a large manufacturing organization. The managing director is bullish about the company's ability to adopt the changes. As such he encourages you to set demanding targets so that the change is implemented in record time. However, the MD is relatively new to the company and does not understand the cultural barriers that exist to this type of change. If the end consumer is unwilling to accept the quality project, it might turn out that you are pilloried for failing to deliver the change and in some cases forced to suffer financially.

So in any case where stretch is being tested, you would be wise to undertake a simple triangulation exercise. Calibrate the capacity of both the client and the consumer to stretch and adapt to the proposed transformation process. You can do this by analyzing the system to be changed and mapping it against the structural factors. For the example shown in Table 7.5, the analysis indicates that the organization is in a highly stressed state owing to an impending cost-reduction and downsizing programme. As a result, the implementation of a new computer system might face problems. The combined problems of cost reduction, suspicion of a new reporting package and people's general unwillingness to help external agents means that real obstacles can occur.

Table 7.5 Structural analysis

Structure factor	Organization	Change impact
Stress	The atmosphere is one of relatively high stress as the business is operating in an increasingly competitive market, and pressure is on to reduce costs across the business	Financial pressures within the business might cause the change to face problems. Unless the system is eased in within existing budgetary constraints it might face problems
Strain	Internal politics form a major part of the company's operating system	It will be imperative to undertake a detailed stakeholder and power broker analysis – otherwise political blockages might occur
Strength	People are willing to make quite large personal sacrifices to ensure that products and services get delivered on time	If the change is positioned as a political and business imperative, then there is greater chance that people will support the change
Surface Tension	The organization has proved adaptable at resisting the recent influx of management fads. They seem content to ignore changing trends and work on their own ideas	The trick will be to sell the change as an internal transformation rather than an external imposition
Stretch	There is evidence that they are not able to stretch with any great ease. They can operate in their own confines, but outside of this, problems occur	The system should be eased in at such a pace that it does not overload the current processes

Change proposition: Implement a new MIS financial reporting package to produce a set of monthly statistics on profitability by product line.

Using this analogy, the solution is to add a restraining process that will remove some of the stress. Like the architect who uses steel beams to support a ceiling when a wall is being removed, you will need to import support forces to reduce the organizational stress. This could involve ensuring that senior managers are on hand to support and coach people through the process or offering to pay people overtime where longer hours need to be worked.

A team or organization is like a house built with playing cards. They are often fragile structures that can be toppled over with relative ease when the right leverage point is touched. The consultant's role is twofold: first, identify the areas that are able to accept and embrace the change; second, avoid those areas of the system that are structurally unsound. There is always a risk that an inappropriate change could inadvertently topple the organization by pulling out the card holding up the rest of the deck. This approach to clarifying the change situation is a simple but effective way to understand where maximum leverage is placed while ensuring that inadvertent damage is not done.

Even more, it is a powerful tool to help the client and consumers to diagnose their readiness for change. Put the client in with a group of consumers and ask them to agree where they fit against the five structural factors. Although they might reach a general accord about the factors, any disagreement will offer valuable information on potential problems. For example, the client might believe that the organization offers little resistance to change programmes and there is little chance of surface tension causing a problem. However, the consumer might offer evidence of previous local initiatives that have failed because people were not willing to change. The simple fact that you offer the two groups a shared language and metal mindset will allow issues to surface that might have remained hidden until the critical point.

> **Back pocket question**
>
> Do I have a clear understanding of the structural make up of the system and how it is likely to react to any changes that are made to its construction?

Stakeholders

Stakeholders have power to influence, enhance or curtail an engagement. They can operate in both an overt and covert manner, often driven by their personal values and goals as opposed to those of the organization. Like beauty, stakeholders are viewed from a subjective rather than objective position. They are only viewed as stakeholders if perceived as having power over the perceiver.

When attempting to clarify the issues that surround any problem, it can help to develop a map that indicates who can influence the outcome of the change and to what extent they might wish to wield their power. Consider the consulting firm about to undertake a critical piece of work with a multinational client.

Although the client might have set out the basic structure of the organization, indicating the key figures involved in the project, the consultant will need to take this a step further and understand who the real power brokers are and to what extent they can amplify or attenuate the flow of the project.

It can pay to map the organization's key stakeholders against the criteria used in the change ladder (see Chapter 5). It then becomes possible to use the five attributes of the change ladder to build a deeper understanding of each stakeholder group and how it might affect any proposed change. By constructing a simple matrix, the consultant can quickly understand which of the key stakeholders need to be influenced.

Table 7.6   Stakeholder chart

	Stake 1 (Key person)	Stake 2 (Loose cannon)	Stake 3 (Little interest)	Stake 4 (Desperate Dan)
Asset	High	High	High	Low
Blueprint	High	High	High	Low
Capability	High	Low	Med	Low
Desire	High	High	Low	High
Existence	High	Low	Low	Low

For each of the four stakeholders listed in the matrix, it is possible to infer what effect they might have on your project. The benefit in producing the profiles is that it makes it easy to quickly share the impact of the stakeholders with other members of the change team.

- **Stakeholder 1** *(key person)*: A critical player. Has both the power and ability to affect the change dramatically. The question is, which way will they choose to exert their influence? Will they act as the powerful benefactor, bestowing their grace and favour on the project and so help speed it to a successful conclusion? Alternatively, have they yet to be convinced about the need for change and so will they be a powerful force to oppose it? The golden rule in this situation is to get to the person as quickly as possible. Make time to meet the individual, understand their orientation and what action needs to be taken to ensure they will support the change.

- **Stakeholder 2 (*loose cannon*):** Such people are a real problem. They hold all the aces in the deck but don't understand how to use them. They manage the assets used in the engagement, the procedures and have a real desire to be involved. The problem is that they don't have the appropriate knowledge and they don't have a real appreciation of the need for the transformation. As such, you might need to make a rapid and effective change to ensure they don't inadvertently derail the process by taking inappropriate action.

- **Stakeholder 3 (*little interest*):** This person is on the fringe. Although they have the ability to affect the change, their interests lie elsewhere and they have no desire to get involved. While in some cases this is useful, the downside is that they can turn into a loose cannon if they choose to get involved later. Like a time bomb, the stakeholder might decide the day before implementation to disagree with the change and withdraw assets from the transformation. Your approach with this person might be classed as softly-softly. A low-key relationship must be formed and maintained over the life of the change, such that you will have the ability to sniff out if the stakeholder is being energized and in what direction their energy will be directed.

- **Stakeholder 4 (*Desperate Dan*):** The stakeholder has a high desire to get involved in the engagement but little capability, power or understanding of the need for change. Depending on how they are used, this person is a liability or an asset. In the way that a willing person is worth ten pressed people, it might make sense to use them simply because of their energy and desire to help. However, if their association becomes too high profile it is possible for the stakeholder to make inappropriate statements that are associated with the project. In this case, you need to make a decision whether their involvement in the project adds real value or could end up taking more time and trouble.

This methodology takes what is a very complicated and emotional process and turns it into a simple but practical diagnostic model. The value comes not from the map but the dialogue you go through with the client in developing the shared model. It helps to dispel many of the unspoken concerns about the stakeholder group and allows the client and consultancy team to operate on a common platform.

> **Back pocket question**
>
> Do I have a clear map that indicates who can influence the outcome of the change and to what extent they have the capability and desire to wield their power?

Life-cycle risk

The fact that consultants have been invited into a change process suggests that risk is an issue. The nature of any change is built on the premise that the future can be envisioned and delivered. The reality is that this is impossible to guarantee. As such, you need to always be aware of the trade-off between the risks being taken and the associated reward.

Fig. 7.8   Trade-off between risk and reward

Any risk/reward balance will fit onto one the four quadrants shown in Fig. 7.8. The first is the commodity quadrant, where the service being delivered is of little risk and any corresponding reward simply reflects the accepted market rate. There is no premium and little opportunity to maximize income. This is akin to the delivery of a training programme or undertaking some desk research on a company's market position. Although this is seen as a low-value area, the benefit is that the effective consultant can use this as a launch pad to sell products and services that sit in the high-reward quadrants.

Next is the safe option, where the company is happy to pay a premium over the standard rate because of their confidence in your competencies. It might be that a relationship has built up over time or that you have a particular niche expertise or that you have a trusting relationship with the client.

The last quadrant is headed as gamble simply because if you choose to take a high-risk contract for a low fee there is a chance that you will not achieve a payback. This scenario is often found with consultants who have just started. As new entrants, they need to gain income streams and market share fast and one way to achieve this is by taking the jobs that other companies won't and in some cases for less money. Although this is a good way to enter a new market, it is dangerous to operate this quadrant for long as eventually the odds will stack up against the consultant.

Wherever you sit in the matrix, there will be two key questions to ask: what chance is there that something will go wrong?; and how can I ensure that unseen problems are managed? This breaks the risk element into two areas – risk assessment and risk management. The scientist who developed the Saturn 5 rocket that launched the first Apollo mission to the moon highlighted these succinctly:

> *You want a valve that doesn't leak and you try everything possible to develop one. But the real world provides you with a leaky vale. You have to determine how much leaking you can tolerate.*

(Anon, 1996)

Your job in an assignment is to determine the extent to which the project might fail and to do everything in your power to ensure that it doesn't.

Risk assessment

Although the issue of total risk is considered at the outset in the construction of the contract, risk in the Clarify stage is more about assessing the dynamics that will have to be managed.

Risk is not a cold probability calculated at the outset. It is a continuous process of qualitative and quantitative analysis of what could happen and what should happen during the project. The key with risk management is often not to try and stop problems from happening; rather it is about determining what problems can be tolerated without damaging the process.

Consider a project where the consultant has been asked to manage a large corporate project. Fig. 7.9 shows that the consultant has thought through the key issues that might affect the change. The reality is that halfway through the process there is an unexpected change of CEO and this results in significant

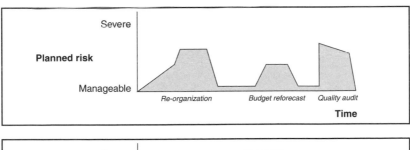

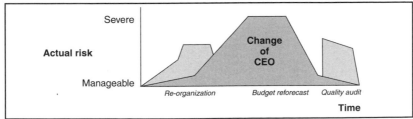

Fig. 7.9   Risk assessment

changes. Replacing the CEO is outside the consultant's control and all he or she can do is ensure that any fall-out from the change is minimized. No matter how much you plan, it is impossible to anticipate all the risk factors. However, you can develop a state of mind that assumes that problems will happen and so be more prepared when they do.

One of the factors that will indicate the degree of potential uncertainty is the extent to which the organization is viewed as risk-averse or risk-seeking. A former will avoid taking actions that have a potential for failure and will tend to take the safe option. The risk-seeking culture values both the rewards that come with risk and possibly the excitement associated with the gamble.

However, there is another factor in the equation that has as much impact on the success of the change – to what extent is the consultant risk-averse or risk-seeking? While the nature of the job might suggest that the consultant will have a risk-seeking nature, this clearly is not the case. Many people turn to the consulting profession as a way to develop a set of latent skills, a way to survive following redundancy or as a hook into a new market sector. This stresses the importance of risk assessment within the consultancy cycle, to understand the risk drivers for the client and consultant and what impact this might have on the relationship.

In clarifying the situation, you need to consider a number of key factors:

- The nature of the organization: to what extent does it adopt a risk-averse style of management?

- The nature of the consultant's engagement: to what extent do you feel that it is regarded as a high-risk venture?

- The personal biases of the consultant: are you risk-averse or risk-seeking?

If these three factors are in alignment then the assumed risk is minimal. However, if there is a degree of misalignment, then issues might start to surface as the project moves forward. The classic problem is a risk-averse consultant implementing a high-risk project in a risk-averse company.

However, once the variables are understood, steps can be taken to minimize the impact of uncertainty. This is risk management, or managing the uncertainty that can affect a successful outcome of the project. Since all projects will have unknown factors, at best the consultant can reduce their impact. At worst, the high-risk factors might cause failure. Good risk management can help to take the luck out of bad luck and build on the random opportunism of good luck.

Risk management

Risk is managed by using a set of tools to manage the issues that surface in the assessment phase. Although which you use will depend upon the context and content of the change, there are three simple tools:

- **Pilot:** For any proposed analytical or change process, it is wise to test the deliverables and variables in a controlled environment, using the process with a small team before rolling it out.

- **Risk list:** In considering the proposed change, you should attempt to agree with the client and consumer the potential risks over the life of the project. The risk list is categorized against a range of variables including probability, impact, owner, etc. Once the risk list is defined then a series of contingency plans are developed for each of the options.

- **Contingency response:** When faced with a potential problem, the best option is to build a planned response to take away the element of surprise. There is a range of generic responses for each of the perceived risk factors:

  - Do nothing: simply ignore the risk in the hope that it will disappear because of other factors.

  - Deeper diagnosis: gather further information on the issue in the anticipation that greater clarity will lead to risk reduction.

  - Alternative strategy: is the risk sufficiently large that an alternative approach is warranted, one that bypasses the problem and does not attempt to tackle it?

  - Ignore and plough through: is the change momentum such that there is a belief that any obstacle will be beaten?

  - Hedging: in some cases it is possible to build a basket of diverse responses so at least one of them will minimize or eliminate the problem.

  - Specific response actions: it might be that a response is built around all of the above, with the development of a highly complex response pattern to what is a highly complex problem.

At this stage in the cycle you will have a real feel for the setting and symptoms to be addressed and the potential risks that will be faced in dealing with them. Managing risk is difficult and more of an art than a science. You will never be able to predict with any accuracy what will happen, but you can ensure that all of the pegs are in the ground to ensure that when unplanned issues occur you will be able to reduce their impact.

Back pocket question

Have I determined the extent to which known and unknown factors within the change process will have an impact on its potential for success?

Feedback

The final part of the clarification stage is to identify how the client and organization wish to be informed of progress. A consultant can often perform miracles, but unless the client is aware of the success there is every chance that the change will fail because of diminished senior management support. Additionally, unless you stay close to the client's team there is a possibility that operational changes will be initiated that have a detrimental effect on your project.

Four things need to be agreed to ensure that the feedback process will be effective: timing, detail, issue management and ownership. If these are defined at the outset of the relationship, then there is little chance that communication will break down. If you don't agree the overall process and structure of the feedback link at the outset then there is every chance that the change will end up out of sync with the needs of the client and consumer.

The timing of feedback depends on a range of factors, but most important is the client's interaction rate. Consider the director who runs a team of ten managers. She might well be responsible for a spread of processes ranging from product design right through to product delivery. The diversity of activities under her command means that at most she will allocate a day or two to each area over the period of a month. Consequently, the time allocated to interact with the consultant is likely to be limited (unless the project is mission-critical). As such, the consultant will probably be able to touch base with the client at most once a month to up-date her on progress and highlight future plans. The alternative example is the director from a financial institution who is responsible for regulatory affairs. In such a highly specialized job, he might have a team of people and can allocate more time to the consultant. Neither option is better, it is simply a case of trying to fit in with the client's needs and work patterns.

As mentioned earlier in the Orientation section, some clients will prefer to look at the big picture, only worrying about what is happening to the total programme. Others will want feedback that offers information on the smallest detail, individual or project task. Although you might have guessed their orientation in the early Client stage of the relationship, at this point you should attempt to derive a clear agreement as to the level of detail the client wants to receive.

Issue management is simple to deal with. At the end of the day, the client either wants to be in the loop, dealing with issues as they arise, or to stay out of the loop, only dealing with problems by exception. Your objective is to agree the trigger point. Do they want to be advised if people don't become engaged; software doesn't work; or when the project is about to hit a major blockage? No one option is correct; it simply depends upon the client's needs.

Finally, it is important for the client to appreciate that the issue of feedback is not a one-way option. Both you and the client are responsible for ensuring a two-way flow. Your responsiblity is to be honest with the client about formal progress and your personal concerns. The client's responsibility is to keep you informed of all the operational issues that might affect your areas of concern.

There is no single model for agreeing the feedback mechanism as personal choice and context drive it. Hence it is important that you specifically ask the client how often they want feedback, what level of detail is required, whom you should go through if the client is unavailable and how problem escalation should be managed.

The following list offers a range of actions to be used during an engagement:

- Breakpoint presentation: proving an update only when a critical milestone is reached.

- Monthly RAG reports (Red for problems, Amber for potential issues and Green for things going well)

- Daily voice-mail or e-mail updates, possibly to act as more of an emotional comfort as opposed to adding any real value to the client management process.

- Board updates. On the upside, these can ensure continued visibility of the project, but on the downside can simply feed the political system's insatiable desire for current data rather than any real desire to understand progress issues.

- Covert client reviews to allow the client to understand and possibly influence progress of the process in the background.

This leads to the final question, what circle of security should be applied to the feedback process? Within any feedback, there is a circle of people exposed to the ongoing flow of information. At the core of the circle will be the followers, those people who the client trusts. This continuum continues out to the opposite extreme, to those people who must never be exposed to the content or process information. Woe-betide the consultant who fails to respect this delicate balance and discloses information to someone outside the trust circle. As part of any discussion about the feedback process, you must get explicit information about who is allowed what information and when.

> ### Back pocket question
> Have I clarified how the client and organization wish to be informed of progress, both in terms of the content and process?

Chapter 8

Stage three: Create

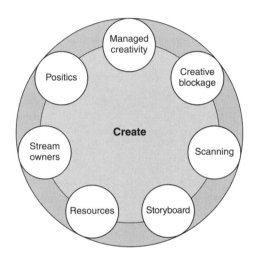

Imagination is intelligence having fun

Anon.

At this stage of the project cycle your aim is to develop a unique and specific solution that will deliver the most appropriate remedy for your client's problem. This part of the process is among the most exciting but also the most frustrating. Like a musician composing a song, an author writing a book or a child building a brick house, your actions will be based on the idea that something new is created out of something else. Here are some examples of what can happen if you fail to manage this process:

- An industrial process engineer has been employed to manage the re-design of a production line. However, he relies on in-house engineers to design the new process and the proposal fails to ignite interest with the board because it lacks any real breakthrough ideas.

- A team facilitator is helping create a new confectionery product. However, the team fails to develop any new ideas because rumours about an impending take-over sap motivation.

- A marketing consultant's assignment is to develop a set of strategic plans but he fails to get them agreed by the board. His inability to gain any close allies on the board means that the plans are presented but do not make any headway because of the lack of political support.

- A strategy consultant has been asked to present a model that will help a company break into overseas markets. But he fails to gain the contract because he has used analytical models that are culturally-focused on the Anglo-American market and do not take into account the different ideas that drive Asian markets.

- An IT project has been designed down to the final detail but then collapses as critical people are dragged away on other corporate imperatives.

- An efficiency expert who develops a unique time-saving process for an organization is unable to make progress below board level because he is cannot find the right people to own and manage the different elements of the process.

- A quality consultant attempts to implement new control procedures but decides to reduce costs by adapting the system from an earlier project. As a result the implementation fails because the project is viewed as inappropriate.

You can avoid these problems by ensuring that a clear line of sight exists between the problem statement outlined in the contract, the diagnostic process and the final solution offered to the client. The issue is how to maintain rigorous continuity while developing solutions that are innovative and free thinking.

The process offered in this stage of the model follows this pattern:

- **Managed creativity:** Use the CREATE model to originate and develop potential solutions for the core issue identified in the Clarify stage.

- **Creative blockage:** Ensure that the blockages to creativity are understood and 'managed out' of the process.

- **Scanning:** To what extent can solutions be found in the work that others have done?

- **Storyboard:** Breathe life into the potential solutions and start to validate their potential to deal with the issue. Shrink to one single action plan.

- **Resources:** Map the resources to the potential solutions to ensure that they are viable.

- **Stream owners:** Identify owners for the consultancy solution and test that they have the capability and desire to own them.

- **Positics:** Ensure the proposed options do not create political problems for the client or consumer.

The whole process should come together to offer a diverse, imaginative but practical action plan. The history of science is full of inventions and ideas that emerged from creative thinking and were managed into working tools. It is also awash with ideas that failed to gain acceptance. The objective at this stage is to ensure that the solutions are not just created but also marketed to the client and consumer. Unless both sides of the equation are carefully managed, the change can easily fail at this stage.

Managed creativity

The development of a competitive advantage in the market place often hinges on creativity and invention – doing what others haven't yet done. Virgin's approach to air travel, Sony's mass marketing of the Walkman, and Trevor Baylis's invention of the clockwork radio are all examples of people using creativity and innovation to break the existing market mould. In most cases, this type of ground-breaking innovation enters market areas that others thought unworkable or unprofitable.

How can you introduce this type of managed innovation into the Create stage of change? How can you help people to escape the attitudes and mind-sets where they currently take the simple, safe and stagnant approach to change?

In many cases, the only reason you will be working with the client is because of the creative value that you bring.

In many cases, the only reason you will be working with the client is because of the creative value that you bring. If all you can offer is a slight variation on the previous offerings then your contribution will at best be marginal. However, by introducing more radical elements of wisdom and creativity, you might be able to help the client deliver a solution that breaks the current management paradigm. Your goal is to help the client move from a world that they know and shift them into the area of unpredictability and uncertainty (Fig. 8.1).

We all have our own mental models of the world and frameworks that we believe to be true. A teenage daughter wants to stay out late at night; her parents want to set a curfew. Each has a set of experiences, beliefs and views as to what is safe, practical and appropriate. But both parties are operating from the world they know and are not prepared to consider other options. Even more, they are not prepared to sit down and think about solutions that neither of them has ever considered before. If you were asked to help resolve this issue, one of the ways that a collaborative solution might be found is by forcing them to move into the 'I don't know what I don't know' area and to generate new solutions to their impasse. This same approach can be taken when working with a client or consumer that has to find a solution to a seemingly intractable problem.

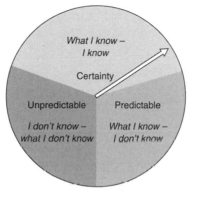

Common sense is the collection of prejudices acquired by the age of eighteen.
– Albert Einstein

What I know – I know

Certainty

The world we have made as a result of the level of thinking we have done thus far creates problems we cannot solve at the same level of thinking at which we created them.
Albert Einstein

Unpredictable

I don't know – what I don't know

Predictable

What I know – I don't know

To raise new questions, new possibilities, to regard old problems from a new angle requires creative imagination and marks real advantages.
– Albert Einstein

Fig. 8.1   Create spectrum

However, simply finding a radical solution to a problem is not enough. Anyone can create hundreds of ways to make their first million, but few manage to turn these pipe-dreams into reality. You might be able to help your client to create new solutions to problems, but ultimately you must also help them to develop ideas that are practical. From this, you can help them to make the final decision on which ideas should go forward for implementation. The bottom line is that innovation is about 'managed creativity', taking the initial ideas and working through a process whereby the change is actually delivered and does not stay inside people's heads or on their lists of things 'to do'.

Thomas Edison, one of the most prolific inventors of the past century, demonstrated the ability to 'manage' the creative process. He credited his success to the fact that he did not wait to be struck by an idea but found the solution through aggressive and careful investigation. He would often decide what he wanted to invent before knowing if it was possible. He would then work on ways to develop the product that he envisaged (Birch and Clegg, 1996). His process of invention was characterized by repeated trial and error and experiment after experiment until these studies led to those flashes of insight known as inspiration. From this comes his well-known comment that genius is 99 per cent perspiration and 1 per cent inspiration (Wren and Greenwood, 1998). The perspiration comes from the process of actively managing the process and not just sitting in a dream-world waiting for good ideas to implement themselves.

Many people might find the combination of the words 'managed' and 'creativity' alien or uncomfortable. They might think 'managed' implies a degree of control and planning while 'creative' signals the need for an intuitive and unbounded framework. However, this is not an either/or situation. To achieve true commercial creativity, both arms must be used in partnership. This means delivering a style of working that I describe as 'loose-tight' in format. Clearly, employing wildly creative people might be fun, but unless they deliver ideas in a working format then it might prove to be fruitless. Conversely, you might know of a consultant who is highly skilled in managing change but who doesn't take time to try to be creative in the way they work. The trick is to create something new and also ensure that it will add value to the client and consumer.

Two essential ingredients fuel the ability to create innovative solutions. The first is the ability to open your mind and remove inhibitions and blockages that prevent the generation of new solutions. By doing this you will be able to create a rich pool of innovative ideas that can be used as a well-spring for the next stage. The second stage is to consider the pool of ideas and filter out those that do not add real value.

Think about the last time your partner asked you to get a bottle of wine. In the space of a few seconds you will go through a complex decision-making process to choose the wine. However, this is something we do intuitively and without any realization of the strategies we use. So, what steps do people actually follow?

The first stage is to have a clear understanding of the challenge: namely to find a wine that matches the meal. The second stage is to look for a store that holds the widest selection of wine. Once the pool of potential wines is identified, you might start to read the labels to explore which wine will be most suitable. Once the options are understood, you move from an exploratory process to a decision-making approach. You might look at each of the labels in more detail and appraise them for suitability with the meal. As you go through this process, you will be testing each bottle against a set of criteria that probably includes cost, quality and reputation. Finally, you will prioritize and evaluate the options to make a final choice. This process might take an hour or it might be over in the blink of an eye. However long, the goal is to follow a journey that takes you first down the divergent path of thinking, closely followed by a style of thinking that is convergent in nature (Fig. 8.2).

The divergent stage of the journey will be driven by three attributes:

- The ability to *challenge* the status quo and break through the mentality that strives for the average level of mediocrity that often drives the creative process.

- Once the desire is in place to reach out for new ideas by *randomizing* potential solutions, a deliberate process to generate a rich tapestry of options.

- Finally, *explore* each of the ideas and see which ones start to offer some real change options.

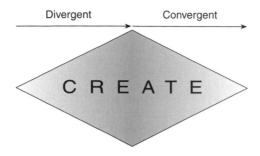

Fig. 8.2 A thinking process

The underlying theme at this stage is to avoid any form of judgement or criticism. It can often be easier to adopt a critiquing role rather than take the position of someone who is being asked to bring forth new ideas. It is essential that you do not allow creative laziness to come into play whereby a judgemental hat is worn as soon as the ideas start to roll. However, once the divergent or dream-like stage has helped to bring out a range of potential ideas, the next stage is to shift into a convergent style of thinking, where the creator can take a more critical role.

The convergent process is used to bring you from a dream state into that of critic or judge of the ideas generated. This process will typically draw upon three styles of thought:

- *Appraise* each one and filter out those that clearly do not help resolve the original issue.

- *Test* the remaining ideas, often by filtering them through a criteria sieve to identify which of them can deliver a valued output.

- Finally, each of the remaining options is *evaluated* against the core requirement to ensure that the end solution deals with the problem.

Although the six stages of the create model are offered in a linear format, this can be difficult to manage, especially when working with a team. There might also be questions as to the extent to which such a linear process can destroy the opportunity to free-form or grab wild ideas that occur in the latter stage of the process.

Finally, you might argue that by using such a methodology there is a chance that people will be put off by its formality. Although all of these arguments are valid, my core proposition is that commercial and practical creativity must be managed and cannot be left to chance. As such it can help to use a process that is simple, logical and easily understood by all. The create model, outlined in more detail below, isn't the only way to manage the generative cycle but its application will help to ensure that ideas are originated and deployed in a practical way.

Challenge

The first stage of the divergent process is to ensure that you are mentally prepared to challenge the status quo. Norms exist in all forms of life: the conventions a family follows at dinner; the way pop songs are written; or the cultural norms that drive how an organization takes decisions. These norms are often so entrenched that people are unaware of their existence. So, when any solution is being addressed it is important to understand the norms that underpin the context and in what way you are prepared to challenge this status quo. All change propositions will have a solution boundary, an implied or explicit limit that sets out how far the consultant, the consumer and the client wish to stretch or puncture this norm. It is important that this is understood from the outset so that time is not wasted and people do not feel let down when the final proposition is rejected.

Wherever possible, try to put a clear objective for the creative challenge in writing. Develop a clear and succinct statement that sets out what you hope to achieve at the end of the Create stage of the change project. This statement will indicate the problem (as defined in the Client or Clarify stage) and the type of solution. By type, I mean that it can help all the people involved in the process to understand the amount of stretch required. It might be a category one solution, where the final resolution will not challenge any of the existing and accepted conventions; a category two solution, where the boundary is stretched but not to the extent that rules have to be re-written: or a category three solution, where the final proposition must break all existing boundaries and set new standards for the industry.

The danger is that without this type of initial focus, the Create process will start to address ideas that are off-centre and have little to do with the client's goal. Examples of this can be found in the US patent office – a diaper for parakeets, an alarm clock that squirts sleepers in the face, a machine that imprints dimples on the face (Mickalko, 1991). Although there is a wild chance that a need will occur for these items at some time, there is a better chance that the inventor has patented an idea that will not generate a great deal of interest.

Randomize

If we are going to originate new ways of thinking, it is important to step outside the box – to take on board new and chaotic ways of viewing the world. The enforced randomization of potential solutions can help to push the boundaries back and also take on a new perspective. Leonardo da Vinci believed that to gain knowledge about the form of a problem you had to look at it from different perspectives. He felt that by simply sticking to the first view, you would be left with a limited impression of what the object is and what it might be. He would restructure his problem by looking at it from one perspective, then move to another and then another. With each move his understanding would deepen and he would begin to understand the essence of the problem (Michalko, 1998).

However, helping people to step outside their normal frame of reference is difficult, as they need to let go of their comfortable thinking styles and practices. One way to achieve this is to use different techniques that force the mind to operate in areas of uncertainty:

- *Randomize:* Take an encyclopedia or dictionary and pick random words. Use these to stimulate new ideas and actions associated with the engagement. Don't try to force anything, just let the back-of-the-mind thoughts trickle through to help originate new ways of working.

- *Connections:* Consider the change process and then link it with another idea. Ask yourself or your team to imagine how the change process might operate like a Chinese restaurant or how they might use the local library as a training location.

- *Opposites:* If you think of many of the new ideas that surface, they are actually the opposite of what is traditionally being used: the shift from fixed phones to mobile phones; private rather than public investment in the transport infrastructure; or disposable rather than long-lasting razors.

- *Explode:* Take one idea and then grow it, like an expanding balloon – see where it goes when self-imposed limits are taken away.

- *Reframe:* Take the issue being addressed in the engagement and reframe from a problem to a golden opportunity. Imagine that what is being offered is actually the solution required and then work through how such an opportunity is used. Alternatively, take the issue and turn it into a negative. If the problem is how to improve morale in the office, reframe the statement into how to make morale worse. See what ideas this type of re-orientation produces.

- *Why, why:* Take one of the issues or options and repeatedly ask why. Force people to dig deeper and deeper into the problem so that new and more divergent solutions are created. This can also be used in a revolutionary mode to encourage a business to break its own rules, especially if they can't remember why those particular rules where instituted in the first place.

- *Reminiscing:* Encourage people to use 'this reminds me of . . .' statements in relation to aspects of the change process. This uses the power of recall to stimulate people to make links with other experiences.

In trying to originate new ideas, the danger is that both you and the client group will sit in a certainty box, offering ideas that don't step outside the comfort domain (Fig. 8.3). However, as you both start to learn from each other's experience, so it becomes easier to shift into the unpredictable area, offering up new and innovative ideas.

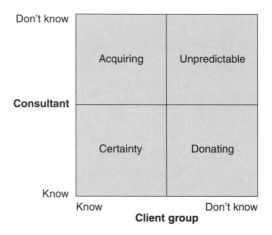

Fig. 8.3 Shared learning

New ideas will emerge as people draw upon the ability to network and inter-act with others. There are times when something exciting happens between two people that would not have happened to an isolated individual. It is very rare that one could explicitly point to an idea that one person solely originated with-out help (known or unknown) from another human being. The development of new ideas will be a buoyant process where one person's thoughts will trigger an idea in another, which in turn leads to a prototype by someone else. So often in a creative process, it is this social construction of ideas that adds the most value.

Explore

Once the wild and random ideas are generated, it is important to play with them and start to flesh out how they might be used. This means that each of the ideas is toyed with in the same way that a baby experiments with a new toy. Question the purpose of the object, see how it might be used and find out what practical value it holds. Try to put some flesh on each of the ideas that emerges from the random stage and really understand how they might be applied in a practical way. While the randomization stage is 90 per cent idea and thought based, the exploring stage is 90 per cent hard effort – actually taking the wild ideas and really trying to understand how they might contribute to the problem at hand. You can achieve this by asking the following types of questions:

- How would it work?
- Can it be used in any other way?
- What happens if it is used with another option?

- How would it be organized?
- What resources would it need?
- Where are the synergies?

The exploring stage is the final element in the divergent process. From this point onwards the goal is to close down the number of ideas. Hence it is important to ensure that all of the ideas are really pushed to their limits to understand what value they might add.

Appraise

Building on the toy metaphor, when a child is faced with a floor full of toys it will naturally start to appraise which of them it will take out to the garden to use with its friends. In the Create model, the appraisal stage is used to make the transition from divergent to convergent thought patterns and so start the closure phase. Your aim at this point is to filter out those ideas that do not add value or are less effective than others offered in the generative stage. Although this stage will often be intuitive rather than explicit, you must ensure that intuitive disposal is not used as an excuse to get rid of those ideas that are too risky or step outside of the normal mode of operation.

The basic process is to take all the ideas that have been generated as part of the randomization and exploring stages and subject them to a first pass of rejection. Using both intuitive and explicit knowledge and experience, take a first pass at all the ideas to weed out those that seem totally unpractical. One way to do this is to write all of the ideas on paper and spread them over a wall or floor. Ask people to go through the list and mark those that they totally reject, are not sure about, and really favour as having potential. Do this individually, without any discussion between the team. In a short space of time you will have broken the ideas into three separate groups. It is then possible to discard those that have been rejected by all the team, set aside those that offer a possibility and focus on the ones that all team members believe might add value. It is important to point out that those ideas in the possibility pile should not be pushed aside in favour of those that have full backing from the team. At some point it is important to test these ideas. But where time is of the essence, this quick appraisal process can highlight the ideas to be focused on initially.

Test

Once the appraisal process is complete, then you will need to be more explicit and rigorous in selecting the ideas that will be used. This is the final gate that the ideas must cross to ensure they offer effective solutions. Although this might be undertaken in many ways, one of the more effective approaches is to use a criteria-based selection model. At the very outset of the exercise, you can determine the criteria that any final solution must meet to ensure that an effective outcome is achieved. This criteria set might be a series of hard financial measures, a group or cultural factors or a stakeholder agreement list. Whatever the format, it is a clear indication of the factors that will ensure that any proposal will be accepted.

Evaluate

Finally, once the number of potential solution is down to a short list of two or three; they can be evaluated against the core challenge set out at the start of the process. de Bono (1992) suggests that the process of evaluation is logical and judgemental and is not directly part of the creativity stage. He suggests that evaluation can be based along four lines: is the idea feasible?; what benefits will it offer?; what resources are required?; and does it fit the need of the end client? When any idea is being evaluated, it can fall into a range of camps:

- Directly usable now;
- Good idea but not for us or not for now;
- Needs more work to bring it into a usable form;
- Has value but cannot be used because of regulatory, environmental or other reasons;
- Interesting but unusable; keep around for future investigation;
- Weak value when really put to the test;
- Unworkable because it has fundamental impossibilities that prevent it from being delivered.

The essential point at this stage is to ensure that emotion does not creep into the decision process. Although emotions are critical throughout the creation process, at this stage they become dangerous. If people are allowed to push their personal fads or projects then the creative rigour of this model can be compromised.

One of the most important objectives in any consulting engagement is the drive to create a solution that is both innovative and practical.

One of the most important objectives in any consulting engagement is the drive to create a solution that is both innovative and practical. It is essential to ensure that the full creative processes are stimulated but with the caveat that any idea can be delivered within the given constraints. To achieve this delicate balance it is important to ensure the managed creativity rather than freewheeling creativity is adopted.

Back pocket question

To what extent have I ensured that solutions will be innovative and original?

Creative blockage

Anyone can be creative. It is no different to breathing, eating or drinking in that it is something we do all the time without thinking. People are creative in the way they paint a house, choose a meal in a restaurant or select presents at Christmas. The problem is that when they are placed in a situation where they feel they have to be creative, blocks come into play. These creative blocks are generally self-imposed barriers that can be broken down. The trick is to recognize the blocks and then understand what strategies can be used to overcome them.

There are too many reasons why blocks occur to summarize here. However, it can help to consider creative blockage using the change ladder introduced in the Client section. In simple terms, the act of being creative is one that requires the individual or team to think of something new, essentially to change how they view the world. It can help to focus on the idea of factors that drive personal change rather than creative blocks. When this view is adopted, then it can help to use the change ladder as a framework to understand the creative blocks and how they might be managed.

For each stage on the change ladder, the following blocks can be identified:

- **Asset:** One of the more common reasons why it can be difficult to develop a creative atmosphere is the environment in which the process is taking place. Although it is possible to originate new ideas in a damp basement, the middle of a field or on top of a mountain, in a business context it can help to have the basic tools. These include plenty of floor and wall space to spread the ideas out, electrical equipment that works and has spare parts in the event of a failure, compatible computer software. It is these seemingly small factors that can lead to irritation and frustration that lose time and block the creative juices. Alternatively, the importance of the work place asset is now high on the agenda for many companies. The rise in the use of in-house coffee bars as places where people can foster accidental creativity through chance meetings is now common. A more radical agenda is offered by companies that use assets in a radical way to drive up the sense of creativity. This includes meetings rooms with waist-high tables and no chairs to limit the time that people spend in the room; the replacement of personal desks with hot desk or mobile work stations; or the use of wireless computer networks to facilitate a greater flow of knowledge over the company intranet. There is clearly no right way that assets can be deployed to enhance the creative process but the first step is to understand just how important they can be.

- **Blueprint:** Teams can suffer creative blockage because each individual has a preference in the way that the creative process is managed. Just consider how many brainstorming sessions you have been to where people start to argue the 'rules' of brainstorming. Where this happens, they are not arguing the need for creativity, they just need to develop a common mental model about the rules. In other cases, the way the people frame their world will affect the creative process they prefer. The person who is outgoing, data-oriented and heavily into planning might prefer to develop ideas on the run with a team. The natural introvert might choose to develop their ideas in isolation and then present them for comment. Bringing these two types together can cause problems. If the preferred creativity blueprints become incompatible then people might clash over the process rather than the content of the session.

- **Capability:** An individual may have all the necessary desire and need to be creative but has simply not been trained to follow a process. There are a host of different creativity models that will help people to follow a creative pattern or process. One blockage in the team sense can be when certain members suggest that a specific tool that other members have never used before. Do the people that know how to use the framework teach their peers and lose valuable time or do they lose the opportunity to use the technique? There is no right answer but it is important that teams are aware of the potential blockage before they enter the creativity stage.

- **Desire:** Asking a person or team to 'be creative' is like asking someone to cheer up when they have just lost a winning lottery ticket. Since the early stage of the creative framework is driven by the need to be open and divergent, this is the moment where emotions and feelings need to have their head. But if a person is not in the mood to be creative, it can be hard to suddenly turn on the tap. One way to deal with this is by using the force of the low emotional ebb as a trigger for new ideas. Use the antipathy as a frame to consider potential solutions. Another barrier at the desire level is the unwillingness to break with the status quo. When things are flowing in a certain direction and everything feels quite comfortable, it takes a brave person to say let's stop what we are doing and do it differently.

- **Existence:** An individual's inability to think creatively is often linked to self-limiting beliefs. People are often placed in situations where they have the opportunity to create new ideas but feel unable to do so because of a sense of inadequacy. You may, for example, create action groups consisting of members from different levels as part of a quality drive. However, after many years of being told that their ideas and thoughts are not as important as those of senior managers, the clerical and field staff can withdraw and offer only simple suggestions that they believe won't make them look silly. The other block at this level is where people have a rigid belief. Consider a managing director of a financial software house who attributes lack of market growth to a looming recession. He believes that the company's future lies in targeting small but high-value customer who will pay for unique software solutions. However, the software developers feel that the company is overly exposed to one segment of the market and that they should be able to hedge their bets by operating across a range of sectors. The large gap in these perceptions of the company's direction will act as an initial block to any creativity.

Trying to offer blanket solution for each of these problems would be naïve. Creative blockage is a complex and difficult thing to overcome and cannot be fixed by dispensing a creativity pill. You can invite someone to a brainstorming session but you cannot make him or her come up with new ideas. Any fix must be done inside out, by first understanding what the blockage is, how the individual or team feel about the blockage and what action they are prepared to take to overcome or eliminate it.

> **Back pocket question**
> Have all the potential creative blocks been cleared away?

Scanning

Sometimes it can be difficult or impractical to come up with totally new ideas. You might need to look outside your normal surroundings and scan the market. Although this can be done in a variety of ways, there are a number of common approaches. These are built around two key variables. First is the breadth of the search: is the search based within the same industry or does it move into a totally different area? The second variable is the balance between a passive and active search. For the passive, systems are put in place and then left to react to ideas as they surface. Alternatively, you can search in a proactive way. The relationship between these two produces the following activities which can generate a matrix (Fig. 8.4):

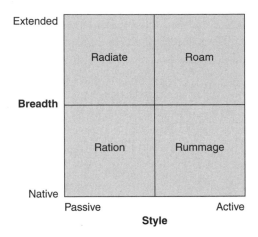

Fig. 8.4   Consultancy scanning model

- **Ration:** There is only limited interest in searching. This is seen in only a passing desire to subscribe to journals, join committees or scan the Internet.

- **Radiate:** Ideas from other areas are of interest but little positive action is taken to pick up on them. Benchmarking is one example of a positive process for identifying new ideas, although the extent to which other people's ideas are actually adopted will indicate whether a reactive or proactive stance is being taken.

- **Rummage:** The creative team will take the time to interact closely with new people but the search is still limited to the local area. New ideas are forthcoming but they are likely to be in use already.

- **Roam:** A positive decision has been taken to look aggressively for inspiration beyond the local area and to actively look for ideas from counterparts in other industries and across more diverse fields.

It is important to keep a balance. The danger is that people can be lazy and might try to simply transplant what other people have implemented. It is this approach that is seen in the way that companies blandly climbed on the total quality, reengineering and downsizing bandwagons.

A crucial part of the scanning process is to develop the ability to recognize ideas that occur naturally. Stories abound of the various inventions that have emerged from the process of serendipity, such as Goodyear's accidental discovery of the vulcanization process for rubber or Fleming's accidental discovery of penicillin. All of these originated because someone (apparently) happened to be in the right place at the right time and was observant enough to notice something out of the ordinary. However, simply being around when an accident happens is not enough to bring about new ideas and discoveries. It is important that the development team is in a state of constant preparedness and able to recognize the difference between an accident and when fate offers the chance to create something new. A discovery based on serendipity is the fruit of a seed sown by chance in fertile ground (Chambers, 1991).

The idea of 'fertile ground' is an engaging one. How can a consultant create the fertile ground to allow for surprises or serendipity? The list is probably endless but the importance rests in helping individuals to be in a state of readiness. An eagerness to challenge, desire to learn, a spread of relationships and the ability to reframe all contribute directly to creating fertile ground. It is also important to draw upon the unspoken ideas and thoughts that are held at a tacit level. Tacit knowledge is described as the thoughts, feelings, dreams and intuition that go on in the background while people are performing a task or as the natural acts that people perform without consciously thinking.

In one study, 82 of the 93 winners of the Nobel Peace prize over a 16-year period agreed that intuition played an important part in creative and scientific discoveries (Cooper and Sawaf, 1997). It is just this soft and intuitive part that can help to develop consultancy processes that break the mould. Human emotion rather than any logical cause–effect analysis drives intuition. It is the ability of the individual to have a hunch that something might work, even though everyone else says it will fail. I am not suggesting we try to systematize an inherently soft factor, but I am making the point that people can choose to influence their ability to take intuitive decisions.

However, intuition does not preclude the notion of rationality. Although intuitive insights can appear not to make sense and might seem to be the opposite of a rational response, when brought together they form a more powerful tool. Einstein never discovered anything solely with his rational mind – the principle of relativity came about after he imagined himself travelling on a beam of light. This intuitive idea, coupled with his brilliance as a physicist, allowed him to develop a scientific theory that helped change the world's view of itself.

Once the power of unspoken knowledge is extracted, the tap is turned on from the pool of known explicit knowledge – the clear, known and unambiguous experiences that people bring to work. For example, product managers do not live that role for every hour of the day. They might also be parents who experience products on a personal as well as a professional level. This is just a simple example of the life experiences that an individual will bring to the workplace. The question is, to what extent can the consultancy team draw upon this fountain of knowledge and skills? If you are serious about creating new and innovative ways in which to assist your client, you need to offer freedom for the members of the consultancy team to present their whole self to the change process. You must value the rich diversity that resides within the workforce.

Back pocket question

Have I scanned the market to find out what other people have done to resolve the issue?

Storyboard

You will need to put wild ideas and concepts into a harder context. This can be achieved through the use of storyboards. The storyboard is effectively a sequential model of both text and pictures that describes the journey a change might take. The team will take the ideas generated and use them to construct a number of potential story lines. The idea is to allow people to piggyback and bounce off each other and from this instigate a range of optional stories and patterns. Typically, each story line will follow the pattern used by most good books or films, with a compelling start, engaging middle and a strong ending. Each of the stories offers a potential solution to an issue.

Imagine a team trying to resolve a poor morale problem in a large insurance company. As part of their group session they might identify three different story lines. Each storyboard offers a different approach that might resolve the situation:

- *Story line 1*: Undertake a cultural audit to determine the key drivers for the problem; Map issues and share with selected focus groups to confirm target areas; Create action teams from the focus group members to own and manage the problem; Provide expert support to the teams; Central project management team to oversee and report back to board on resolution of issues.

- *Story line 2*: Run a series of large team meetings and allow people to voice concerns; Allocate project leaders to each issue; Project leaders to report back on progress at regular group meetings, possibly monthly; Publish progress in house magazines.

- *Story line 3*: Invite unions to a meeting to consider problems; Identify what they believe the issues are; Set up union/management teams to resolve issues; If this proves to be successful, consider setting up a joint team to deal with all future staff issues.

Within each of these three story lines, the basic start and end are similar but the content is quite different. However, by building the story lines using words and pictures, the team can quickly understand the total picture and options. In the same way that it only takes a few seconds to draw the essence of a story from the front page of a newspaper, your team can rapidly assimilate and communicate a large amount of data.

This ability to communicate ideas and patterns quickly will allow the team to modify and rebuild the story line in a matter of minutes. As a result the teams are quickly able to test which of the three story lines will be most effective. It also means that the team can readily test the risks associated with each option by pushing each of the story lines through a range of different scenarios. Finally, if the team wishes to involve others in the decision-making process, it becomes quite easy to share the stories.

This approach can also be useful when you start to design the transformation process. Whereas many change programmes use a hard approach (substantial objectives, plans and structures) to build the change plan, in using this approach, you will use a softer style (holistic, loose relationships and metaphors). One of the primary problems with the hard approach is the tendency to mentally lock into the first design that emerges, thus restricting any real opportunity to search for innovative and interesting solutions. With the storyboard approach, the options are framed in such a way that the first plan is not necessarily the final one. The use of pictures framed in a loose structure means that once a story has been placed on the wall, it can be cut and pasted in seconds to create a totally different change model.

Although this approach feels simplistic, it can help develop a complex and detailed framework. Behind each panel in the storyboard there are a series of sub-panels that underpin the ideas and these can in turn hold a greater level of detail. Using this system, quite complex and detailed propositions are framed in such a way that all players can readily understand them.

The use of a narrative style can also help people to make emotional as well as logical sense of the change. Like a cartoon film, powerful messages are delivered in a short time with little embellishment. A good story can bring together diverse elements and help people to make sense of a complicated message. Whereas many project plans can be quite adversarial and impersonal, the storyboard aims to be engaging and inclusive. The idea is to use it as a way to help a group of people design, develop and disseminate a simple story.

Some might view this approach as fuzzy, lacking in rigour and overly driven by intuitive frameworks. However, storyboard modelling is as rigorous as any harder approach because it still includes logical and linear relationships found in formal development systems. It just presents them in a more palatable way. Rather than developing the change plan using dates and numbers on a Gantt chart, the creation process uses pictures, shapes and colours on a storyboard.

At this stage, the team should be able to work through the various options and agree on one single story line that will form the backbone of the consultancy process.

Now, with the final proposition in place, you can start to understand the implications of the decision and test its viability. In particular, understand what resources will be required, who will own the work activities and what specific actions need to be undertaken.

> **Back pocket question**
>
> Have I ensured that the final solution will fit together in a cohesive way?

Resources

There is clearly a big difference between the design and the delivery of a solution. In general, the initial design element is theoretical and idealized in nature, where people work on the basis of what they would like to happen. At this stage, managers are still in the euphoria stage and will possibly offer total commitment and promise to deliver the necessary people, plant and finances. You are the saviour who has arrived on the white charger to rescue them from a dastardly problem. However, partway through the transformation, the promised resources either start to disappear or, worse still, never actually materializes. Like the pull of gravity from a black hole, the energy and resource starts to be sucked off to deal with other pressing issues – 'resource shrinkage'. As a result you are left to deliver the contracted change without the necessary resources.

Although resources are often agreed at a senior level, they will generally be deployed at a lower level. You might have a 'formal' sanction to use a resource but trying to gather and hold it can be difficult. As such, the final delivery of a project is based more upon your ability to bargain for and leverage resources than making a sales pitch to the client. In a perfect world your engagement would be the primary initiative for the whole company and support would be ensured. The reality is that organizations are a boiling pot of ambitions, politics and changing priorities. As such, your initiative will only have a limited honeymoon period, after which you will have to get inside the system to fight for resources.

Successful resource management depends on your ability to negotiate in an internal market. To ensure that the resource stays allocated to the engagement you will have to develop a range of tactical and strategic actions. These include:

- **Amass:** Like the farmer who stores supplies for the winter or the mechanic that keeps a secret stock of parts that he will need when the local suppliers have run out, a consultant often needs to amass a pool of local talent and resources to be drawn upon when sparse times surface. These people will generally be friends who have offered to help or people with a real interest in your proposition.

- **Borrow:** Often, when resources become difficult to hold, you might need to resort to a process of surreptitiously borrowing. The difficulty comes in defining the boundary between borrowing and stealing. It is important that you operate within the spirit and letter of the contract but always seeking to deliver the agreed outcome. If active borrowing outside the agreement of the contract is necessary, then you must ensure that the dominant stakeholder is aware of the situation and is willing to underwrite the action.

- **Complement:** Often, it is difficult to obtain the exact skills to deliver a specific outcome. Trying to find an IT specialist who has experience within the travel industry might prove difficult. However, by adopting a fusion mentality it is possible to generate the necessary resources. Is it possible to identify an IT expert who can work with a travel specialist to create a collaborative partnership?

- **Demarcate:** When you agree the initial contract, it is important to delineate the general broad resources required to deliver the outcome from the core resources that are mission-critical. If this is a core group of people, they must be ring-fenced to prevent anyone from trying to pull them from the project. Where possible, this ring-fenced group must be included as part of the contractual arrangement with the client.

- **Economic:** At the end of the day, the appropriation of human capability within an organization is based upon an economic model. People are traded in the same way as equipment, office space and IT software. As such, you must understand the barter value of the individuals within the project and where necessary trade to ensure that they remain locked into the process. For example, one trade-off might be that you could hold on to a programmer if you are prepared to be responsible for their travel and training costs.

- **Favours:** In Tom Wolfe's book *Bonfire of the Vanities* there is a suggestion that 'everything in the criminal justice system in New York operates on favours. Everybody does a favour for everybody else. Every chance they get, they make deposits in the Favour Bank.' This same principle can be applied to the appropriation and management of resource. People are loaned across functions, teams and geographic areas. Therefore, it can pay the consultant to maintain a log of individuals who are in debit and credit with regard to resource sharing. Although this is an option that might only be used as a last resort, it can help to resolve issues that seem insurmountable.

Resource management will always be complex, because the nature of your relationship with your client is grounded in a collaborative, but competitive framework. Although you have been invited in to help resolve a problem, to the consumer you are probably just a temporary member of the team so they will be loath to offer you access to their scare resources. As such, you must master the ability to acquire, manage, retain and deploy people with all the expertise and guile of a general in battle. However, the moment you actually view the acquisition of resources as a war rather than a collaborative effort, then the battle is lost. You will always be playing against local managers on their home turf and as such they will have the dominant position. It is far better to work at a desire level within the change ladder. Convince them of the need for change and the benefits they will gain from helping you. Then you will be able to resource a team that has the capability and desire to help.

> **Back pocket question**
>
> Have I mapped the resource to the potential solutions to ensure that the option is viable?

Stream owners

Once the plan has been developed, in most cases it will be broken down into work packages or action streams. However, at this stage it will be difficult to decide who should own the various work streams because much of the detail will be uncertain. For example, in a product development project one stream might deal with changes in the engineering department and another will deliver improved bottom-line results for the marketing manager. It is therefore open to debate as to who should be held accountable for delivery of a stream. Do the logical owners accept responsibility for the change? Should it be a shared responsibility? Or do they both attempt to absolve themselves on the pretext that they don't have time or interest in the change? Although as a backstop you might be able to own some of the streams, unless the home players accept some responsibility then it becomes harder to effect a logical hand-over of responsibility at a later date.

You should aim to move to a position where both the design of the change stream and the owner are clearly understood. As the ownership of the stream becomes clear, this will lead to a deeper understanding of the design issues. However, as these become clearer so the issue of ownership comes into question, as seen in Fig. 8.5. The end result is that you might need to allow time and space for people to accept ownership of a work stream. If you can sit back and let the ball bounce around, when it finally settles there will be a greater chance that it has fallen into the right home. If you try to force the issue and end up allocating the work stream to an owner, there is a greater chance that game playing will emerge later.

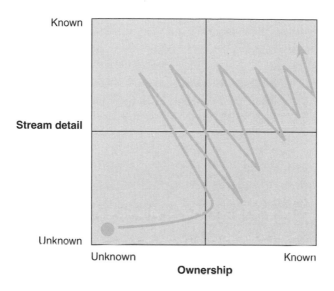

Fig. 8.5 Ownership of streams should become clearer

Imagine a project designed to reengineer a manufacturing process. At the outset, ownership of the work stream might be allocated to a director on the main board. Once he or she looks more closely at the issue, they might decide to pass it to the engineering director. This person does some work on clarifying the issues that drive the change and then passes it to the technical design team since they control the necessary levers to effect the change. Finally, once they have mapped out the change levers, it might end up with the plant manager to oversee the implementation.

These ownership transfers are legitimate and make sense in isolation – the problem is that with each transfer energy is diffused and lost. Like a raindrop rolling down a window, as it falls lower it gets smaller and loses energy. Whereas at the outset the goal was to reengineer the whole manufacturing process, it might end up that local changes are made to the flow mechanism – possibly things that the plant manager had planned to do anyway. The end result is the delivery of a safe change, one favoured by all stakeholders.

Ensure that authority is firmly tied to accountability. Like the bungee jumper who dives off the bridge parapet, always know that the elastic is anchored.

To avoid this dilution, you must ensure that authority is firmly tied to accountability. Like the bungee jumper who dives off the bridge parapet, always know that the elastic is anchored. The same applies here, no matter how far the natural owner chooses to devolve authority, they must still hold on to the accountability. Without this anchor, the stream can lose energy, direction and focus, resulting in only partial delivery of the goals. If circumstances dictate the initial owner must let go, then the recipient must be made aware of the fact that they are being handed both aspects and will be measured accordingly on the end result.

Back pocket questions

Have I found clear owners for the solution? Do they have the capability and desire to own them?

Positics

One of the biggest problems for any change is the frustration caused by internal politics. Often you might be frustrated at the inability to move forward and your client irritated by your failure. However, anyone who suggests they can or should try to eliminate politics is naïve. Political action forms the lifeblood of any group. But it is possible to redirect some of the selfish energy and turn the negative aspects into worthy ones, i.e. 'positics', the positive application of politics.

If you want to understand the political orientation of an organization, look at its normal behaviour and ask two questions: whose interests are being promoted?; and how visible is the action? By considering these two issues, it might be possible to determine the organization's political style. Response to the first question will indicate if behaviours are focused around self-interest or shared interests. The second question will indicate if actions take place in the hidden or shadow areas or are out in the open. The result is that the target audience will potentially sit in one of the four quadrants offered in Fig. 8.6. The result is that an individual's, team's or organization's natural orientation can fall into the politics, patronage, promotion or positics quadrant.

Organizations that sit in the politics quadrant can be recognized by the way that people jockey for position to advance their own interests and make their own claim on the organization's resources (Kanter *et al.*, 1992). This behaviour is driven by self-need and often takes place behind closed doors, deep in the shadow world. The end result is game playing, conflict and significant levels of mistrust. This is a style of behaviour that can limit the performance of an organization and inhibit the progress of a project. Although political action is by its very nature hidden and intangible, it is possible to determine the level of political activity. Just look around the business and see how it is built. Are there barons controlling empires, are there pay rates that seem out of alignment with market rates and do the cultural norms of one group dominate the organization?

Fig. 8.6   Positics framework

One quick and dirty way to assess the political balance within an organization is to use the change ladder as a comparative framework. Take each of the five layers in the model (asset, blueprint, capability, desire and existence) and compare who holds dominance in each of the functional disciplines. As seen in Fig. 8.7, you might ask who controls the business assets and whether they also own the blueprint that drives how they are used. From where does the soul or existence of the organization emanate? Does it align with the ideas of other groups? To what extent do one group's desires align with company goals and objectives? Any mismatches in these areas do not necessarily mean that political action will be taken, but it certainly provides the climate for such action.

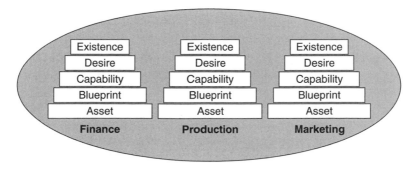

Fig. 8.7   Cultural comparison

The patronage quadrant of Fig. 8.6 offers a slightly different set of behaviours. This might be seen as a style where people operate from a positive frame but don't want the action to be too public. This is almost a philanthropic or altruistic approach, where action is taken for the good of the group in a private and reserved manner. This style might be found in an organization that is at ease with itself and possibly has a secure position in the market. Look at blue chip companies and this type of behaviour will probably be found in pockets. The optimist might suggest that this behaviour emerges from the natural soul of humans and is a style to which all people aspire. The cynic might suggest that it is a sign of a lazy organization and one that is due to lose market position or be taken over in the near future. Your concern will be to understand how you can use this supportive tendency to assist change. Can you find background benefactors who will support the change or people who are willing to offer their time to help others through the transition?

The promotion quadrant is quite different. Here people are driven by self-interest but are quite open and public about it. The classic example is the sports or music promoter who campaigns for his client on the basis that he will take a commission on any income. Interestingly, the way that people view this type of person will depend on their need for the services he provides. In a war, black-marketeers are vilified as selfish wide boys out for their own interests, but also seen as meeting the needs of people who want food and petrol. You must tread a careful line with these people. Clearly you might need to enlist their support when looking to find scare resource or influence certain people. The downside is that your association with such people might taint you. If you enlist the help of such a promoter, you should do it with the full knowledge and backing of your client.

The final quadrant, positics, is the one that you should aspire to operate from personally. Behaviour from this area is visible to everyone and is seen to be taken for a shared rather than selfish success. The intent is to still intervene in the political system but to do so in a manner that is both visible and seen to deliver a win–win outcome.

You may, however, face problems when you try to understand and use the political system within your client organization. Although the client and consumer may operate out of the positics model, your change might well be the trigger that pushes them back into the politics quadrant. You must be sensitive to the alignment between all five levels on the change ladder. If you are trying to change one of the levels, consider the political implications and how it might cause problems for the whole organization, not just your client area.

> **Back pocket question**
>
> Have I considered if it is possible to redirect some of the selfish energy, and turn the negative aspects into worthy ones?

Chapter 9

··

Stage four: Change

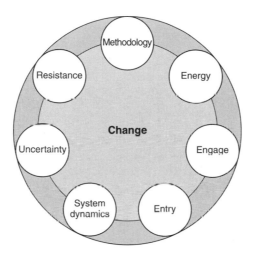

Consider how hard it is to change yourself and you'll understand what little chance you have of trying to change others.

Jacob M. Braude

Change is the fun part of the whole process. This is where the action takes place, careers are made and reputations destroyed. At this stage, as a consultant you might put on your project management hat, pull out the 25-page work structure breakdown and launch into a rambling discussion about milestones, critical paths and percentage completion factors. Clearly, these issues need to be included, but this aspect of the process has been sufficiently well documented elsewhere so it has not been covered in this book.

The focus is on the meta-level factors, the issues that have a subtle but significant impact on the change process. It is these softer factors that can often be pushed to one side. However, only by taking care of the soft issue will the hard deliverables be achieved. The impact of missing these issues is seen in the following examples:

- An engineering company brings in a change consultant to help shift the management style from autocratic to collaborative. The problem is that they try to use their old command and control style to implement the changes. The result is that staff react against the change, suggesting that it is only a fad and that when the next downturn comes the company will revert to the usual style of management. The company cancels the contract with the consultant on the basis that the people are unable or unwilling to accept any reasonable change.

- The IN-Ovation consulting company is employed by a marketing director to introduce a number of new and radical creativity models into the product management teams. However, the daily rate that IN-Ovation charges is twice that of the nearest competitor and the finance director is not happy about such a large expenditure, especially at the end of the financial year. The end result is that the finance director has sufficient energy and power within the company to persuade the CEO to pressure the marketing director to employ a company that operates in a lower price bracket.

- As part of a reengineering project, a consultant is asked to design and manage a workshop for senior managers. The goal is to present the findings of the early research team and get people to support the next wave of changes. But the event is ill-thought-out, people don't understand why they are at the workshop and there is little follow-up action. The result is that when the managers are asked to nominate people to get involved in the next phase, they have little belief in the change process and so hide their best people and offer the low performers. This corrupts the development phase and causes major problems for the consultants in the next wave.

- It was the second progress review with the board and things weren't going too well. At the beginning of the project, the consultant presented a clear, concise and detailed project report. It spelled out the core change streams, who would own them and gave specific milestones. The problem was that following a reorganization in the IT and accounting departments, several of the stream owners had moved on and the consultant was having problems finding new owners. This resulted in three of the key milestones being delayed, which in turn pushed the final date of the project back. The problem was that the board had been sold on the idea of a highly controlled change process and the slippage after only two months meant that they were beginning to investigate the idea of bringing in a new project manager to bring the engagement back on track.

As Senge *et al.* (1999) suggest, most change initiatives fail. In many cases the supposed failure rate for total quality and reengineering initiatives is around 70 per cent. Kotter's study of a hundred top management-driven corporate transformations concluded that more than half did not survive the initial phase (Kotter, 1999).

The failure to recognize or resolve this problem is often shielded by the cloak of political intrigue or the simple fact that organizations change so fast that the failures are lost in the mists of time. The premise is that effective change is not about increased technical or project management capability, it is more about the need to understand the meta-processes that drive and support change. These are the actions that need to be understood irrespective of the nature of the change or the industry. However, these factors are often viewed as the soft processes, the intangible elements that get left aside once the ball is in the air and the crowd is baying for blood.

My underlying message is that often within an engagement, the soft issues are the hardest. Although the development and management of the project plan, along with the associated task activities is difficult and often labour intensive, it is important to ensure that the more intangible issues are not overlooked as the heat gets turned up. The Change stage of the Seven Cs model includes the following themes:

- **Methodology:** Determine from the outset what methodology will be used to drive the engagement.
- **Energy:** Change is driven by energy; the consultant must have a clear appreciation of where the energy will come from and how it will be dissipated across the different stakeholders.
- **Engage:** How can people be encouraged to be involved in the transformation?
- **Entry:** What is the best level of entry to effect a long lasting change?
- **System dynamics:** How will the system respond to change?
- **Uncertainty:** How is it possible to construct a plan that has the capacity to operate in a dynamic and complex world?
- **Resistance:** Undertake a reality check to see how people will react to the proposed action.

Methodology

In this context, methodology refers to the underlying ethos and approach that will be used to underpin all of the decisions and actions taken by the consulting team and client group.

In recent years, change has become a discipline in its own right. It is now recognized that it is important to pay attention to the underlying dynamics that drive successful business transformation. In particular, understand what choices you have when faced with change issues. Although these choices are many, two factors should be taken into consideration.

- First, to what extent will the programme be planned in advance of the change? Should every detail be strapped down well in advance or can things be left to chance?

- Second, to what extent will receivers of the transition be aware of what is happening? Is it to be conducted in the public domain or will it be hidden from view, where any shift is viewed as happening naturally as opposed to an external change?

In considering these two drivers, it is possible to identify four schools of change management that are commonly seen in industry, namely accidental, backstage, controlled and debate. In looking in more depth at each of these four styles, it becomes possible to develop a simple change management matrix (Fig. 9.1). Each of the four quadrants is seen to have a particular management style that may be applied in different circumstances.

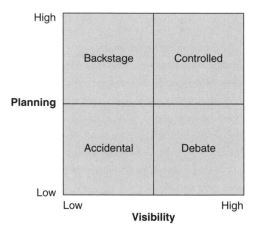

Fig. 9.1   Change matrix

Accidental style

When a group of young children play together, the way they interact, the games they play and the overall behaviour of the group has a chaotic feel. An observer sees the chance of anything productive coming out of the antics as accidental in nature. It is often left to the capability of a single teacher to manage the demands, tantrums and excesses of over 200 apparently wild animals. However, within this zoo-like scenario, there are a number of powerful rules that control how the group operates.

The children are effectively operating as a self-organizing system. Although the head teacher has set out ground rules, within these the children operate as free agents. Examples of these rules are: keep on the hard surface; no swearing or fighting; and everyone must line up for dinner at a certain time. Since the teachers are also aware of these rules, they can initiate a change and within reason guarantee that a desired outcome is achieved.

For example, if a football is left in the playground at the start of break then within minutes a football match will start and will keep the children amused for the duration of the break. Alternatively, just drawing some white lines will trigger specific games associated with the patterns. The children also understand that if the head teacher suddenly walks out into the middle of the area and blows a whistle, they are expected to stop what they are doing and listen for instructions.

Let's assume that organizations can operate in a similar fashion by conforming to a shared set of common rules and norms. As a result, rather than trying to dominate and deliver an outcome, some consultants might choose to spend their time trying to understand the rules that drive an organization. Once understood, they can make engagements that might seem chaotic or random but which will deliver the desired outcome. The engagements are not highly planned and have little visibility – but they still have a clear purpose.

A regional manager within a retail organization might have a level of stock wastage higher than the industry norm. She must reduce it to an acceptable level. Clearly one option is to issue dictates, discipline people or change the formal stock control procedures. Now this might 'apparently' work but the ingrained behaviours are likely to surface once the manager's attention is focused elsewhere.

However, by using the accidental methodology, the manager might attempt to understand what rules or norms drive the wastage to happen and why it is seen to be acceptable by local managers. It might be that at the store level, wastage costs are attributed to a hidden budget line, visible only to the regional manager and the finance department. This rule means that the operational managers are not actually affected by the wastage, so it is not part of their frame of reference. By simply changing the bonus indicators, for example, the regional manager might be able to deliver a radical reduction in wastage. The change will have been managed without any real control or planning and its visibility would have been limited, but the end result is a successful change.

This is clearly a high-risk strategy and is reliant upon the trust of the organization to adopt any changes that are promoted by the management team. The consultant's role in this management style is more about helping to develop a suitable environment for the change to occur rather than formalizing any direct approach.

Backstage style

Millions of people have seen the movie *Titanic*. The boat scenes are amazing, to the point where the audience believes they are actually part of the production. Although star actors play a critical frontstage role, it is often the backstage people that can make or break such a film. Compare the technical prowess of *Titanic* with the out-takes shown on television: doors won't open, walls fall over and props fail to perform. When you think about these two scenarios, the power of the backstage processes is apparent.

The key to managing any backstage process is preparation, preparation and more preparation. Just to generate a simple scene in a film will take hours of pre-production effort. This process is invisible to the audience since they just see a two-second jump off a cliff. The same idea is seen in the way that some transformation programmes are stage managed by consultants. The installation of a new IT system, the shift to a new quality directive or the adoption of a new legal ruling: all of these will be highly managed and planned but will in the main be invisible to the end user until the point of handover.

The process is often concerned with the exercise of power, persuasion and political skills. It involves intervening in political and cultural systems, influencing, negotiating and selling ideas and meaning to the owners and recipients of the change and mobilizing the necessary power to effect the backstage activity (Buchanan and Body, 1992).

Imagine that you are to install a new quality system into a medium-sized manufacturing company. You might choose to operate across a number of backstage areas. The first step is to agree the content of the system with the directors of the company since the structure of any quality system will potentially lock in a set of standards and processes. Next you might need to undertake a degree of negotiation with all the key stakeholders to ensure that the content of the system fits with their map of the world. Last of all, much of the backstage work will be focused on managing people's feelings. The quality system is right for the business, but if people 'feel' upset or concerned about its adoption then the whole change process will be fraught with problems. So, although there will be effort applied in developing the new system, a large chunk of the work will be focused on the backstage issues, the unseen aspects that will never be apparent to the end user.

The backstage model is one that people use intuitively every day. Persuading the child to eat her cabbage; hiding a pill in the dog's food; or flirting with the boss's PA so as to get some time in the diary. The question to consider is the extent to which it is undertaken as a manipulative tool for personal gain. When it is overtly used, you must be careful that you are not seen as using the process in a duplicitous way just to further your personal goals. In working with a client group, there will always be a degree of suspicion about your actions.

When this model is used it is imperative that it is used openly and without any hidden agendas. This doesn't mean that you go round telling everyone what is happening, simply that if people ask about the process being used that you take time to explain it.

Controlled style

This type of change is like the processes used to manage a large construction project such as the Channel Tunnel. The scale and risk mean that everything down to the last nut and bolt must be forecast and controlled to ensure that the change is managed to time, cost and quality.

The control model is based upon a deterministic framework. This means that the consultant makes the assumption that it is possible to predict and control the future according to a set of rules. Plans are made, resources booked and people hired all on the premise that the change will follow a known path. The change is then managed using the exception method, where the goal is to minimize any variance or disturbance in the system. Accidents will be frowned upon, deviation is not allowed and failure to hit a milestone will cause apoplexy.

Where the surrounding issues are managed by the consultant or client then this is clearly effective. However, where you or the client do not control all the levers then it is quite dangerous. In building a rigid plan and locking people into a controlled system, all of the eggs are definitely in one basket and sudden changes in the environment can result in costly and time-consuming last-minute actions.

This methodology is perfect for the delivery of fixed outcomes, particularly where the plan is built using logical cause and effect reasoning. This is why it is used with such success in the construction of missiles, houses and a host of other projects. The crucial aspect is that (barring the weather) it is dependent on your ability to control all the environmental factors.

Debate style

Think about the case of a merger between two large organizations. Project managers, probably using the control methodology outlined above, will wrap up all the mechanistic issues. However, there will be elements of the merger that cannot be managed using a highly planned style. In particular, how will the two cultures come together?

When you try to merge cultures, the desired outcome is reasonably clear but it is very difficult to plan down to the last detail what will happen and when. People are people and have their biases, preferences and particular styles of thinking and behaving. Any action plan will have some critical milestones or tasks but there is likely to be much debate as people struggle to come to terms with new ways of working. Only through a process of sharing and working together will people start to understand what value their new partners will be able to contribute.

The debate style of change is seen in many areas. Think about the traditional way that a senior team will develop vision and values. It often falls to a consultant to organize a workshop. This will be preceded by a meeting with each of the directors to develop an understanding of their beliefs about company values. This initiates the debate process, whereby each person is encouraged to talk about their views on what the company values should be. This offers people the necessary time and space to share their schematic view of the world. As they talk to the consultant, they start to firm up their beliefs so that once they get to the workshop they will have a firmer view of their desired outcome. At the workshop, these personal schemas are displayed, shared and (if all goes well) will merge to become a shared schema, one that is communicated to a wider audience.

Another example is the way strategy can slowly develop within an organization. One view is that the control approach should be used, where logical processes are used to build a corporate strategy. Another view is that strategy emerges from dialogue and debate that goes on between the key players in the business. This might happen in formal meetings but in many cases is the odd comment as people meet in corridors or coffee rooms.

The end result is that the debate model happens all the time but is often not recognized. As a process, it is difficult to recognize because it is so natural and embedded in the content of the change. Trying to understand how a decision was made, or a mission or strategy developed can be quite painful as people struggle to understand how the change took place. However, the benefit is that when the change is used, it is locked in at the desire level in the change ladder. As such it will have a greater degree of passion and permanence.

Four-quadrant model

In bringing these change styles together, the resulting four-quadrant model is seen in Fig. 9.1. In this simple matrix, it is seen that each quadrant aligns four styles: accidental, backstage, control and debate. This suggests that in many cases you might have to take a decision to use one particular style. Should the change be controlled or is it best to take the accidental route? Should the development of the outcome be through open debate or is it more appropriate to push the discussion into the backstage and develop answers that people are mandated to follow?

However, it is possible to offer a holistic framework, a hybrid model that builds on the strengths of each of the four quadrants and yet tries to avoid their weakness. In drawing upon each of the four quadrants, it becomes possible to develop another option, that of the emergent style – a fifth way that sits in the middle of the matrix (Fig. 9.2).

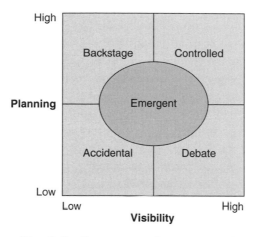

Fig. 9.2   Emergent change matrix

Emergent style

If a group of people decides to travel around the world on a back-packing holiday, which of the four styles would be appropriate? The accidental approach is exciting but could leave them sitting as hostages in a war zone. The backstage model would be ineffective because only the travel agent would know the itinerary. The control model seems to be the most practical but using a deterministic approach in a chaotic world will only lead to frustration and cost increases as they struggle to get back in line with 'the plan'. Finally the debate model is pretty inappropriate since the group might have fun discussing where to go next but the trip will probably take three years longer than expected. The option is to adopt a change process that allows for clearly defined outcomes but with the flexibility to be adaptive.

The emergent model allows an agreed outcome to be delivered through people interacting according to their own sets of behaviour and to create a framework for action without specifying the action to be taken. As consultant, you will set the goals, boundaries and basic operating rules but leave the action and detail up to those directly involved in the engagement. The benefit is the development of a flexible plan that allows people to respond to changes.

This type of approach is often seen in culture development programmes where the end goal may be understood but the deployment process needs to be flexible enough to cope with the needs of different managers. Imagine that you have been asked to deal with a problem of poor morale in a large corporation. You might have agreed a measurable outcome with your client but the actual processes and tools can only be determined once you are inside the system. This is because the needs of the group rather than your client's needs drive the choice of a change tool. For example, if the morale issues are in the open and being discussed at a team meeting then it is useful to rely on peer review and open events between people and their managers. If, however, the issues are buried deep in the culture then focus groups and one-on-one coaching sessions are more appropriate.

In considering the five-segment model, each of the four primary models (accidental, backstage, control and debate) has a clear role to play in managing change. However, emergent style is practised widely but not knowingly. I use the word 'knowingly' quite deliberately. When change is being managed according to one of the four primary styles, any deviation from the preferred approach is viewed as a failure. Hence, the person running a project using the control model might view deviation and variability as a problem. Conversely, someone using the accidental style might forcibly resist any attempt by the organization to impose formal controls or milestones on to the engagement.

The emergent school of change is something that people use all the time – namely in their diary system. A manager's life is often in tension between planned and unplanned events. It is a battle between order and disorder seen in the deletions and changes to most people's diaries. However, it is the practised ability to manage unplanned and emergent interactions that allows a manager to respond to changes in the market place. Once the boundaries are set and simple rules are understood then it is possible to create a balance between accidental and controlled change.

Although this model segments your approach into five different methodologies, clearly it is never so simplistic. Any change methodology must be focused entirely on the needs of the client and the context, as such each one should be unique. However, what this model does highlight is that there are alternatives to the more typical command and control approach to managing change.

Usually the change process will use all of the options at different times. Imagine you have been asked to lead a project team to develop a new Christmas toy. You only have nine months left to design, develop and deliver the toy to the shops. Clearly with such a tight deadline, and with the fact that the environment is under your control, you may well opt to take a control approach, clearly setting out the goals, milestones and delivery dates for each of the project teams. However, you should also recognize that this is a creative as well as a delivery process and as such it would be unwise to constrain people's freedom to innovate and make mistakes. You try to ensure that the lower-level change processes have a degree of freedom and space so that people can experiment within the teams. A map of the change style used for different elements within the project might look like the list set out in Table 9.1.

The decision to adopt a particular change style is not black and white and in many cases might not actually be a decision that has to be taken. In some cases, it is best to let things happen naturally and simply be aware of the choice that is made in case things start to go wrong.

Table 9.1 Change types

Project activity	Change type
Project plan	*Control:* primarily because of the fixed delivery date and the ability to manage the close environment
Review meetings	*Debate:* allows the necessary flexibility to find out how the project is progressing, but with space for some of the shadow issues to surface
Design meetings	*Accidental.* the need to offer the designers space to innovate is paramount at this stage
Customer focus groups	*Accidental:* again the primary goal is to understand customers' expectations and to give them the space to talk and describe their feelings
Pilot trials	*Control:* since this feedback will affect the launch decision, the marketing data must be very accurate and controlled
Measurement process	*Backstage:* the primary focus should be on delivery of the product; the goal is to keep any project measurement procedures to a minimum. They will only operate in the background, using exception reports where issues surface

Back pocket question

Do I understand what methodology will be used to drive the change process?

Energy

By definition, change is about modifying the status quo, managing a shift from one state to another. This transfer requires energy. It might be the energy required to climb on the exercise bike; that burst of energy to read the latest management book; or the physical and emotional energy required to run yet another quality workshop. Alternatively, it is the energy required to stop something or someone from taking action when they want to be a change inhibitor. Just think how often you work with an organization where people spend more time stopping action from happening rather than making a change work. When thinking about the idea of energy, you need to have a clear appreciation of where it will come from, and how it might affect the change. Carter (1999) makes this point when he suggests that:

> The energy that people put into organizations is absorbed in a number of ways. Some of it is used for actually doing things for the customer, such as adding value to a product or service, but little of it is directly productive in this way. Much of it is spent communicating with other people within the organization, co-ordinating activities, planning, motivating, managing, being managed.

When understanding how this energy can affect a change, you might map three aspects:

- The source.
- The mass.
- The direction.

In understanding these issues, you can set out a strategy to harness the power and use it to support the change. Or you might develop counteracting energies that will help to overcome any resisting forces.

Energy source

This is how and where energy is dissipated across an organization. Simplistically, power is bestowed as part of the formal governance system (in reality power germinates and accumulates in a range of areas within any system as a result of energy used). When you are dealing with an organization, you must determine where the power lies. Then you must use this knowledge to determine what strategy will be appropriate to influence how the energy is directed and applied.

Consider a touring group performing Shakespeare. If you look closely it would be possible to deconstruct the energy within the group, to identify who owns and dispenses different type of energy and so power. One of the group might manage the finances; another interaction with the various theatre managers; yet another might act as the group's soul, with the energy to ensure that effective relationships are maintained within the group. It is possible to map the various energy levels and, more importantly, how the energy is deployed within the group.

The same idea can be applied to an organization change. In looking around any organization, it is possible to see where the various streams of energy sit. Here is an indication of some of the possible groups:

- **Financial:** In many organizations you only have to walk through the door to realize that the financial controllers have their hands on the tiller. The construction of the tender documents, the people that have to sign off your contract or the extent to which financial prudence is seen in the building decoration.

- **Operational:** In some types of business, the operations managers are seen as the gods. Possibly where production lines are key to the business, they will dictate what changes are acceptable and how programmes should be implemented.

- **Professional:** In some companies, the professional groups hold control over the key decision-making processes. The lawyers, IT specialists or marketing groups often feel that they are above transformation programmes and don't need to be involved.

- **Interest groups:** Sometimes the power actually exists outside the organization. In the UK, for example, government regulatory bodies hold sway over the regulated industries. In other countries lobby groups have amassed power over the petroleum industry.

- **Customer facing groups:** In professional service firms there is often an absolute focus on the customer experience. In large consulting or accounting firms, the core driver for all resource allocation and decision making takes place on the yield figure. The billable time booked to the customer is the core driver. Any transformation programme will take people away from this billing activity and so you will have to justify the true business value of any change.

I am not trying to indicate the absolute sources of energy within an organization, simply to highlight how it can surface in different shapes and forms. Your role is to build an intuitive ability to smell out where the sources of power originate when developing the change implementation programme. However, simply understanding where the power resides isn't enough. You also need to determine the extent of the power under their control.

Mass

The mass of a body in terms of the physical world is its weight and is measured in terms of its inertia or resistance to acceleration. This mass is actually nothing more than a bundle of energy and even when an object is at rest it has energy stored in its mass. In understanding this idea, it is possible to consider the energy sources within an organization in terms of the ability to release energy.

However, within any organization, different functions will have differing energy levels. So for one company it might be that the finance department has a significant mass of energy and is able to exert a great deal of influence over the business. In another business it might be that the IT group has a significant energy level but their true ability to exert a force over the company is limited because the real energy is held by the customer-facing teams. When trying to understand the mass within a system, it can help to calibrate it against a set of levels:

- **Dense:** absolutely power and energy to drive or resist change within a business.

- **Medium:** some energy to effect a control over the change process but subservient to the dense groups.

- **Light:** limited energy to effect change and will always lose to the medium and dense groups.

This suggests that the IT department with a light mass level will not be able to force through an idea in opposition to a finance department that has a medium or heavy mass. Although many groups in this position do attempt to take on the stronger opponent, the reality is that unless they are adept political animals they will waste their time and energy in a fruitless battle.

Trying to find a way to accurately map these energy levels is difficult. However, one way is to look at the profiles that the groups promote within the organization. Who is featured in the internal house magazines?; What people sit on the financial approval committees?; Who has the ear of the managing director? Finally, and most indicative, whose budgets gets cut first every time there is a reduction in expenditure? Across most industries, training is the first budget to be reduced when a downturn comes – this is indicative of the limited mass that the personnel function is seen to have. This approach does not offer the definitive answer but it might help to point you in the right direction. The other approach is to follow the money. In the majority of cases the dominant group will have a significant amount of influence over the way that cash is received and distributed.

Direction

The final issue to consider when mapping the energy sources within an organization is their direction. Imagine a company facing a crisis. Sales are falling, costs are rising and the market doesn't look rosy. In the midst of this the marketing director suggests that part of the problem is the fact that the espoused brand values are not being lived by the customer-facing teams. So while the company sells its products on the basis of 'a quality product with a quality service', the service end is not being delivered. There are reports of rudeness and inefficiencies from customers, and the marketing director believes this is causing sales to fall. He therefore proposes that the company embark on an organization-wide 'living what we value' programme, where everyone goes through an intensive series of workshop and coaching session. Clearly, in such a difficult time, this individual might find it difficult to introduce a change programme that will temporarily raise costs. The key point will be what energy other directors have in resisting his proposal and in particular where the energy is directed. If the finance director has sufficient mass, and chooses to focus it in his direction, then he might well block it outright. However, it might be that he has the mass to stop the proposition but his energy is actually focused on the engineering functions in the belief that their costs are the cause of the problems. If this is the case, then the marketing director can use this space to push his proposal through.

So when trying to understand how any one person or group is targeting their energy, it is possible to allocate it to one of three categories:

- **Driver:** A positive force that is supportive of the change.

- **Doubtful:** In-between. Not quite a supporter but not quite willing to resist any change process.

- **Driven:** An energy source opposed to the ideas put forward by the consultant and as such has to be pushed to take every action.

Although allocating such a category to any person or group is bound to be at worst a guess and at best open to contradiction, it does have some major benefits. The first is that it offers a benchmark against which other stakeholders can be calibrated. Although as an absolute measure it is inaccurate, at a relational level it is possible to build an accurate picture of your supporters and opponents. Second, it offers a dialogue tool that helps to gel the views of different individuals. Often when people come together to effect a change, each will have different experiences of the various power brokers and independent views of their orientation towards the project. Bringing these views together into a single picture helps to create consistency within the project team.

Energy map

By now you should have calibrated where the energy is contained within the organization. This will indicate both the energy level and where this force is directed. Now you can construct a map, one that will bring this knowledge into a single view.

Imagine a company is being pressured into adopting an environmental quality programme. Fig. 9.3 shows how an outside pressure group is threatening to take the company to court if it does not implement a new environmental directive. The legal department realizes that the company must take urgent action, but the work will incur significant cost and disruption. The net result is that the legal department is applying pressure to three key organizational groups: the finance department, the operations managers and the customer service groups. The legal department has sufficient mass within the business to drive the latter two groups to change without much resistance. However, in dealing with the finance team, they are tackling a group that has more mass and as such they will have a problem in trying to effect a change.

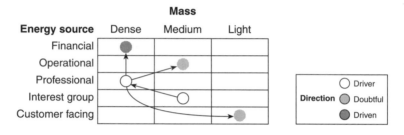

Fig. 9.3   Energy map

The map indicates that in trying to take on the finance team, the professional unit is unlikely to succeed. However, if they use the additional energy contained within the operations and customer facing groups, the combined force might well offer sufficient power to effect a change.

I am not suggesting that energy within any group must be mapped in relation to another group. I am, however, proposing that it should be possible to intuitively calibrate such detail and use it to ensure that blockage does not occur.

Back pocket question

Do I have a clear appreciation as to where the change energy will come from, and how it will be dissipated across the different stakeholders?

Engage

At some stage in the change the people who will be involved have to be engaged. They will need to understand at a personal and emotional level what they will have to deliver as part of the transformation. Czerniawska (1999) makes this point:

> *What some consultants have neglected is the fact that people – at whatever level in an organization – become resistant to change where they do not understand what is happening. And this is a problem which, as companies become increasingly internationalized, is only going to get much worse, as cultural diversity creates new barriers.*

Consultants often seek to deliver this through workshops, team events or other group occurrences – any event that brings people together to share a common change experience. Examples include:

- Project design workshop to bring together the various stakeholders to prepare the business plan.

- Training session to help educate operational groups on a new process design.

- Learning reviews where you can work with a pilot team to understand how successful a small-scale engagement has been.

- Directors briefing where the CEO and his or her team will update people on the current progress and successes of the change processes.

All of these processes are grouped under the ICE banner; they are designed to involve, communicate or educate people who are recipients of the change. One example of this type of event was highlighted by Tichy and Sherman (1993) with General Electric's use of the 'work-out programme' to spread new organizational values. These events offered the opportunity to meet and discuss issues, which would in turn create a process to act as a catalyst for change.

In any such change event there is a strong suggestion of a (actual or virtual) platform or theatre, a place where traditionally there will be those who deliver messages and those who receive them. Typically this is in a single direction (presenters to receivers) but this is modified at times to develop a two-way approach. 'Event' is very much about a notable occasion that will result in a defined outcome, where the suggestion is one of excitement and energy.

Often these types of events can seem to be effective at a superficial level but when the outcomes are tested for depth or robustness, they can slip away and little change will have been made. Common problems include:

- **False questions:** A consultant or senior managers, concerned that people either won't ask any questions or will ask the wrong type of questions, dummy up a few people with pre-prepared questions to help make the process roll.

- **Toilet talk:** All discussions at the event operate at a superficial level, where no-one is prepared to raise issues or concerns that take the session out of the comfort zone. Only once a break is taken, or the session is over, do people rush for the privacy and seclusion of the toilets to talk and moan about the real issues that surround the engagement.

- **Self-segmentation:** In considering the people who are at the event, a kind of self-segmentation takes place, where the people who don't want to be involved (but possibly should) always find a way to avoid it. They will cry off session after session until they are all forced to attend and inevitably they all have to turn up to the final event. This means that the final session is an almost riotous assembly, where the real issues are raised, but which is dismissed as just a bad bunch and not truly representative of the people and their true feelings about the change.

To ensure such problems are reduced, there are a number of factors that should be considered to help ensure that the event has meaning and is not seen as just a 'just another consultant presentation'!

All staged events may be considered in three steps: pre-event, event and post-event activities (Fig. 9.4). And within this there are ten key stages that need to be considered if not actually undertaken:

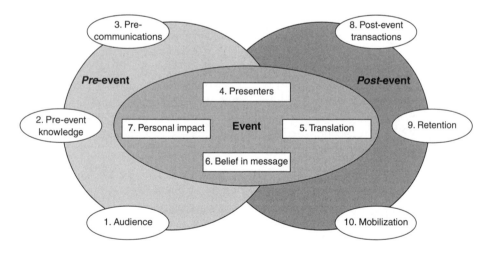

Fig. 9.4

- **Target audience:** Have the delegates some purpose in attending, and do they understand the purpose both for themselves and the business?

- **Pre-event knowledge:** How will what the audience already knows affect the process?

- **Pre-event communications:** It should be possible to use internal communication processes to send messages out that raise people's appreciation of many of the factors and dilute some of the rumours and scare issues.

- **Presenter:** The style adopted, the words used or the perceived credibility of the presenters affect the willingness to accept the change message.

- **Theory translation:** At some stage the event needs to help people to take any conceptual or theoretical ideas that have been offered and transform them into tangible actions to be taken after the event.

- **Belief in the message:** If the participants do not appear to believe the key messages delivered, little will happen to effect the necessary changes.

- **Personal impact:** Without a clear personal buy in, there is little chance that the change will ever take place.

- **Post-event language:** If any change is to take place after the event then the participants' language must be modified.

- **Story retention:** Can the delegates clearly describe the key messages or the story line? If not, is it possible to reinforce the story after the event through the use of in-house communication systems?

- **Mobilization:** At the end of the day, has the event made a difference?

This involvement, communication and education process is critical. As news of a new idea or change spreads, people begin to talk about the events that are used to diffuse the idea. However, in many cases, rather than describing the content of the event, they will focus on the smaller issues – spelling mistakes in the call-up letter; insincerity in the presenter's voice; failure to ensure that action takes place after the event. All of these subtle messages will circulate around the organization and can potentially disrupt or stall change.

> **Back pocket question**
>
> Do I know how people will be encouraged to get involved in the change?

Entry

There are few change projects that don't require people to modify how they think, feel or behave. Unless you understand the people issues, then the chances of carrying out a successful engagement will be limited.

The key question to consider is what is the level of entry to make with this change? I suggest that changing how people operate can take place at one of the five levels on the change ladder:

- **Existence:** what people believe in or use as their core purpose for taking a set of actions.

- **Desire:** the extent to which people are motivated to take a set of actions.

- **Capability:** the competencies or skills that people have to undertake a set of actions.

- **Blueprint:** the guidelines or procedures used to make decisions about the actions they take.

- **Assets:** the assets, tools, instruments or techniques that people use to do their job.

You must decide at which level of the ladder the change will be delivered. The problem is that so many changes have aims that are delivered at the wrong level. Many organizations believe that a change in the office environment (assets) will miraculously clear all the morale problems (desire); that sending people on a course (capability) will improve the effectiveness of the processes (blueprint). Unless your change is positioned at the appropriate level it will at best deliver a short-term gain and at worst fail miserably.

The existence level is the core of the individual, where spirit and soul are held. In working on this level a consultant is helping individuals to change goals, what they believe in or what they see as their purpose. In real terms this might be running a self-development workshop where people are asked to think through their goals in life and how they will achieve them. It might be helping people to understand the importance of their role in the context of the wider organization, for example, customer service programmes where the goal is to get people to see the customer as the core rationale for the business. This is the hardest type of change to effect. I don't mean hard in the sense of designing or managing the engagement, just difficult because people shield their goals and feel uncomfortable about telling other people what their purpose is in life. In many cases people actually don't know what their goals are since society tends to place people in stereotypical packages that do not encourage people to focus on what they really want out of life. The key problem for the consultant is that this type of chance nearly always requires a great deal of time – something that few clients are willing to give. Often the drive is for a quick fix and it is this factor that causes pseudo change – where people simply pretend that they have changed their personal focus but in reality hold on to it like a hidden jewel in a precious box.

> *People simply pretend that they have changed their personal focus but in reality hold on to it like a hidden jewel in a precious box.*

144

The desire level is the area where you might wish to change how people feel about a particular situation. This might involve taking action to improve staff morale, changing customers' perception of a product, changing financial markets' appraisal of a company's stock value or helping senior managers to take a more collaborative approach in a joint venture. The type of changes that you might use include: 'scare workshops', where the senior team are shown the dire position that they are in and are driven to take immediate action; 'Dr Feelgoods', where the organization uses internal journals, intranet sites or promotional material to make people feel good about the company and development programmes. These are commonly used where the client needs to change the feel of a company – how people feel about themselves, how they feel about their peers or how customers feel about the company. As a change process it is relatively easy to design and implement but there are still problems associated with the fact that it very much an intangible, so it is difficult for the client or consultant to really define the change and measure the success of its delivery.

At the capability level, the change is more tangible in that other people see it. This is concerned with how people do things. How well does the mechanic fix a car? Can the manager run a project? Can the field technician repair a fault? The change for this will be based on giving people the appropriate knowledge or skills to do a job or might be focused on behaviour modelling where people are being coached or coerced into changing their behaviour. Examples are customer care courses, appraisal systems that reinforce certain behaviour or system training for a customer service representative. The change process is explicit and is designed, delivered and measured with relative ease. The problem is that because it is visible, uses off-the-shelf packages and is seen to give a short-term fix, it can in many cases be abused with the client assuming that just by putting people through a training course the problems will go away.

Change at the blueprint level doesn't directly instigate a change in someone's behaviour but it can have a significant influence. Simply changing a few lines on an organization chart can have a notable impact on people's behaviour. Alternatively, simply increasing what someone is expected to deliver can bring about a radical change in their output. However, because such changes are so easy to achieve in the short term there is a tendency to use them as an easy way to behavioural change. But just because it is quick and easy doesn't mean it will be sustainable. Transformation at this level will often require additional action to take place at the desire or existence level to ensure that it becomes permanent.

The asset level is the most extrinsic and visible. Assets might be a computer for the programmer or a social network or the senior manager. It is everything that the individual uses to do their job, including the accommodation, marketing material and communication systems. Change engagement at this level might include new IT systems, relocation projects, plant upgrade or new corporate clothing. In this case, the engagement is akin to simple project management. The end goal is clear. All that has to be done is to make a physical change within agreed limits. The problem is that simply changing the apparatus for something new will offer little payback if the actual problem is more to do with the ability, attitude or aim of the individual. In using this model to understand the change process, there are three key points to consider:

- The pressure for you to deliver quick and tangible results can drive the project to the lower level of the ladder where the outcome is visible and is measured. But unless the upper issues are resolved then the problem will resurface.

- It would be a brave person who promised to tackle all five levels in one strike. Like any assignment, the best option is to focus on the root of the problem. Once this is addressed it makes sense to come back to resolve the additional issues. If all levels have to be dealt with in one change cycle then care must be taken to understand how they interrelate and affect each other.

- Where change is taking place in a large organization, beware of portfolio clash. A company will often be operating in the asset level in one part of the business and the capability level in another, in some cases offering conflicting messages. There is a significant risk of this in large companies where it is possible for a range of different consultants to be employed at any one time.

This model does not attempt to encompass all the different levels that a change may be aiming at but it will help to create a greater sense of alignment within the engagement.

> **Back pocket question**
>
> Am I clear on the most appropriate level of entry to effect a long lasting change?

System dynamics

Look at the list of words in Table 9.2. Why is it that so many consultants sell their services using words from the left-hand column while so many clients believe that the words on the right are more indicative of the outcome? Wherever you go, whatever industry, the role of the consultant is generally under attack. People moan about doctors, householders complain about builders and directors moan that yet another consultant has left them with a mundane solution. Clearly the consultancy industry might have a few rogues and the odd bad apple but the huge growth in consultancy spend over recent years seems to run counter to the view that consultants do not add value to the client and consumer.

Table 9.2 Consulting aims

Consultant's intent		Perceived outcome
Action	——	Abort
Better	——	Bluff
Cure	——	Chaos
Deliver	——	Delay
Easy	——	Embarrassment
Faster	——	Fails

One of the reasons is because so many consultants do not pay sufficient attention to the nature of the system they are working with. They act on the evidence of a single event and give little consideration to the deeper issues that underpin the system. Consultancy projects are often designed on the premise that the issues revolve around a simple, predictable component. In reality, it is the tip of a problem that involves a complex, dynamic and integrated system. As Senge (1990) suggests:

> *Business and human endeavours are systems . . . they are bound by invisible fabrics or interrelated actions, which often take years to fully play out their effects on each other. Since we are part of that lacework ourselves it is doubly hard to see the whole pattern of change. Instead we tend to focus on snapshots of isolated parts of the system and wonder why problems never seem to get solved.*

For example, the incident the police most dread is a family dispute. In this situation they are being asked to dive into a situation that is volatile, emotional and unpredictable. There is often no 'solution' since the issue is possibly about a perceived rather than actual problem. As such, no matter what action they might take they are likely to end up in the firing line, often being abused by both parties. They are effectively being asked to intervene in a system where they have little or no control over the process or outcome.

As a consultant asked to help resolve a problem within an organization, you are often in a similar position. You will be asked to unravel problems to which people are emotionally attached and will defend against outside interference. Even more difficult is the fact that you will rarely have to resolve an issue that involves just one person.

In all cases the effective consultant will focus less on the issues (tasks, content or facts) than on trying to understand the relationship between them. For example, the only way a marriage guidance counsellor will be able to help resolve a problem is by understanding the nature of the relationship between the husband and wife. Just understanding each of them in isolation will only produce a rubber band solution, where the old problems bounce back after a few days. In the same way that 2+2 is vastly different from 2×2, the relationship is as much a part of the system as the component parts. In other words, the whole of the system is more than the sum of its parts. Unless you are able to see this then any project will be flawed from the outset.

You must see (and help others see) the big picture. The view that an individual, team or organization can be improved by focusing just on one part in isolation is seriously outmoded. Senge (1990) makes this point when he suggests that:

> From a very early age we are taught to break apart problems, to fragment the world. This apparently makes complex tasks and subject more manageable, but we pay a hidden, enormous price. We can no longer see the consequences of our actions; we lose our intrinsic sense of connection to a larger whole. When we then try to 'see the big picture', we try to reassemble the fragments in our minds to list and organize the pieces.

Once this dissection has taken place it can be difficult to resolve the problem. Actions are taken on the separatist's principle with the result that a short-term fix might be delivered but with a bigger long-term problem planted. Generalization is dangerous because the exception can generally be found, but I suggest that the consultant's failure to take account of the total system will lead to one of the following scenarios:

● **Action/Abort:** Systems that are made up of people do not react passively to an outsider. They will fight back with all the energy they can muster. The result is that the change makes things worse. The reason is that it is difficult for a stranger to fix a problem because they do not have sensitivity to the context and situation. The reality is that it is impossible to make a change in one area without some impact being felt elsewhere. The end result is that the consultant has to close down the project or call in other people to help untangle the mess. The interesting thing is that in many cases consultants will make a good living on the back of projects that previous people have failed to resolve.

● **Better/Bluff:** Things often get better before they get worse. Like the car mechanic who changes the spark plugs when your car is running rough, you might get a short-term improvement in performance but in reality, unless he resolves the fact that the clogged-up spark plugs are caused by excessive oil being burnt, then the issue has not been resolved. The real problem is that the piston rings are worn and no amount of short-term fixes will produce a long-term improvement.

- **Cure/Chaos:** In this case the cure is worse than the original problem. A doctor may happily prescribe Valium for a depressed patient. But unless the doctor tries to understand the root cause of the depression, he or she is leading the individual down a rocky road to possible long-term addiction. An insidious cycle of shared dependency can be generated with this approach. As the system falls into chaos because of an inappropriate cure, so managers look to the consultant to help them resolve yet another problem. Dependency is created between the consultant, client and consumer, with each believing that the real cure is just around the corner, if only they can have just one more fix of the latest consultancy bauble.

- **Deliver/Delay:** Clearly, when a change causes a problem for the system you can take immediate action to resolve the issue. The difficulty comes when a time delay creeps into the reaction and problems are caused downstream. You might make a change on the assumption that it has been effective. The problem is that you might not be around to see the impact of your actions. In 99 per cent of projects the consultant is not around after six months to understand the impact of the change.

- **Easy/Embarrassment:** If you are asked to help resolve a problem, the temptation can be to use the tried and tested techniques on the basis that what worked before will work again. You are like the man with a hammer who believes that all problems can be fixed with a nail. The danger is that after trying for the fifth time to push 'a square peg into a round hole', you might have to accept (with some embarrassment) that the easy, quick-fix solution might not be the most appropriate. Just because one system looks like another, it doesn't mean that solutions can be easily replicated.

- **Faster/Fails:** The pressure valve on a cooking pot or the governor on a steam engine are examples of the way that things are set to operate at their optimum level. In the same way, any system will have an optimum level at which they will operate and any effort to push this over the limit will be frustrating for you and damaging for the system. This can be seen in the way that people try to resolve difficult issues. Rather than stepping back from a situation to consider what deep structural issues are causing the problem, the tendency is to work harder, do more research or involve more people. In many cases, it might be that the slower or smaller action would actually deliver the desired outcome. Rather than trying to overcome resistance and force a change through, it might be easier to understand what limiting factors are causing the resistance and try to eliminate them by more subtle means. You can spend an hour arguing with your daughter about the need to keep her bedroom tidy, but it might be simpler to suggest that the tidiness of her bedroom will be directly linked to her pocket money.

Although each template tells a different story, they have a common theme that has a serious implication for any consultant. They suggest that when embarking on an engagement, you need to ensure that the situation is understood from the whole perspective and not in isolation.

There is no simple answer to this problem as my whole proposition is that each change must be treated individually, in the same way that each system must be regarded as unique. When undertaking a project you can consider the system to be made of a number of forces that either aid or oppose your change proposition. These forces can be seen to act at each layer of the change ladder and can both amplify or attenuate a change process. E-mail can be a positive force when implementing a large multinational project, but can also be used to counter change through subversive messages. At the blueprint level, positive forces can be seen in the rapid time to market processes that organizations develop and resisting forces can be seen because the process might be overly locked-in and unable to respond to market changes. For each step on the change ladder, it is possible to see forces that can enhance or inhibit the change.

Where a change force is applied, the resistance of an opposing force at the same level can be understood and managed. However, problems occur when negative forces respond from a different level. This can be seen where a new asset is introduced to a system (computer or production capability for example) and the opposing force comes from the capability or desire level. Even worse, when this opposing force has an associated time lag, then the real problems start. So while change at the blueprint level with the imposition of a reengineered process might seem to work in the short term, over time resistance might grow at the desire level and people might become concerned about imposed changes that detract from the company mission statement.

This can be seen in the change ladder of Fig. 9.5, where the engagement is out of alignment. No matter how hard the consultant pushes at the blueprint level, equal forces can be returned at the desire and existence level. It is this misalignment that can trigger the unease and frustration that accompany so many consulting engagements. People might feel uneasy about the proposed change but are either not allowed to express their feelings or express their full support for the change while inside they hold on to a level of discomfort.

When undertaking any change engagement, you must pay careful attention to the relationship between the five levels. The systematic relationship between these levels can either fuel the drive towards a successful engagement or leave a problem legacy for the future – a problem that you, a colleague or client might be forced to resolve.

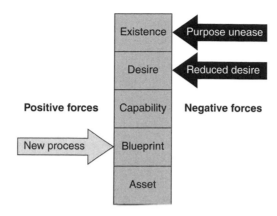

Fig. 9.5   Change forces out of alignment

Back pocket question

Do I understand how the system is likely to react to my proposed changes?

Uncertainty

You need to understand that the plan you set at the beginning of a project is unlikely to be the one delivered at the end. All too often we design plans on the basis that rationality prevails, order is desired and uncertainty is banished. However, how will such a style and structure fare in a world where change is discontinuous, random and complex and unexpected market shifts occur at global rather than national level? The notion of predictability and stability are false idols and many consultants need to become more adaptive within the engagement. This state of constant unpredictability is driven by the following factors:

● **Non-linear:** The traditional mechanistic model assumes that life is a linear process, one that is predicted, directed and controlled. A look in the newspapers or a glance at the stock market will immediately highlight that this is not always so. Life and organizations are built on a set of constructs that use chance, random disturbance, changing dynamics, turbulence and interconnectedness as the base presuppositions. Non-linear systems are nothing new and consultants should recognize that life is not an orderly system. You must be able to recognize non-linear undercurrents and not be surprised when things do not go as planned.

- **Interacting structure:** Often, you might be invited to undertake a project in one particular part of the business. However, you need to recognize no system acts in isolation. Through this interconnection, changing a variable in one area will in some way affect other areas. Identifying this interconnection is easy where the impact is seen, the problem comes when the impact surfaces in other areas of the business or emerges months, or years, later. It is important to be sensitive to this interrelatedness and to be prepared to modify the plan if it turns out that the engagement is causing problems in other parts of the business.

- **Self-organization:** When you try to change a system, there must be an appreciation that change will occur on its own as a result of the interaction between different parts of the system. Beneath the polished veneer that all organizations present to the world, there exists the potential for spontaneous self-organization. Within the stable mechanistic business processes that organizations typically adopt, there is a living force that drives and supports the business but in ways that are not always obvious. To ensure that the assignment is controlled, it is important to appreciate the nature of complexity and self-organization and not necessarily regard unplanned activity as a failure. In many cases it is the spontaneous action that emerges from interaction between different parts of the system that enhances the change process.

Imagine you are part of a consultancy team replacing a customer service computer system within a telemarketing centre. The team has developed the overall schedule and is in the process of finalizing the project plan for the implementation cycle. Overall the project has gone well but there are a number of issues that could affect its success. First, the senior management team is in the process of being changed and the IT director is likely to be replaced by the deputy IT director. Second, the finance director is concerned about this year's budget and might need to reduce some of the system's frills. Lastly, the existing IT system has been in place for 15 years and has multiple connections with internal and external MIS systems. Hence the team is not convinced that they have a truly representative data flow map. On a positive note they are experienced in installing the new piece of kit and have a solid reputation with the client for delivering on time to the agreed standard.

In considering this scenario you might consider the following:

- What are the core activity streams in the change programmes?
- What external factors are likely to alter over the life of the change?
- To what extent should the streams be strictly planned and to what extent should the fine detail be left to emerge as the project rolls out?

These three factors can then be used in a matrix that will give a feel for the variability within each stream and over the whole engagement (Table 9.3). Each cell on the matrix should be assigned a value that represents the extent to which the external factor will change. So a figure of 1.0 means that the stream is planned on the assumption that no emergent factors will cause the team to modify its approach, whereas 0.1 means that there is a strong chance that emergent factors will affect the delivery of the change stream. Hence, the fact that the budget is cut part way through the programme might well cause the training programme to be slimmed down, thus giving it an emergent score of 0.7.

Table 9.3   Variability matrix

Change stream	Change factors		
	Senior team change	Budget review	System link uncertainty
System implementation	0.9	1.0	1.0
Training	0.8	0.7	0.9
First MIS run	1.0	1.0	0.5

If an average of the various scores in the matrix is taken, the result is 0.86. As a consulting project, the vast majority of the transformation processes can be assumed as safe. However, there is a chance that some emergence will occur that will affect the plan. Your team would be wise to allow sufficient flexibility in the process to make changes as turbulence surfaces.

It is important to emphasise that we are not trying to apply rationality to an irrational process. The future cannot be predicted and this tool will not guarantee that the beast of uncertainty is tamed. It does, however, offer a vehicle by which the consultant and client can have a clearer understanding of the degree of uncertainty that exists within the project. Simply helping the client to consider the fact that the future cannot be determined will help to ease relationship problems if the project starts to run into bumpy waters.

You will only be able to predict with any certainty how a change will turn out if you have absolute control over all the variables. Since this is impossible, it is important to factor in the emergent variables in order to ensure that the engagement delivers a value-added output.

Back pocket question
Does my plan have the flexibility to operate in a dynamic and complex world?

Resistance

Resistance to change is one of the most significant but least understood issues. This is because many people view opposition as a negative issue, something to go into battle with and defeat. However, unless people are already moving in the direction of a proposed transformation then it is natural to expect some form of resistance. This might be minimal, such as the odd joke or sarcastic comment about the new corporate uniform; or major, such as company-wide industrial action triggered by proposed downsizing. Although these two examples are different in scale, they follow the same underlying process that is a natural response in reaction to something people regard as unfair or inappropriate.

The first reaction to such resistance is to question 'how do we minimize any response to the proposed change?' But all this means is that valuable time is spent on avoidance routines, trying to work out ways to hide the elements that people might not like. For example, think about the hours people spend trying to find a politically correct way to present an idea that is obviously not politically correct. Hence the rebadging of 'downsizing' to 'rightsizing' or 'decruit' as a way to manage people out of a business in a controlled way. All of these actions indicate a change process that is being squeezed through the back door rather than being presented honestly.

Natural resistance

It is normal for individuals, teams, organization or even nations to react adversely when faced with something different or unexpected. This reaction can be mapped in the form of a chart, one that maps time against the emotional stages the individual(s) will pass through, as in Fig. 9.6. The U-loop is a powerful and effective change model that clearly maps many of the feelings associated with change and learning. People will especially feel these emotions where the change process affects their self-esteem or position in an organization. The suggestion is that there are five major stages in the process of change (Carnal, 1995):

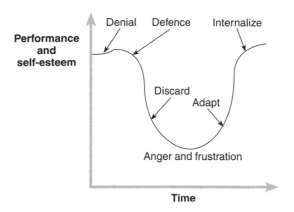

Fig. 9.6 Change U-loop

- **Denial:** Many people feel uncomfortable with change. Often the typical response to any change is to ignore it. People either do not believe that it will affect them or are resigned to the idea that there is nothing they can do, so it is best to ignore the threat.

- **Defence:** This is where people might take action to try to prevent the change from taking place. It might be simply withdrawing from the process or in some extremes taking pre-meditated guerrilla or political action to stop the change.

- **Discard:** All change is about shifting people's schema or view of the world. To move forward, one has to discard past behaviours, feelings and consequences; to let go and be happy with what has gone.

- **Adapt:** At this point the past has been left behind so people can begin to explore new ways of working. This is a confusing time, as the old and new are still likely to be in conflict. However, with the correct support, the individual can quickly shift to the next stage of commitment.

- **Internalize:** Once the change has been accepted, the individual can adopt it as the norm and internalize it as the current way of operating. At this point the energy returns, the process is owned and the individual will, in many cases, try to convince others of its benefits.

These stages can be found in all situations where change is required. From the way that people react to a change in their job description; the suggestion that it is time to lose some weight; or the pain associated with enforced redundancy. Although each example is different, all the players will follow the pattern outlined in the U-loop.

It is important that you understand the process and implications of the U-loop at a deep level. Once understood, you will be able to rapidly assess where individuals, teams or organizations are in the transition.

Although it is impossible to identify every type of behaviour where resistance is being enacted, there are a number of common reactions that are observed as people experience the adaption process (Kubr, 1976).

- Lack of conviction that change is needed. If people are not properly informed and the purpose of change is not explained, they are likely to view the present situation as satisfactory and any effort to change as useless and upsetting.

- Dislike of imposed change. In general, people do not like to be treated as passive objects. They resent changes that are imposed on them and about which they cannot express any views.

- Dislike of surprises. People do not want to be kept in the dark about any change being prepared; changes tend to be resented if they come as a surprise.

- Fear of the unknown. People do not like to live in uncertainty and may prefer an imperfect present to an unknown and uncertain future.

- Reluctance to deal with unpopular issues: Managers and other people often try to avoid unpleasant reality and unpopular actions even if they realize that they will not be able to avoid these for ever.

- Fear of inadequacy and failure. Many people worry about their ability to adjust to change and to maintain and improve their performance in a new work situation. Some of them may feel insecure and doubt their ability to make a special effort to learn new skills and attain new performance levels.

- Disturbed practices, habits and relations. Following change, well-established and mastered practices may become obsolete and familiar relationships may be altered or destroyed. This can lead to frustration and unhappiness.

- Lack of respect and trust in the person promoting change. People are suspicious about change proposed by a manager whom they do not trust and respect or by an external person whose competence and motives are not known and understood.

The core problem with all of these issues is that resistance often occurs when people do not feel engaged by the change process. In general, people can live with what they know but find it difficult to live with the unknown. This resistance can be managed using a range of strategies (Kotter and Schlesinger, 1991).

- Facilitation and support: Give people time and space to acclimatize to the proposed change.

- Education and communication: Help people to understand what is coming and how it might affect them.

- Participation and involvement. Involve the potential resistors in the engagement to get them involved.

- Negotiation and agreement. Offer incentives to change in exchange for a shift in position.

- Manipulation. In some cases you might need to take a more aggressive stance by using a judicious use of information and conscious structuring of events.

- Explicit and implicit coercion. Force people by threatening them with loss of job, status, etc.

Ultimately, if you treat people as though they are children, and give them tit-bits of information covered in sugar then you are forced to bluff and bluster your way through the change process. The suggestion is that it is best to tell people the truth and avoid the complexities of deceit and game playing.

Change segmentation

There will be occasions when resistance starts to stall change. All consultants will have war stories of the time they spent battling with a group or individual that refused to change. If this happens, it can help to segment the target audience to ensure that energy is applied in the right places. The worst thing that a client or consultant can do is to spend time and resource trying to change someone if they don't really contribute to the end transformation process.

The change process can be considered along two specific lines of interest. First, the extent to which people are actively involved in the change. For a retail organization about to implement a new stock control system, it might be that certain groups of people are critical and need to be introduced to new ways of working at the outset. However, there will be people that might need to know about the system but whose training can take place at a later date. Second, consider the level of resistance to change. This is high (where there is a real blockage to the change), down to low (where the people are really quite happy to take on board the new ways of working). The end result of combining these four approaches is seen in Fig. 9.7.

The 'leaders quadrant' includes those people who are viewed as the early adopters, people who will respond to the change initiative in a proactive and visible way. They have a critical role in the final change outcome and have a low resistance to change. Hooking in these people early gives a clear signal that the project is serious, people are buying into the new ways of working and the new model is socially acceptable.

As a example, consider the cable TV company that has merged with another similar group and needs to re-locate to a site over 100 miles away. Resistance to this shift is likely to be fierce and could lead to protracted negotiations and

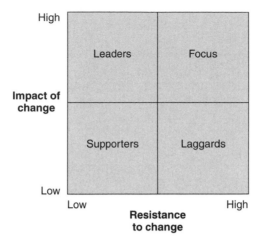

Fig. 9.7   Change segmentation model

conflict. However, it will be useful to identify one or two people who are happy with the change and are willing to support the strategic need for relocation. Their visible support sends a positive signal and other people will be more amenable to the change.

The 'supporters' quadrant includes those people who have limited involvement in the change but are committed to its success. They are people that enthuse about the change but in reality it makes little difference if they decide to change or not. In the case of an IT upgrade, the small customer services team may be enthusiastic about the proposed shift to a new platform. However, the shift has actually been proposed to reduce the product delivery time. So their gain is only a limited by-product of a shift elsewhere. However, if this team is committed then it makes sense to use their enthusiasm. You could use them as internal communicators, trainers or facilitators. Although their involvement might add little to the formal engagement, it might have a substantial impact on helping others to see the need for a system upgrade.

The people who fall into the 'focus' quadrant will resist the change but must be converted to ensure success. They are the key players. If you don't identify these people early on then there is a chance that valuable resources will be deployed elsewhere. As a result, you will not be able to spend time and energy working with them to help them make the necessary change. This is seen in the case of a project to implement a new financial package within a local government office. It might be that the government has mandated a system change to deliver the necessary data to the Treasury. However, if the chief executive does not accept that the system will add value in her domain then she will have the capability to put every possible obstacle in the way. You must put every available effort into working with the individual and her team to convince them of the benefits. Failure to shift their viewpoint will turn the project into a nightmare and might result in a loss of your future income.

Lastly, the 'laggards' segment highlights those people who will fiercely resist the change but have little involvement in the outcome. In many cases it is better to say, 'fine, we will make the change in your absence and when the time is right you can make the shift in your own way'. An example is a technical department that refuses to accept the need to attend customer skills training. While the chief executive has decreed that everyone should attend a two-day event, this group has little contact with other people. While the consultant could force the situation, the end result will be a great deal of game playing by the unit manager and a disruptive crowd of people at the change workshop. By giving them the option to adopt the new techniques at their own rate, they are able to do so in a way that suits their needs. As a result, they might become leading exponents of the need to adopt a more customer-focused approach within their work and actively start to promote this ethos to their suppliers.

Back pocket question

Do I know how people will react to the proposed action?

Chapter 10

Stage five: Confirm

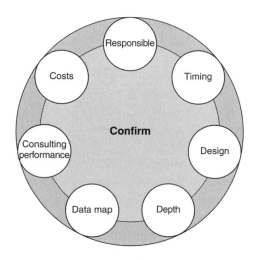

***Not everything that can be counted counts, and not
everything that counts can be counted.***

Albert Einstein

With any new engagement, passion flames when you first met the client, curiosity emerges in the clarification stage, adrenaline gets running when creating new ideas and the real buzz emerges when making a change. However, when the excitement is over, someone has to confirm that what was wanted has actually been delivered. At this point, everyone looks around to find a willing victim, someone who is prepared to put his or her neck on the line to measure the outcome.

Your motto must be 'start to measure before you start'. You wouldn't start a diet and then wait three weeks to see if you had lost any weight. Unless you take an initial measurement, there is no way to confirm that the change has been effective. So although the Confirm stage is shown at a relatively late point in the cycle, this doesn't mean that you should wait until the change has been completed before thinking about the issue.

Unless you take an initial measurement, there is no way to confirm that the change has been effective.

160

Even when you first agree the contract, it will have insufficient bite to make it worth signing unless you have thought about the measurement process. As an ideal the contract should have both the process of measurement and the targets that are to be achieved. However, if the contract is one where a degree of uncertainty exists about the outcome at the start, then the measures will be implied in the goal and objective statement used in the contract.

Failure to address any of the issues considered in this stage can result in the some of the following problems:

- A consultant has not thought through the measurement process and agrees that his client can use an internal audit to confirm that change has taken place. The problem is that political bias sets in and the client uses his hold over the resource as a way to leverage more work out of the consultant. The audit team is told to look under every stone for unresolved issues and problems and the consultant is pressured into redoing much of the work, even though people within the company caused the failure.

- As part of a product re-launch assignment, a consultant had been asked to advise on what design modifications would give a distinct edge in emerging markets. Following the consultant's advice, the product is re-launched to critical acclaim and sales triple overnight. However, once the consultant has closed the contract, sales suddenly start to fall, to the point where the product has to be re-launched again three months later. The consultant had identified the new market niches, but failed to accurately forecast the volumes that they could sustain. The client's failure to put a delay clause into the terms of payment meant that they had paid for a service that was not sustainable.

- Coaching for a telemarketing centre seemed to have been a great success. People were buzzing and there was a sense that the management style was changing. To save time and money, the consultants decided to measure the change by sending an e-mail to everyone rather than running focus groups. The message thanked people for attending the event and asked to flag up any complaints. Two months after the consultants left, performance fell, customer complaints increased and dissatisfaction surfaced among staff. The problem was that the measurement failed to pick up some of the deep personal concerns that people had about the new ways of working. As such, without the external support from the consultant, people reverted to their normal ways of working.

- In running the confirmation stage, a consulting team assigned a couple of junior members the task of gathering the necessary measurement data. The problem was that they each went off on their own to gather data based upon their respective experiences. One used a highly qualitative process, using focus groups and open interviews techniques, whereas the other used survey techniques. The end result was that the final data sets they delivered to the senior consultant looked incomplete, did not align and didn't really tell them anything new. As a result the whole process had to be re-run, a cost that had to be borne by the consultancy team.

These examples indicate some of the costly and damaging issues that can surface if the confirmation or measurement process is not taken seriously. It is not something that can be left to at a later date and it is not something that can be brushed aside if everything looks rosy. It is a fundamental part of the process and as such must be high on the client's and consultant's list of things to discuss at the outset.

The following seven steps are offered in the clarification stage:

- **Responsible:** Agree who will own and manage the measurement process.
- **Delay:** What impact will the timing of the change have on the perception of the outcome and your final remuneration?
- **Design:** How should the clarification process be designed and what should the relationship be between qualitative and quantitative measures? How should this balance with the relationship between outcome and process-based measures?
- **Depth:** Will the measurement be focused on extrinsic issues or will it deal with intrinsic issue such as attitude, motivation and beliefs?
- **Data map:** How can the various measurement activities be controlled and managed to ensure that an integrated approach is taken?
- **Consulting performance:** How can you ensure that your performance has been up to the standard expected by the client?
- **Costs:** What impact will cost have on the different measurement processes and what types of costs are found in the clarification stage?

All too often, the charge levelled at the consulting profession is that its people don't stop around to see how any transformation process turns out. Although the outcomes of the change are not expected until a later date, you need to ensure that the measurement phase is clearly designed and locked in as part of the cycle. In applying the seven clarification steps, you will ensure that real clarity is gained and that your client understands the process by which the outcomes will be measured.

Responsible

The first step is to agree who will own and manage the measurement process. The client, consumer, external verifier, stakeholders and yourself all have a valid reason for owning the measurement process, but all might have a hidden agenda as well. It might be your need to prove that the change has been a success and the client's need to identify areas that have not worked so as to question the amount being billed.

There is no one answer to this conundrum as it will always depend on the context in which the confirmation process is taking place. However, the crux is not to get 'the' answer, more to offer a model by which the debate can take place in a structured and controlled manner.

It is important to appreciate the importance of schematic variation and the need to bring together people's separate mental models. An individual's schematic map acts like a filter, letting some things through and screening out others. It helps to bring certain elements of the world into focus while making others blurred and fuzzy so that they are ignored or overlooked. It is this screening process that causes a problem with the measurement stage since two people staring at the same object or issue can view it from totally different perspectives. While one person might think that the quality project has resulted in a reduction in faults, the other might feel that training costs were so high that it will take years to recover the investment.

Your goal is to ensure that all of the players' perspectives are brought into alignment to give a sense of balance to the measurement process. As any boating enthusiast will appreciate, it is impossible to get an accurate bearing by taking a single point of reference, since a true position can only be determined by taking two independent references. It is through this process of triangulation that a true position is derived and it is by the same process that you can confirm that the correct output has been achieved. When confirmation of the change process is required, as least two of the players shown in Fig. 10.1 should be involved.

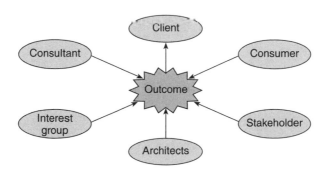

Fig. 10.1 Schematic views

This triangulation process can include any mix of players. The most common triangulation will be one that uses you and the client. The problem here is that the real issues that are being faced by the consumer are potentially left out of the equation. For example, in reviewing the outcomes associated with reengineering, your view might be that you have delivered the agreed reduction in time to market and the client's view is that the overall costs of the business will be reduced. The problem is that no-one is around to voice the issues that have surfaced as a result of the your change. The increase in sick leave, reduced quality and general cultural dissent are all potential issues that would not be picked up in this triangulation.

The natural response is to include the consumers in the confirmation process. However, who then raises the concerns of the interest groups and the fact that the change might result in a serious gender or racial bias within the company? You must understand this problem and be able to take on a multiple personality role – to be able to objectively represent the views of the various actors and in doing this ignore the subjective personal interests within the engagement. Although this is difficult in the short term, by presenting an approach grounded in integrity, the long-term payback more than covers any losses. If you are able to demonstrate the capability to deliver a reasoned and impartial view on the success of the change then this increases the chance of gaining further contracts.

So at the end of the engagement, your aim must be to stand in the shoes of each of the various groups and experience how the change might look and feel to them. So for the reengineering project, there might be real evidence that the social structure of the organization has been damaged; for the consumers a fear culture has surfaced; and for the financial stakeholders an indication that the financial investors are not happy about the change strategy. However, just because you decide to ignore these feelings and thoughts, it doesn't mean that they will not create problems in the future. If there are confirmation issues for any of the players, then it is better to deal with them online rather than waiting for them to fester.

> **Back pocket question**
>
> Do I know who will own and manage the measurement process?

Timing

The measured success of a project is often linked more to the timing of the assessment than to the delivered benefit. Some change processes will kick in overnight; others might take weeks or months and some large-scale processes might take years to realize a payback for the company. As Senge *et al.* (1999) stress, don't judge the ultimate success or failure of your efforts based solely on early results. Managers often want to pull up the radishes to see how they are growing and pushing the measuring process can disrupt the delivery of the desired outcome. As such we constantly disregard the importance of time delays in the engagement and assume that we live in a mechanistic society where an input leads to an immediate output. The possibility that we actually live in a complex and dynamic world, where change is unpredictable, is seemingly forgotten in the rush to deliver hard outputs.

Consider a trainer who has been employed to introduce a culture change programme into a medium-sized organization with the goal of improving performance in the customer service department. She decides to run a series of workshops that introduces some new human resource processes, specifically team meetings, appraisal system, upward feedback meetings, etc. The programme is launched in a blaze of publicity, with the active support of the managing director and the board. All goes well until news comes in that the company will be purchasing a smaller competitor in order to rapidly grow its market share. Although the MD and the board believe in the need for a cultural shift in the business, their time begins to be taken up with the acquisition. The result is that many of the people start to doubt the senior team's belief in the changes and stories start to circulate about how the new appraisal system is being abused in some departments.

Clearly the consultant has delivered the changes specified by the client. The problem is: when does the measurement take place to confirm that the outcomes have been achieved? Through no fault of her own, factors have conspired to affect the assignment to the point where major remedial work will be required to bring the transformation back online. The timing of the change will affect the perception of the outcome and might well even affect the final remuneration that she receives. Consider the four different time slots where confirmation might take place (Fig. 10.2):

- (T1) Shooting star: Any consultant who wants to impress the client will measure the change when the momentum is at its peak. At this stage both desirability and capability to become involved in the change is quite high, hence the confirmation process is likely to show it to be a raving success.

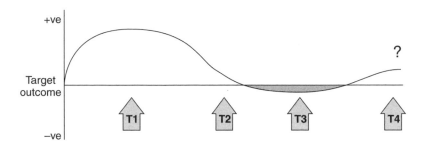

Fig. 10.2   Confirmation time slots

- (T2) It wasn't me: As new toys and interests come along, the organization will eventually tire of the change. Undertaking the confirmation process at this stage will be the kiss of death. The negative bias that people put on failed projects will potentially put the chance of any further work in jeopardy.

- (T3) It's over: In many cases, the negative spin applied to the change can actually result in the view that the company should never have embarked on the change and that it caused more problems that it cured. Measuring the transformation at this stage would be akin to committing professional suicide.

- (T4) Never give up on a good thing: Once the dust has settled and a sense of reality returns, most change projects are seen to have added something. As such it is possible to measure a residual outcome, one deeply embedded in the culture of the business.

Clearly this model takes a pessimistic view. I am not suggesting that this cycle will happen in all change processes, but it will happen in a number of them. Your goal must be to ensure that the dips at T2 and T3 are never actually reached and that sufficient energy and momentum is maintained to hold the gains.

Your goal should be to develop a process that truly measures the value of the change as opposed to the impact of the uncontrolled extrinsic factors. Unless you have the ability to see into the future, you will never be able to predict where your change is on the curve. As such, you must build in as many measures as possible to ensure that you obtain a true picture.

Back pocket question

Have I decided when the confirmation and measurement will take place?

Design

When you start to design the measurement process, there are primarily two things to consider. First, there is the extent to which the measurement is qualitative or quantitative. The second concern is are you measuring the process or outcome of the engagement? By pulling these two dimensions together, we can construct the matrix shown in Fig. 10.3. From this, four types of measurement are developed that can be used to confirm progress.

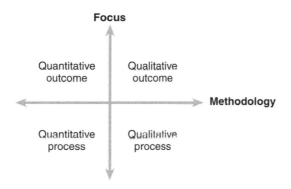

Fig. 10.3   Measurement matrix

Quantitative outcomes

Against this, it would be practical to set many of the factors that may have contributed to the approval for investment in the strategic engagement. For example, the number of people undertaking external training programmes, cost of internal workshops, increase in intellectual capital, etc. However, this is a dangerous measure and one that is abused. The use of quantitative measures can lead to people trying to achieve the measures rather than trying to change the culture. It can also create a false sense of end goals, e.g. 'well we meet the 75 per cent criteria so we can back off now'. Finally, any manager with a degree of common sense can meet targets by simply juggling resources and spreadsheet data.

Quantitative process

This includes many of the standard project management measures: achievement of milestones, number of completed tasks, cost overrun, etc. As a tangible measure, it is very effective for keeping minds focused on the process of change and ensuring that resources are carefully managed. This is fine if the organization is installing a new computer system or building a new extension, but people are not plant or equipment. People are unpredictable and social change is uncertain. The idea of hard measures for the process is entirely correct but there has to be a degree of care to ensure that the measures do not become more important than the desired outcome. If this were to happen, the measures tend to take the focus away from the end goal and act as an attenuator that restricts the change and learning process. The old adage that 'what gets measured gets done', often becomes 'what gets measured gets bluffed'.

Qualitative process

This approach is concerned with understanding how people feel about the engagement. It is driven by how people perceive the change at an intuitive and emotional level. The difficulty is that there is nothing that an accountant can really get a handle on to produce a cost benefit chart and little for the whole business to get a hold of to get a feel for the change. The only way that people can really get a feel for progress is by becoming a part of the change itself. In doing this they will also derive an intuitive appreciation of the progress made and where the change is heading. The key point is that businesses are not run for pleasure – they are run to maximize the profitability of shareholder investment. If shareholders cannot be satisfied that the investment is worthwhile, there is always a chance that any resources allocated to the engagement will be withdrawn.

Qualitative outcomes

This section is virtually the same as the qualitative process, except that it is concerned with the change in daily life as perceived by people in the business. These measures might be drawn from interviews with people after they have been through some experiential parts of the change initiative. They will help to understand how the deeper issues around the culture are transformed. One approach is to map people's perception of the changes in the cultural artefacts within the business against the stated outcomes.

The measurement process is a minefield. However, always remember that measurements exist to gauge progress, not to drive change.

The measurement process is a minefield. However, always remember that measurements exist to gauge progress, not to drive change. The push should come from people's desire to make the change and the pull should be driven by an agreed outcome, not the numbers on a spreadsheet.

Depth

When confirming that a change has taken place, you must determine how deep to measure. Do you need to determine the extent to which the environment or behaviours of the target audience have changed? Or do you need to measure the change in people's mindset and feelings? It can help to use the change ladder to understand the type of measures to be applied.

For change focused on external factors at the 'asset' or 'blueprint' levels, the measures will be focused on tangible deliverables: is the system in place and working, have the tools been provided or have the marketing recommendations been implemented? For change at the 'capability' level, the measure will be around change in behaviours, skills or competencies. When measuring the 'desire' level, the focus will be on changes in the way that people feel or think about themselves, the company or colleagues. When confirming change at the 'existence' level, the measure is focused on people's beliefs, team mission or company vision statements.

The key thing to appreciate is the difference in methodology or approach required when developing a confirmation process for each of these levels. The variations in style are shown in Fig. 10.4, where the dynamics between the various levels are indicated. When the change is measured at the existence or desire level, the methodology is likely to be subjective and focused on long-term change, concerned with invisible factors and with an emphasis on long-term transformation. This is often difficult to measure because of its intangibility. At the other end, confirming that change has taken place at the asset or blueprint levels uses methodologies that focus on visible transformation, objective measures, short-term change and quantitative process. It is relativity easy to do because of the tangibility of the elements being measured.

In summary, the pressure to deliver change in a limited time, at the cheapest rate and with the highest quality will conspire to press the confirmation to take place towards the bottom of the ladder. The aspiration is often to confirm that the change is delivered and then move on to the next project. While in many cases this is viable, there is a danger that the true essence of the change is never being measured – and as such the heart of the individual, team or organization is hidden because measurement is focused on the espoused rather than the actual change.

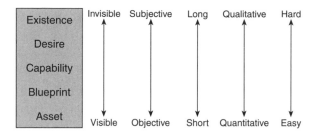

Fig. 10.4 Confirmation level dynamics

People will focus on delivering what is measured rather than what is needed. If short-term fixes are what the client requires, the lower-level measures will be appropriate. But if the client is looking for a deep, long-term sustainable change, then the confirmation must deal with those issues at the upper end of the ladder.

Back pocket question

Have I decided if the measurement is focused on extrinsic issues or will it deal with intrinsic issues such as attitude, motivation and beliefs?

Data map

One of the potential problems in the Confirm stage is data overload and mis-alignment. There are numerous ways in which to measure how the client system has changed, and there is every likelihood that the confirmation team will consist of people from a range of areas. The use of such a diverse team of people can lead to political in-fighting, data discrepancy and inefficient resource allocation.

Imagine the case of a call centre computer system upgrade. The IT team might be focused on measuring system performance by monitoring the transaction speed across the network. The client will want to conform that the new system has increased the call-handling rate. You might want to ensure that the people have received effective training in the new system. Finally, the finance director has decided to use the audit team to guarantee that financial integrity has been maintained. Unless all these activity streams are managed cohesively, then it will be difficult to agree if the change has fulfilled its objectives. One solution is to trace the various measurement activities on to a common map, one that indicates the type of measurement, who owns the activity and why it is being taken.

When building the data map, it is important to ensure that people are clear why the data is being gathered. Usually it is for one of these five reasons:

● **Augment:** This is used to create the initial data set or build or expand upon the level of knowledge about a particular area. So if the data indicates that certain issues within the engagement might have been less than effective, the choice is to re-visit to get more data on which to take a decision.

● **Broaden:** It can help to gather broader-based data, possibly about other parts of the organization, benchmarking against other businesses or wider academic views on a particular subject.

● **Confirm:** To verify that a particular data set is giving accurate information, possibly by triangulation or by a repeat process in the same area.

● **Depth:** The goal is to develop a more detailed picture about a topic. This might be where you mine deeper into a financial report, gather more data on people's views about a subject or run a focus group with customers to verify that a product enhancement is adding value.

● **External verification:** You can use external agents to verify that bias or corruption has not crept into the change. They are able to verify that the process and the content of the findings are accurate and reflect the true outcomes. The term 'external' might mean independent consultants or agency groups or simply a separate department within the company that hasn't been affected by the transition.

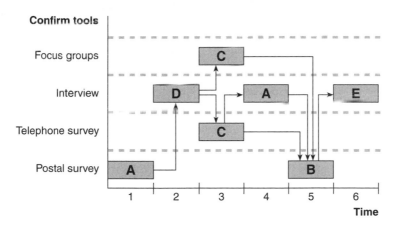

Fig. 10.5   Data map for customer service confirmation

Take as an example a customer service programme implemented in a national fast food chain (Fig. 10.5). In building the data map, the steps are:

- *Augment* the limited data by running a postal survey. The aim is to build the first data set to ensure that all people have attended the programme and to gather their initial thoughts.

- Gather information in more *depth* about some of the issues raised in the feedback through a series of random interviews.

- To check this data to *confirm* the outcomes with a number of focus groups and a limited telephone survey.

- The results would then be *augmented* by specific interviews.

- All of this data are used to build a customer survey questionnaire and so *broaden* the information by undertaking a postal survey with a selected range of customers that have used the service since the programme has been introduced.

- Finally, the results from the confirmation process are *externally* verified by asking the company's internal audit branch to confirm that the change has been successful.

Unless the data are sourced with care and control, there is a chance that the confirmation will be superficial. The data map helps to ensure that alignment is maintained and also helps clients and consumers to understand how confirmation of the change will be managed.

> **Back pocket question**
>
> Do I have a plan to ensure that an integrated approach is taken to the clarification stage?

Consulting performance

Of all the different measures that you will instigate, one of the most important is to confirm your personal effectiveness. For this you will need to gather some quite specific and detailed feedback from the client and consumer on your performance. Although the feedback can take many forms, one effective process is to gather it on three fronts: how the process was managed; the delivery of the task; and what feelings the client has about the project. As with the principle offered in other areas of this section, wherever possible the measures should be triangulated with data gleaned from as many interest groups as possible. The questions framed as part of the review will depend on the context and project but generic issues to be considered are covered in Table 10.1.

Table 10.1   Performance issues

	Self	Client	Consumer
Task ● Delivered what was promised – both explicitly and implicitly ● Costs managed within budget ● Expenses managed within budget ● Able to respond to unforeseen changes in the project ● Anticipated the needs of the client and consumers			
Process ● Always kept others aware of progress ● Meetings managed effectively ● Flagged deviations as soon as they emerged ● Ensured that the appropriate decision-making style was used throughout the engagement ● Understood and positively used the network of stakeholders			
Feelings ● Had confirmed that the project would be delivered ● Felt able to talk about deep issues that were of concern ● Able to adapt and blend in with the local culture ● People believed in the competency to effect the change ● Managed the needs and feelings of all stakeholders			

Back pocket question

Has my performance been up to the standard expected by the client?

Costs

Safety is a difficult issue for an airline. Although the ultimate goal is to spend as much money as necessary to ensure the safety of the passengers, there is a break point on the expenditure curve where it becomes uneconomical to invest any more money. The same applies to the investment in the measurement process. Clearly you, the client and the consumer all need to have a clear appreciation of the impact and value of the change. But there is a cost associated with any measurement process. At some point you will need to agree with the client when it becomes uneconomical to measure.

Consider the implementation of a customer service-training programme within a large organization. While the client might wish to undertake a full measurement and evaluation process to confirm that the engagement has worked, there is a downside: the cost of developing the confirmation system; the cost of taking people away from dealing with customers; and the potential cultural corruption that is incurred as people play games with their responses. The alternative view might be that if the programme has worked, then any change will be apparent in the way customers are dealt with – so why bother with a grand confirmation process? Neither argument is right, but the client must understand the two extremes in order to develop an appropriate and cost-effective confirmation process.

However, in making this decision you need to have a clear view as to the various costs:

- **Design:** These arise from the initial front-end work that takes place in the confirmation process. This might be sizing the market to be measured, designing the survey criteria, developing the questionnaires and arranging for people to attend a focus group. Depending on the process being used, this is biased heavily towards the use of a professional to design or administer the process.

- **Deploy:** These are the direct operational costs incurred from running the measurement process. This includes printing and mailing questionnaires, paying for meeting rooms, paying professional interviewers and telephone charges. In the main these will be quite predictable.

174

● **Deliver:** These costs are associated with taking the primary data from the measurement process and turning it into something that has value for the consultant and client. This can be data modelling with a software package, aligning the data with industry benchmark information or preparing a slide presentation for the client. These costs might have a tendency to overrun, as they are difficult to pin down. Just one stray comment from the director who wants a 'bit more information on the slides' can result in cost overrun.

Table 10.2

	Design	Deployment	Delivery
Postal survey	Standard costs, most of which will be in the design of the questionnaire	Just mail and admin time. Money is saved if an e-mail system is used. This can also indicate if people have received and read the survey form	So long as the questionnaire has been designed properly and is quantitative in nature, then analysis is relatively easy and cheap
Open interviews	Limited up-front costs, but is high in preparing people for the interview process	High costs in taking people away from their jobs and the costs of the interviewer	High potential costs in coding and analyzing the final data. Time is saved if interviewee does partial coding
Telephone survey	Questionnaire design	Telephone costs and interviewer's time, also takes people away from their jobs	Analysis should be relatively low-cost, especially if response is fed online to a computer system
Observation	Low up-front costs, but assumes that observer will have necessary skills and knowledge to do the job	No direct costs from people being observed, just observer's time	Potential high costs associated with coding and analyzing what is apparently wild and diverse data
Diary	Low up-front costs apart from diaries	Just the person's time who is filling out diary	Potentially huge as data is random and diverse
Focus groups	Some up-front costs in design and administration costs for getting people together	High time costs of facilitator and participants	Potentially high costs of analysis and presentation

When you discuss the costs associated with the Confirm phase, you should have a few facts and figures ready to answer questions from the client. Typically the 'what happens if' type questions can end up either costing you a great deal of money or put you in the embarrassing position of having to tell the client the confirmation costs are much higher than anticipated. As a result, you must consider the measurement processes that are available and start to understand what cost drivers will affect the final figure. A few examples are shown in Table 7.4.

Although there will always be pressure to reduce confirmation costs, there is a risk that too much downward pressure will increase the level of errors within the process. A decision to reduce expenditure in any of the confirmation areas will increase the error cost. These errors arise because the returns are not truly representative of the final situation or the data are incorrect and have to be gathered again. You must always be attentive to the fact that at the run-down stage of a project people's minds will be elsewhere, the budget will be drained and careers are always made on the next project. Hence there is a tendency to cut corners. This is a false economy and every effort should be made to ensure the robustness of the confirmation process.

Back pocket question

Have I a clear view of what impact costs will have on the different measurement processes?

Chapter 11

Stage six: Continue

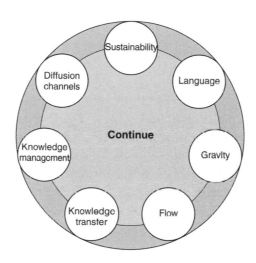

Many receive advice, few profit by it.

Publilius Syrus

The most common criticism of consultants is that once their report has been completed it is put on the shelf to gather dust along with all the other consultants' reports. As a result, the change is only short-lived and the problem returns. Imagine if you went to the dentist only to find that your toothache returned the following morning or employed a builder to construct an extension and found cracks appearing two weeks later. The goal is real long-term results, not short-term fixes. Czerniawska (1999) aptly makes this point:

> *Although as a consultant, you recognize that the prime responsibility for implementation lies with the client, you also know that your job is not done – or not done properly – until you have helped the client achieve real results.*

The key question that the dentist, builder or consultant must ask is: 'How can I ensure that any changes or recommendations that have been offered will continue following my departure?' Failure to consider the issue of continuance can result in the following:

- A strategy consultant has worked furiously for six months and finally delivered his report to the board. It offers a highly elaborate review of the current market position and the company's capability to move into new markets. However, the one thing he forgot to do is get the emotional buy-in of the key stakeholders. The report is warmly accepted and endorsed by the board but fails to be implemented because it doesn't align with the background political issues.

- A quality programme had been underway for some time and senior managers were keen to see the benefits. A consultant was employed to implement a rigorous tracking system that could highlight progress. The problem was that people were asked to fill out countless forms that detailed all their actions. The end result was that in some cases over a third of their time was spent on administration, thus preventing people from actually delivering the quality improvements.

- As part of a system integration programme, consultants were brought in to manage the design process. All went well and the transfer to the new systems went without any problems. However, once the consultants left, the managers realized they had a problem, the consultants had effectively taken the expertise with them and there was little within the company to maintain the system. As a result, they had to agree a new contract with the consultants to come in and train the local IT staff on the new system.

- As part of a marketing director's brand development programme, consultants wanted to ensure that people were encouraged to live the company brand values when dealing with customers. The first thing they did was to communicate the brand value and what was expected of the people. However, other directors did not really agree with the brand formulation being suggested and when the information came into the communication channels under their control, they augmented it with the brand aspects that they wanted to see included. The end result was that the programme became diluted and corrupted to a point where the whole initiative had to be re-launched.

Clearly, sustainability is difficult. You need to ensure that the following actions are considered from the outset of the change process:

- **Sustainability:** Ensure that slippage does not occur once the project has been closed.

- **Language:** Part of the way in which continuance is made possible is by modifying client and consumer language as part of the transformation process.

- **Gravity:** You must always make sure that any supporting administrative system does not end up as a bureaucracy that will strangle it.

- **Flow:** Make sure the organization learns from the change experience as well as the final outcome.

- **Knowledge transfer:** If the benefits are to be maximized, both the client and the consultant must ensure that a learning transfer takes place so that key elements of the consultants' competencies remain in the business following their departure.

- **Knowledge management:** Any knowledge created as part of the consultancy change must be embodied as a tangible asset for the business.

- **Diffusion channels:** You must undertake a practical analysis of the client's capability to diffuse new ideas across the organization.

The continuance of any change is based on the fact that it will become embedded in the client's system. However, you cannot do this in isolation. In the same way that a doctor cannot resolve a patient's problems without their support, you must work with the client to ensure that they take ownership of the outcome. Working through the ideas covered in this stage with the client will help to ensure that the change will continue once you have moved on.

Sustainability

For the majority of change programmes, you must help the client to hold on to the gains. Slippage is one of the most difficult issues to resolve. People may have the necessary energy to deliver the transformation but they do not all have the power and desire to continue through until the end of the engagement. Even when change is complete, many tend to drift back to the initial state after a short period.

Change is often not sustainable because it has been enacted at the asset, blueprint or capability level of the change ladder, but not locked in at the desire or existence level. Imagine a racing car driver who is unable to attain peak performance on the track. His car has been re-tuned, he has been on a development programme to enhance his driving skills and has been coached by the best guru possible in order to develop a positive mental attitude. The unspoken problem is that he has reached a breakpoint – the thought of speeding around a track at 200mph no longer appeals. His real personal goal is to become a teacher, specifically to help young teenagers to learn how to drive. The end result is that any action to improve his performance might work in the short term, but will eventually fade away because there is little deep desire to change. In the same way, any organization that tries to install a quality culture, create a customer-focused ethos or develop a cost-focused culture must ensure that it aligns with the basic purpose of the business.

The second point to consider is the extent to which the change is driven by extrinsic or intrinsic forces. Imagine you are trying to encourage your child to brush his teeth every day. One option is to stand over him every morning and force a change in behaviour. However, until the behaviour is locked in, the moment that the parent is away the child will forget or choose not to brush his teeth. For the organization, if the managing director drives the change then the moment his attention is diverted, people will ignore the change and revert to type.

You must also understand how change fits in with the political system. When individuals operate in teams or organizations, they will be attuned to the political shifts within the business. The political actors, who either use the energy behind the change to further their political agenda or to resist the change because it potentially erodes their power base, will eagerly seize upon any new initiative or project. For the change to be sustainable, you must be able to present it in a non-threatening way to people who may damaged by it. If you are designing a new computer system that will reduce the headcount in the IT department, then you must market the change in such a way that the systems people recognize the opportunities that will emerge. Otherwise there is every chance that the teams most affected by the change will do everything in their power to sabotage the process once you have left.

You must also develop a deep appreciation of the governance system: how are decisions made?; how is the management board constructed?; what is the process for logging actions?; who has control over the deployment of resources? All these factors can either drive or kill a change process. You need to understand both the overt and covert governance system and ensure that the change being proposed is able to operate in such a system.

Suppose you have been hired to install a new stock control system that allows requisitions to be managed at a local level. The governance system might react badly to this model if financial control is normally held with a financial director who likes to get involved in all the purchase decisions. There is every chance that once the system is installed then the first action that the financial director will take is to bring it back in line with the existing control systems. The consultant has two choices: to either work closely with the financial director to change his or her values about the level of financial accountability with the organization or, second, build in sufficient low-level system controls to ensure that management of the system will be held at the devolved level.

Sustainability is not something to be considered at the end of the cycle. Although it is positioned in stage six of the framework, you must be tuned into the potential for sustainability from the very outset. When addressing any of the other six stages this issue must be at the forefront of your mind:

- **Client:** If there is a risk that the project is a stopgap and cannot be sustained, then it is better to say no to the project. Although rejecting potential income will always be difficult, the danger is that in accepting a non-starter, the client will eventually regard your input as worthless and may even say this to other people.

- **Clarify:** The cultural and political issues need to be brought out in order to find the basis for longevity. This might include aligning the change with the organization's strategic goals; embedding the transformation into the company HR systems; or modifying the reward system.

- **Create:** Develop ideas and process that align with the organization values and do not work in opposition to the natural forces. If a revolutionary rather than evolutionary change is required, make sure that the engagement has plenty of supporting hooks to lock in the transformation once you have left.

- **Change:** When you map the energy being used to drive change, ensure that it will continue after your departure – if not, then try to lock in alternative energy sources to maintain pressure on the organization. If, for example, the change is the installation of a new accounting system and you think the IT group will lose interest, prepare the accounting team to take over once the system is installed.

- **Confirm:** When you design the confirmation process, the tendency is to measure how things work now – especially if your client is looking for proof of output to guarantee payment. However, it is also important to look for proof of sustainability – have people really accepted the change and is it embedded into the behaviours or management systems?

- **Close:** Ensure that the client is aware of the sustaining hooks that have been used in the engagement and what action needs to be taken to ensure they hold in place.

Sustainability will always be a factor of the structural surround that supports change. There is little point in pushing one department to reengineer its systems and processes if the rest of the organization continues to use out-of-date processes; and there is little chance that a new accounting system will be used if people are not trained. If change is to be sustainable then is must be in alignment with the structure where it sits and the appropriate hooks and links must be tied in with the transformation process.

Back pocket question

Do I have a plan in place to ensure that slippage doesn't occur once the project has been closed?

Language

The extent to which change has been baked in can be determined by the shift in people's language. The quality consultant will hear a greater use of words like customer needs, cost of quality or agreed standards. The market strategist will hear words like customer segmentation, value chain or brand development. In changing the language, you will help ensure continuance of change. Although this is not guaranteed in all contexts, it does offer a good indication as to the effectiveness of the transformation. Just listen to the way that children will adopt the language of their favourite cartoon character. The ability to mimic and copy the latest buzzword offers the child membership of a select band of friends and peers.

This power of language to influence how people behave should never be underestimated. We often think that language is simply a way of describing something to another person. However, communication is a magical process that takes the ideas and schematic models from one person's mind and creates them in someone else's. By the use of words, patterns, inflections and sounds an individual builds something new and original in someone else's mind when they speak. So as an idea is socialized through an organization, it is not the case that it is being passed from one person to another like a relay race. At each juncture, the idea is reborn and re-created in another person's mind. Each time this creation takes place, it will be subject to amplification, distortion and attenuation. Like the game of Chinese whispers, the language element of the socialization process can have a significant impact on the way in which knowledge is received and changed behaviours are eventually delivered.

This power of language to influence how people behave should never be underestimated.

The embodiment of new language into the culture of an organization is seen and heard in many different ways. The use of shared metaphors can help to explain a particular idea in terms of another experience. The metaphor is used in two ways: first an implied analogy, where comparison is drawn between two similar things (say, Ford and General Motors); alternatively, it is in the nature of a figurative analogy that draws a comparison between two seemingly different things (musician and manager). You can often use these when trying to explain a complex subject. The test is when you hear the same metaphor being passed on to other people. Alternatively, jargon and catch phrases help to frame the idea in a set of words or context that help the recipient feel comfortable.

Finally, think about 'spin'. Spin is a process whereby you can take an idea and deliberately offer it in a positive or negative light. This is used sometimes (over zealously) by politicians as they try to angle a story so that it looks favourable to their party. It can also be seen in programmes where people talk about the role they took in the transition programme – often escalating their importance when the change has been successful.

The ability to lock in change through the modification of a company's language base can offer immense value. In changing how people talk you are effectively modifying the corporate DNA. So in effecting a change in the client or consumer language, you will be seen to modify the organizational genes that describe how the business operates.

In summary, as changes become embedded in language, so will the associated behavioural transformation. This changed behaviour becomes the norm and is accepted as part of how things are naturally managed. The net result is that continuance is locked in through the shared language and mental models, rather than having to create any overt control system to check that people are changing their behaviour.

> **Back pocket question**
>
> Have I been able to modify the client and consumer language as part of the transformation process?

Gravity

In ensuring the continuance of the change, it is important to focus on the intent driving the transition. For example, in writing this book, there was a clear intent to produce something new and original about the field of consulting and change management. In theory, fulfilling the intent is quite easy – just sit down and write a chapter every month and out pops the finished book. However, nothing is quite so simple. Along the way different things occur that both slow the process down and cause energy to be diverted from writing the book. The children's homework, family problems, boredom and so on all conspire to drag the author away from the original plan.

In the same way, your client might have an overt goal to implement a new programme but along the way things occur that cause a deviation. The greatest cause of 'intent' corruption can be the organization itself. In many cases, the weight of the structure and bureaucracy built around a change process can take energy away from the transformation.

In the case of the sole trader everything that the individual does contributes to the declared goal to deliver a profitable return on the investment. Effective management of the customer interaction generally delivers this return. There is a straight line that connects the energy of the individual to the customer and the intent is clear and understood. Once the business starts to grow, people will be recruited and the birth of a new organization takes place. However, at this point it is possible to see activities that are not directly related to the delivery of customer service. This will include the occasional meeting to discuss missing stock, forms to fill out to satisfy tax officials and agreeing who will provide cover when people are ill. The end result is that the intent is still in place, but the energy is being drained (Fig. 11.1).

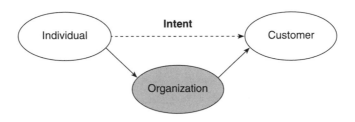

Fig. 11.1   Company growth drains energy

After a year or two, a full-blown organization is in place with a hundred people and all the associated trappings that go with it. Now it is possible to see the effect of organizational gravity acting on the planned intent. The weight of the business systems makes it harder for the service to be delivered. The business has people whose sole responsibility is to deal with internal matters – half-day meetings on budget preparation, two-day workshops on setting the vision and resolving problems that the organization created for itself. It is at this stage that the weight created by organizational gravity can stop the change process from taking place. Fig. 11.2 shows how the energy is focused more upon the needs of the organization than those of the intended outcome. This is seen in many change programmes. Supporting bureaucracy often surrounds total quality and cumbersome systems are regularly built to achieve ISO 9000 registration.

You must ensure that the change intent is always at the forefront of people's minds. If someone wants to install a bureaucratic system then challenge the need for such systems. Every time that a participant is asked to fill in a form or report on progress to the board then this is energy being taken away from the desired goal. You must make sure the client and consumer are aware of the impact of such activities and how they can destabilize the change process.

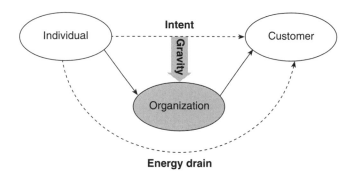

Fig. 11.2   Organizational gravity can kill change

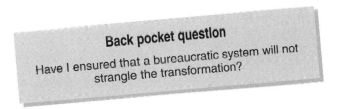

Flow

Many of the gains from change projects can be found in the learning and knowledge that develops as part of the change process. For example, a company might be in the process of upgrading its local network. There will be the chance to look at the alignment between the organizational structure and the network configuration; the opportunity to meet and learn from external agents and contractors; a chance to experience the customer experience from a personal perspective. The problem is that organizations can become so engrossed in the tangible outcome that they fail to take the opportunity to learn from the experience itself.

Although you will obviously be focused on the end delivery, there is also a requirement to ensure that people take time to reflect and learn. For each deviation or problem that emerges during the project, people will normally go through three distinct phases. The first stage is to undertake an action as set out in the plan. As a result, the client will have something that they can reflect on. This reflection might take the form of what happened, did it go according to plan, what action did I take to make a correction? From this reflective process, the client will have ample data on which to base conclusions and so create new knowledge. This is then pushed back into the change, to either ease the change process or to store away for use at a further date.

One other factor that can affect on the sustainability of change is your behaviour. In many assignments, consultants (without realizing it) can ignore the fundamental principles that are being introduced within the transition. How often are quality programmes implemented without any process controls; management development programmes run by untrained facilitators; and cost-cutting exercises led by expensive consultants? Whenever you make a change, even the slightest deviation from the principles being delivered causes the consumer to question the viability of the change. A passing derogatory comment by a behavioural consultant, an incorrect slide during a presentation on quality or the introduction of a new consultant who hasn't been fully briefed. Any agents that are opposed to the transformation will use all of these factors as ammunition against the change process.

Rather than the client learning from their experience, they will feed your behaviour into a loop, draw conclusions from action and form the view that the change is not worthwhile. This can have a disastrous impact on the flow of the change and in many cases reduce any chance that the client will use you for future contracts.

> **Back pocket question**
>
> Do I know what learning has taken place from the experience?

Knowledge transfer

In many cases, you might have been employed because a company does not have the necessary skills or knowledge. Both you and the client have a responsibility to ensure that a learning transfer takes place during the change cycle so that the benefits of the contract are maximized. Your goal is to make sure that the essential elements of your competencies remain in the business. There are three types of knowledge that the client should seek to retain once you have left:

- **Tacit:** the skills and knowledge that are used naturally without any overt thought.
- **Explicit:** the codified skills and knowledge that you bring to the business.
- **Relational:** wisdom that emerges as a result of the social interaction between the client, consultant, consumers and any other players in the engagement.

You must work with the client to understand what skills they want to retain and how best that transfer can be made during the engagement.

Tacit knowledge

Tacit knowledge is formed by the thoughts, feelings and intuition that go on in the background while people are performing a task. At an organizational level, it is characterized as routines, which are the rules, procedures, conventions, strategies and technologies that act as building blocks for an organization (Levitt and March, 1996). It might also be regarded as the beliefs, frameworks and general cultural artefacts that make up the softer elements of an organization.

Although the creation and exploitation of tacit knowledge is desirable from a commercial viewpoint, it does have a major drawback in that it is difficult to transfer within an organization. There are many reasons for this, including:

- Context dependent: the musician who is only able to shine with a certain group of other musicians.

- Difficult to articulate: the chef unable to describe what makes the difference between a good and a great meal.

- Hard to facilitate collaboration: since tacit knowledge is often thought of in terms of personal metaphors and symbols, a metaphor shared between two people might have a totally different connotation to each.

- Requires presence: although it is possible for a skilled pilot in a control tower to talk down a novice in a plane, it is very difficult. Some skill and knowledge are not readily transferred without immediate and close visual contact.

- Emotional barriers: tacit knowledge has a deep personal meaning. For an expert to share knowledge they have spent years gathering means the recipient must be trusted not to abuse the learning.

- Complex: knowledge is not always readily identifiable in a distinct form. It is like a pot-pourri, a mix of different sets of knowledge, experiences and feelings.

Although these factors can make it difficult to transfer, tacit knowledge is the fountain of wisdom. A large element of knowledge innovation will originate from a tacit level and it grows in value as it is transferred from tacit to explicit level and from person to person.

Explicit knowledge

Explicit knowledge is something that is easily talked about, codified and documented. It is a commodity that is readily shared with other people, stored, retrieved and embodied in tangible products, services or processes. Examples that display the attributes of explicit knowledge are:

- training manuals;
- newspapers;
- equipment user guides;
- college lectures.

While explicit knowledge has the benefit of being readily communicated, stored and retrieved, the downside is that it is easily lost to competitors. It is transferred over the Internet at the touch of a keystroke, overheard in a bar or simply deduced by analyzing a company's products. One common example of this is seen in the automobile market. Companies will regularly purchase their competitors' products, rip them apart and extract the embedded knowledge for their own products.

Relational knowledge

Knowledge is created or discovered when you interact with your client. There are times when something inexplicable happens between two people – a manifestation that would not have happened to an individual. Every time you sit down to discuss options and ideas with a client, you have the chance to create new relational capital. It is the existence of this social asset that offers so much hidden value. All organizations have particular capabilities for creating a market advantage and this is often found in the space between the people. Your role is to grab the capital that exists in your relationship with your client and use this to fuel change.

All organizations have particular capabilities for creating a market advantage and this is often found in the space between the people.

The relational discovery process can take place in two forms, either at the tacit or explicit level. Tacit relational knowledge exists where people that work together over a period of time will improve their working methods but may not recognize or discuss the improvement. Examples are musicians who play together for a long period or comedians who intuitively grow their appreciation of each other's style and preferred methods of working. Alternatively, relational knowledge can exist at the explicit level. Examples are researchers writing a paper together or a project team where people share ideas in building the project plans.

You need to constantly monitor your relationship with the client and consumer and grasp knowledge opportunities wherever you can. This might be the fact that you have a shared friend who might help develop a new operational procedure; that your shared interest in sailing can be used to develop a team-building event; or that you both studied at the same college and look at problems in a similar way. Whatever the capital asset, just ensure that you activity use it to aid the change.

Back pocket question

Have I ensured that elements of my competencies will remain in the business?

Knowledge management

Once you have ensured that any necessary tacit, explicit and relational knowledge has been passed to the client or consumers, the question is: how does this knowledge get transferred to the rest of the organization? The first step is to map and understand the organization's knowledge infrastructure so that you appreciate how any knowledge created as part of the consultancy change can be embodied into a tangible asset.

The creation of intellectual capital is based on the successful discovery of knowledge and its embodiment into an organization's systems, processes and products. This process of embodiment is widely discussed, analyzed and pronounced upon but there is little agreement (and is unlikely to ever be) on its delivery. Fig. 11.3 offers a simple but effective knowledge management model.

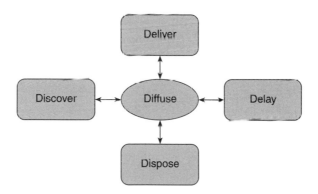

Fig. 11.3   Knowledge management model

Within any organization, knowledge is processed through five stages between discovery and delivery to the end customer:

- **Discovery:** This is where the knowledge is unearthed through a range of processes, including personal invention, group socialization or recruitment of external agents.

189

- **Diffusion:** Once discovered, the knowledge has to be diffused. This is through formal systems such as intranets and journals or through the social network of team meetings or workshops.

- **Delivery:** Once the knowledge has been discovered, it can become embodied within the organization's product or processes. This is as a new piece of software code, an enhanced product design or a new customer service programme.

- **Delay:** However, it might not be practical to embed it immediately into the products or services. In this case the knowledge is (intentionally or unintentionally) held in storage.

- **Disposal:** Although the knowledge is likely to become redundant at some stage it might have some residual asset value to the business. Depending upon its half-life, this might be overnight or it may be a century. The key is to ensure that the disposal process is controlled and the financial gain for the organization is maximized.

As an example, a consultant has been asked to develop a new strategy for a medium-sized company. It is important that the knowledge infrastructure is clearly understood, otherwise the company will be unable to maintain the process once the consultant has left. So the goal is two-fold. First, clearly deliver a change that the business can accept. Second, understand how knowledge is diffused across the business. In this example, the consultant might ask the following questions:

- **Discovery:** How is strategy currently developed? Through a series of company plans, business projection and budget forecasts or is it something that people instinctively know and is held tacitly in people's minds?

- **Diffuse:** Once company strategy is developed, how does it gain approval? What are the processes that enable it to be locked into business processes? What happens if the ideas are not seen to be appropriate for the business? Who has the power to decide on any proposed strategy?

- **Deliver:** You must be able to clarify what your client means when he or she talks about 'the strategy'. Is it a restricted document circulated to the board, an open site on the company intranet or a set of beliefs that are embodied in the organization's culture?

- **Delay:** In developing any business strategy, scenario planning is often used as the diagnostic tool to prepare the potential options. As part of this process, there is a natural redundancy of data as different scenarios are deemed impractical for current market conditions. The question is, how can the organization hold on to this knowledge for use at a later date? Does it have a managed archive process whereby potential future strategies are retained for future use or will it be held in the minds of the participants?

- **Dispose:** You must understand how obsolete strategies are disposed of. Does the company formally close down previous plans or is it a grey process whereby it gradually slips from consciousness? If it is a gradual process then the consultant must make sure that the adoption process for his or her proposal is well managed and integrated into the company's communication channels.

In the majority of cases, any change you make will have a knowledge element within it. As such, you need to understand how the various elements of the knowledge infrastructure will impact upon their ability to deliver and, more important, the extent to which they are seen to deliver.

> **Back pocket question**
>
> Has any knowledge created as part of the consultancy change been embodied as a tangible asset for the business?

Diffusion channels

Building on the theoretical model offered in the previous section, you might need to undertake an analysis of the organization's practical capability to diffuse ideas. Ideally, you should map the transport mechanisms and consider how effectively they will expand and share knowledge. Consider the product team that has discovered a great new method for reducing quality costs on the production line. In an ideal world, this innovation would be rapidly transported across the business so that other teams can reap the benefits. Although organizations might suggest that their internal communication processes are open, speedy and flexible, they are often clogged up and slow. It is important to develop a clear picture of the channels as they are, not how the client or consumer thinks they are.

When trying to map how new ideas or knowledge will flow across a business after the consultant has departed, it can help to consider the impact that the various channels will have on the diffusion process. The definition of channel is any system, process or medium used to transport a piece of information from one part of the organization to another. It might be an internal newspaper, monthly team meeting, intranet system or grapevine. All will be tools to help continue the work undertaken by the consultant in the change project. The question you must ask is: what affect will the channel have on the knowledge as it is dispersed

191

around the business? The following list takes the example of the introduction of a new quality programme and how the different channels will modify the knowledge flow:

- **Amplify:** Knowledge channels rarely transmit information without changing its intensity. Often what is a relatively innocuous piece of information will be exploded beyond all expectation. The fact that the quality programme will include an audit process might well be interpreted by a militant staff association as a way in which senior managers will subject their members to oppressive supervision.

- **Attenuate:** Conversely, some channels will take a relatively important piece of information and cause it to lose power and energy. Although the quality initiative might be commissioned as a way to respond to market pressures, this message might well be lost as the communication channels place greater emphasis on the practical aspects of the change programme. The commercial imperative that has driven the programme becomes overtaken by the project management aspects, thus diminishing the power of the original message.

- **Adapt:** Any newspaper or in-house journal will adapt and modify a story to fit the profile of the target audience. The engineering journal will offer details on the project in relation to the quality targets that have been set for the engineers. The marketing division will sell it on the basis of 'it is what our customers want'. Although this adaptive process is useful in diffusing the knowledge, you must be careful that the information does not become overly diluted or distorted.

- **Accelerate:** Some processes will change the speed of diffusion of knowledge. If you are working in a more traditional organization, then diffusion will probably be through paper-based systems and the transmission time will be measured in terms of days rather than minutes. In an organization that has adopted IT within its core infrastructure, the diffusion of knowledge will be measured in minutes and hours. So whereas the time between a quality audit and the final programme assessment being presented would have been measured in weeks, with many new systems the board can monitor the result dynamically, mapping how different business units are faring in the quality assessment process.

- **Abuse:** Lastly, many channels abuse the knowledge as it flows through. One prime example is seen with the political systems that fuel the grapevine. As people become aware of the impending quality system, so they will reinterpret the message to favour their position. The senior manager who is opposed to the rigour that the system will bring might choose to spread rumours about problems with it and in particular how it will drive up costs.

As these examples indicate, to make sure that the engagement continues after their departure, consultants must pay close attention to the channels within the business and attempt to map how they affect the change process. Wherever possible, your goal must be to understand how the change will be affected and to put in place compensating action to ensure the messages are not corrupted.

	Channel 1	Channel 2	Channel 3	Channel 4
Outcome 1				
Outcome 2				
Outcome 3				
Outcome 4				

● Abuse ● Attenuate ● Adapt ● Amplify ● Accelerate

Fig. 11.4 The channel matrix

One tool that might help is the channel matrix (Fig. 11.4), a simple process by which you can set out what core outcomes need to be maintained after you have closed the contract. With this, you can map the primary channels that will be used to share the knowledge. So for each cell on the matrix, you will attempt to indicate how the channel will deal with the change outcome.

For example, assume that outcome one is head office relocation complete and delivered within the financial year. The consultant considers the various channels, and maps the impact that three of them will have on the process as seen in Table 11.1. The conclusion might be that further work would have to be undertaken with the staff association. Unless they are convinced of the wisdom of the relocation, then problems might be stirred up that could affect the date of the final move.

The effective diffusion of ideas and knowledge will have a critical impact on their sustainability. Like the commuter running to catch a train, chasing through corridors that are clogged up with debris and people heightens the risk of missing the train. Your role is to ensure that the communication channels are free of such debris and that knowledge will flow through the organization and underpin and sustain the transformation.

Table 11.1

	Company newspaper	Staff association	Project instructions
Relocation delivered on time and to budget	*Amplify:* as with most good internal magazines, there will be a positive spin applied to the change, with the up-side issues promoted	*Abuse:* this is only likely to happen where the staff associations oppose the relocation project. In this case, they have significant power to distort the message	*Accelerate:* a good set of project instructions will help to speed up the rate of transmission. The use of e-mail, team meetings and project reviews can ensure that news is speedily transmitted around the team

Back pocket question

Have I undertaken a practical analysis of the client's capability to physically diffuse new ideas across the organization?

Chapter 12

....

Stage seven: Close

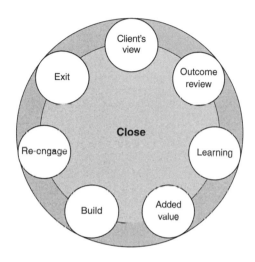

This is not the end.
It is not even the beginning of the end;
but it is perhaps the end of the beginning.
Winston Churchill

So the contract is over, it is time to say goodbye and move on to the next client. But like watching a good play or tasting a fine wine, it is that last memory that will remain and which may cloud the recollection of the total experience. As any psychology student will explain, the 'recency' factor means that the last items presented are more likely to be recalled than those that went earlier. As such it is important for you to carefully manage the exit and not just assume that it will be OK to ask for the money and leave.

Failure to stage-manage the closure process has led and will continue to lead to many disasters:

● Consultants were convinced that since the project action had been completed no formal review was necessary with the client. Although they were paid, no further contracts were offered because the client felt that they had not been prepared to listen to his view of the outcomes.

- Although the board was happy with the new processes that a consultant had helped to deliver, they were starting to question the real value of the change. They believed that they could have made the change themselves and so saved substantial amounts of money. The problem was that the consultant focused on telling the board what had been delivered. If he had communicated how the company had changed as a result, they might have understood that there were elements that they could not have delivered themselves.

- A consultant had finished a great piece of work and the client and consumer were happy and keen to build on the work. However, the consultant was relatively new to the consulting world and felt that she should not be trying to sell on the back of success. She believed that if the client wanted some further work they would indicate that as part of the relationship. The end result was that both parties spilt with an unspoken desire to work together again and hence there was a lost opportunity.

- A consultant closed his project down and left to work on another project. But many parts of the client's organization had built a close working relationship with the consultant and tended to call on him for advice on many of the core issues within the project. His departure meant that people felt slightly let down and were not keen to make use of his services again.

So, in closing an engagement, I suggest that you must avoid the entirely natural urge to say goodbye with a cheery wave on the assumption that everything will be all right because the project outcomes have been achieved. There are many tangible and intangible issues that need to be addressed at this stage and you must work with the client to ensure that time is made available for the closure process.

Within this stage of the cycle, the following issues need to be considered:

- **Client's view:** Encourage the client to reflect on their view of the world before presenting your view of the outcomes.

- **Outcome review:** Work with the client to use all of the available data (objective and subjective) to determine the success of the programme.

- **Learning:** Encourage your client to consider what has been learned over and above the planned outcomes of the change.

- **Added value:** Where applicable, it is important to understand how the outcomes from the change have tangibly delivered improvement to the operational or commercial viability of the organization.

- **Build:** On the assumption that the consultancy assignment has been handled professionally and delivered the appropriate outcomes, then it may be appropriate to investigate what opportunities might exist for further work.

- **Re-engage:** At this stage, you will start the exit process and prepare to either leave the client or begin work on further projects.

- **Exit:** The onus is on you to ensure that at the point of departure all unnecessary levels of dependence have gone from all sides of the relationship.

Like leaving a friend at the station or saying goodbye to someone at a club, it is the last point of meeting that will be remembered. In the same way, how you leave your client and consumer will always affect any future relationship. The danger is that once the excitement is over, you might let your guard drop and mistakes can start to occur. It is at this point that you must take the utmost care to ensure that silly mistakes do not get made and that the change finishes with style and grace rather than on a low note. On this basis it is important that all of the steps outlined in this stage are at least considered if not enacted.

Client's view

When you close a project, really listen and take time to understand your client's perception of what happened over the total life cycle of the change. When people are in the flow of the change process, they are often blind to the problems, changes and surprises that emerge. The nature of memory and the recency factor means that some of the early decisions and panic reactions are forgotten. It is therefore important to encourage the client to reflect on the programme and recall some of the unexpected events. In doing this, you will be helping the client to build a truer picture of the programme and learning prompted by the change, before you present your views.

In trying to get the client to give their perception of what has happened, there will be a number of problems:

- The person who is future focused might not see any value in the exercise.

- Depending on the time taken to deliver the project, they may have forgotten most of what happened.

- It will be difficult to separate what happened within the remit of the project and what factors were actually beyond its scope.

- It becomes a chance for the client to remonstrate about the things that went wrong rather than really reviewing what happened.

If the result is to be positive and add value to your client, it is important that you tightly manage both the process and the content that emerges. This is not to restrict your client's opportunity to say how they feel, but to ensure that the discussion is value-based and not a boxing match.

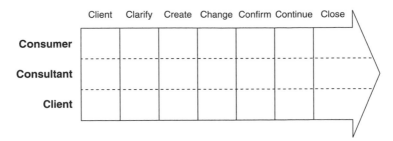

Fig. 12.1   Life cycle review model

It can help to base the conversation around a visual model, one that will help all the parties to suggest how they feel and also to see how other people felt about the engagement. The meeting could be managed around a life cycle model (Fig. 12.1). The goal is for everyone in the review process to talk through the stages of the consultancy project, indicating how they felt about each stage. Although the model only shows three players, the process should be open-ended so that all interested parties are able to give feedback. In asking people to share their mental map of the change cycle, several things can happen:

● What people might have believed to be isolated issues may turn out to be recurring themes throughout the cycle, possibly issues that the organization has to deal with regularly.

● It might indicate where blockages remain. If two or more people feel that one of the stages has issues that are unresolved, then it might suggest that future work is needed before the programme can be closed down.

● It might raise critical differences in the way different groups view the project. If the client perceives that one part went well but the consumers suggest that it had major problems, then there is the suggestion of a cognitive disconnection between the two groups. As such, further work will be required to ensure that a shared mental model is built.

The ultimate goal at this stage is to get the various parties to share their view of the world. However, in sharing their view, you might feel you are being attacked, with the result that your defensive routines kick in. If this happens, then there is a chance of a battle breaking out – something that would be destructive at this stage of the game. What the client believes is true – *is* true (from their perspective). Although you might see it differently, a view is neither right nor wrong. Although it is tempting to argue your position, this might end up souring what had been a positive and

In sharing their view, you might feel you are being attacked, with the result that your defensive routines kick in.

198

effective relationship. The goal is that by the end of the closure phase, you have reached a shared and fair view of what occurred over the life of the change.

Back pocket question

Have I encouraged the client to reflect on their view of the world before presenting my view of the outcomes?

Outcome review

At this stage you need to pull together all the data to determine the success of the project. This review is important for a number of reasons:

- It provides an emotional closure to the prolonged action so that each side can let go;
- It offers factual evidence to ensure that the terms of the original contract have been fulfilled;
- It provides the bedrock upon which all communication messages are shared across the firm;
- It helps to provide some of the high points that are used to celebrate the successful conclusion of the project.

In reviewing the outcomes, the measurement must be against the original contract specifications, including any changes over the life of the programme. The key factors to cover in the outcome review will include:

- **Outcomes:** Have the high-level goals and specific objectives been achieved and is the client happy that the measurement process is valid and reliable in proving the outcomes?
- **Engagement:** Did the engagement take place according to plan? Was it the right change methodology, were resources used effectively and were milestones and breakpoints achieved?
- **Responsibilities:** Did all people conform to their agreed responsibilities and did the sub-contractors fulfil their part of the contract?
- **Boundaries and scope:** Were the agreed boundaries maintained and did any of the change spill into areas that were defined as being separate from the project?

- **Confidentiality:** Have all confidentiality clauses been maintained and are there any additional ones that need to be included as a result of any changes to the project process?

- **Specifics:** Have all the financial considerations been locked in place to ensure prompt payment according to the contract?

Although the review process will draw upon the views of many other players within the engagement, you should aim to close the project by a private session with the client. If other people are included in the outcome review, alternative perceptions, political agendas and shadow issues can start to surface, thus disrupting the closure. The loop should be closed at this point without any external factors to cause a deviation from the contract review.

Finally, you should ensure that no shadow issues are left unresolved. The formal aspects of the project may have been closed but the client may remain unhappy about certain seemingly inconsequential matters. Unless you take the time to raise these issues they will remain hidden. Issues such as the behaviour of the consultants on site, problems with contacting the consultants when away from site or complaints over the competence of the junior members of the consulting team can often fuel antagonisms if they are not dealt with before departure.

> **Back pocket question**
>
> Have you gauged the success of the programme against clear criteria?

Learning

At the conclusion of the outcome review, you still have a responsibility to help the client and the client's organization understand what they have learned from the change experience:

- For the change that culminates in the presentation of a strategy report to the board, it is about closing the presentation with a summary of what the new knowledge will offer to the company.

- In the case of a new IT system, it is a report that details the learning that has emerged from the hand-over process and what action the client can take to better prepare themselves for future upgrades.

- With a culture change programme, it is a review workshop with the internal change facilitators to help them to reflect on what changes have happened in the culture and how they need to modify their style to support the transformation.

Whatever the process, this can often be the added value that the client had not thought about. The result is that if undertaken effectively it can leave your client with a positive view and can potentially lead to the generation of future contracts, either with this client or from ongoing recommendations.

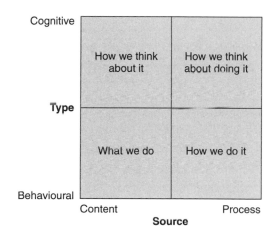

Fig. 12.2 Learning review matrix

One way to give feedback to your client on learning is through the matrix shown in Fig. 12.2. Here, learning is broken into four categories:

- **Behavioural/Content:** this is quite simply the fact that people do things better – customers are handled with more sincerity, data is clearer, transactions are quicker.

- **Behavioural/Process:** in this case the improvement is focused on the way that people manage the process – reduced time to market, improved senior management visibility of the process measures, or just getting to meetings on time.

- **Cognitive/Content:** this might be people thinking through how they will respond to customer complaints before actually taking the telephone call, programmers who have a better understanding of the software, or engineers who understand the technical configurations of the telephone system.

- **Cognitive/Process:** this is related to the way that people plan or think about how they will manage an action. This might be deciding to use a project management system to roll out a new product launch, deciding to involve all the stakeholders before a procedural change, or just trying to agree the agenda with people before starting a meeting.

> **Back pocket question**
>
> Have I helped the client to consider what has been learned over and above the planned outcomes?

Added value

The bottom line for any change must be to add value to the system being changed. This might be through modifications in people's behavioural routines, implementation of a new information system, or completion of a strategy to meet an international standard. If the core value cannot be extracted from the outcome then it becomes difficult for the management team to justify the time and expense to the stakeholders of the business. In the closure stage, you must ensure that the added value is clearly understood by and communicated to the client and the end consumer. The notion of recency is paramount at this stage, in that their lasting memory of you and the consulting engagement will be heavily influenced by the final messages and signals that you send out. Hence, you must ensure that the message of positive added value is included in all interactions with the client (Lascelles and Peacock, 1996).

It is important that you present your role in developing this added value in as simple a form as possible. Developing grand outcome statements or strategic presentations is useful for those people who have been involved in the change, but will mean little to those in other parts of the organization. It is essential that you leave the client with a simple message that can be readily shared across the organization. There are two aspects to the value management process. The first is to clearly communicate in what area of the business value improvement has been managed and, second, to counteract the impact of value shift in the mind of the client and consumer.

Value management

Value management is about the ability to understand clearly and communicate where value is being created. Value in this sense is a tangible function, something that the client will receive benefit from, be it commercially, emotionally or physically. Nagle and Holden (1995) define it as the total savings or satisfaction that the customer receives from the product. Economists refer to this as the use value or utility gained from a product. In consulting terms, it might be defined as the benefit or gain that the client receives following the change engagement. Although your contract will clearly indicate the change that must be made to satisfy the commercial or social relationship, it might not include a specific focus on the value that will accrue on conclusion of the change.

Although there will be commercial consulting engagements that fall outside this limited boundary, the vast majority of programmes will realize value from this area. As an example, the typical consulting actions have been listed in Table 12.1. Although some action will fall outside these four areas, by allocating them

Table 12.1   Value-added categories

Added value	Consultant action
Increase revenue	• Product enhancement • Selling/Marketing strategy • Competitor response • Business acquisition
Reduce costs	• Buying policies • Operating strategy • Process simplification • Use of materials • Reduced overheads • System integration
Effective people	• Organizational effectiveness • Work scheduling • Headcount levels • Pay rates • Training and development
Effective assets	• Use of fixed assets • Gearing levels • Stock levels • Credit control • Material management • Interest levels

to simple headings it allows a consistent message to be communicated to the client and consumers. Although your engagement might be highly complicated and detailed, unless you are able to offer the end consumer (and other stakeholders) a clear and succinct reason for the change, then your action might fade into history along with all the other change programmes.

Value differentiation

In many cases, just offering the customer a review that sets out the value delivered is not sufficient. As considered in the opening section on the nature of the industry, consulting is a trade-based operation where the ability to sell products and services is a core competency. You must ensure that the closure process not only reinforces what you have delivered but how it stands apart from what a competitor might have delivered. The art of the closure is in reinforcing the factors that differentiate your outcome from that of your competitors as well as confirming what might be perceived as the commodity element of your proposition, as seen in Fig. 12.3. Value differentiation might be seen as the difference between the value of the work that you have undertaken and that which might be delivered by a comparable competitor. Value, like beauty, is in the eye of the beholder and is not always an absolute element. Although value might be defined as the savings or satisfaction that the client and consumer receive from the engagement, there are many factors that drive this level of satisfaction.

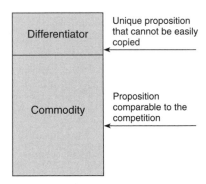

Fig. 12.3 Differentiated delivery

Consider the cost of a litre of petrol. This is a commodity that sells within a narrow price band no matter where you might be. As such you might quite easily define the value of the product and equate it as being equal to the economic cost. Now switch to a different scenario: you have run out of petrol and the garage is a mile down the road. How much would you be prepared to pay for the fuel now? The guess is that most people would be prepared to pay a price premium of 50 per cent to save the effort of walking down the road to get some more fuel. Now consider that you have run out of fuel on the way to an important client meeting. This is the final clincher in what has been a prolonged and difficult sales process and unless you are there to close the sale there is every chance that the client will switch to a competitor. Now consider what value a litre of fuel would hold. In cold economic terms, it can be equate to a percentage of the revenue that you will receive from the client contract, which in many cases might be the price of a new car.

The message in this analogy is that value must be measured from the perspective of the client and consumer, not from your perspective. Value is driven by the availability of comparable alternatives. So even if you have delivered exactly what has been specified in the contract, if the client feels that they could have achieved the result at lower cost via an alternative route, then your sense of value contribution will be minimized. In a simple world, this wouldn't be a problem as the client's view of the perceived value would be constant over the course of the change. However, the reality is that over the life of any change project the client's perception of the value that you are adding could well change. By the end of the project they may be willing to pay the bill but do so with a sense that true value has not been delivered.

Imagine you are walking down the high street and you see a shop that is selling your favourite brand of jeans at a third discount to the normal price. You decide to buy a pair and at the moment of decision you are convinced that this is a fair transaction and one where you will receive value from the purchase. However, as you walk out of the door, you notice that the shop on the other side of the street also has a sale but it is offering the same jeans for half price. Your sense that the jeans were a good purchase will be immediately reduced and in many ways you might blame the shop for ripping you off.

The same can happen in one of your consulting assignments. You begin the engagement on the clear understanding that you are responsible for reengineering one of the company's core processes. All goes well but at the end of the assignment, the client starts to ask questions about the bad press that process reengineering has received. They even start to question if the change was really necessary after all. Although they know in their head that you have delivered the agreed value, their heart tells them that something doesn't feel right and the only person they can blame is you. Here lies the quandary. From your perspective the appropriate and agreed value has been delivered but from the client's perspective the value is suspect.

Clearly, you can't prevent a change in the environment or how the client sees the world, but you can have an array of arguments that will help to ensure the client and consumer are made aware of the unique value that you have offered as part of the transformation. These arguments can be used to help the client to realign their understanding of value and in particular to see the value that your project has realized – even if there has been a significant change in the environment. Examples of the differentiated propositions might include:

- Service performance guarantees so that if the client is not satisfied with the final outcome, any part of the delivery will be re-worked free of charge.

- Faster delivery from the ability to mobilize resources such that any client demands are met without delay.

- Licensed proposition whereby you own the rights to the intellectual capital and no other provider is able to deliver the same product.

- Trusted client relationship where the closeness of the relationship means that no other supplier is able to get close to the client.

These differentiators are crucial because they offer options that the competition might not be able to replicate. Although they are not in themselves unique, any competitor wishing to replicate the proposition will have to mobilize the necessary resource – and this takes time.

So, when an engagement is being closed, it is important to ensure that the core added-value elements are communicated. But it is more important to ensure that the client understands how your particular differentiated proposition is embedded in your delivery. This reinforcement must be communicated on a logical and emotional level. The client must understand the cold logic of your differentiator, such that they are able to rationally compare it with the competition. Second, they must feel how your service is different so that they can sell you and your ideas to others with a sense of passion. Finally, wherever possible, get them to touch the difference. Wherever your solution has a tangible factor, ensure that the client touches, smells or feels how it is different from your competitors' offering. By ensuring that they understand the differentiated value there is a greater chance that the closure is successful and further repeat business can be won.

Wherever your solution has a tangible factor, ensure that the client touches, smells or feels how it is different from your competitors' offering.

> **Back pocket question**
>
> Is there a clear indication of the tangible and differentiated improvement to the operational or commercial viability of the organization?

Build

....

Assuming you have delivered the agreed outcomes, this is the best time to investigate what opportunities might exist for further work. At this stage the relationship with your client will be at a peak. He or she will have direct personal experience of the fact that you are trustworthy. Against the other forms of entry, this is the best time to enhance the relationship and discuss what future work opportunities might exist.

The sales or marketing models that are applied in this situation are numerous and well documented in a range of other books and journals, so they are not covered here. However, I offer one proposition, the idea that in developing a sales transaction the customer must be encouraged to walk through a series of adaptive stages (Fig. 12.4). In taking the client through these steps, you will take them: from generic curiosity through to specific interest; and from cognitive awareness to behavioural action.

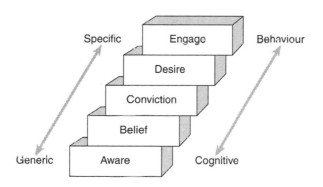

Fig. 12.4   Marketing steps

Consider the case of a senior manager interested in the Internet as a commercial proposition for his company. He is aware of the Internet and understands that it might be used as a sales medium but has not actually taken any action:

- **Aware:** The Internet is a vague thing that holds little interest for the individual. Although the client is aware of the Internet as a growing medium for e-commerce, he has yet to investigate the option. At this lower rung, there is a vague cognitive awareness about the broad issue but no intention to take specific action.

- **Belief:** At this stage the individual starts to develop a personal view about what the product or service can offer. It forms a schematic model that sets out if they are for or against the product and they will use this to define any decision that they are starting to form. At this stage, the client might develop a belief that the Internet will grow and is likely to become a leading channel to market for the company. But this is still a cognitive viewpoint and little behavioural shift has taken place.

- **Conviction:** He has now formed a belief that the product or service will add value and that a purchase will be made at some point in the future. At this stage, the client wants to hook into the Internet and is actively scanning the market to evaluate and assess which option will be best for the company.

- **Desire:** Now he has shifted from general need to conviction that this one product has to be purchased. Now there is a relationship forming with one brand and the client is starting to engage in discussion with the supplier about potential benefits and costs.

- **Engaged:** The individual is now engaged and committed to a purchase. The client has signed a contract with the supplier and has developed a strategy for marketing the company's services on the Internet.

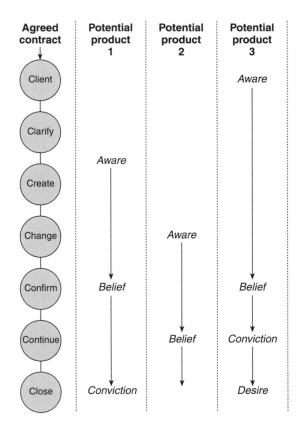

Fig. 12.5 Build portfolio

These five stages effectively take the customer through two different journeys: from broad generic up to a specific desire for one brand; and from a cognitive awareness through to direct behavioural action. The duration of the process might take months, as in the purchase of a house or car, or seconds as in the case of a child's impulse purchase in a sweet shop.

You should be aware of this process and also take the opportunity to subtly introduce the client to new ideas and products over the entire life of the change. So even when operating at the early stages of the consultancy life cycle, you can gently take the client through the awareness and belief stage regarding your other products or services (Fig. 12.5). Your underlying objective should be to reach the Close stage of the life-cycle model with as many potential contracts at the conviction or desire stage as possible. When your client is at this stage then you can position yourself as responding to the client's needs rather than attempting to overtly solicit sales.

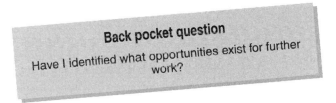

Back pocket question

Have I identified what opportunities exist for further work?

Re-engage

So, the change is nearly over and you have to carefully manage the closing stage. There will be four options:

- **Re-engage and modify:** The review process has identified where certain parts of the change programme have either failed to change or have reverted to type. As such you have been asked to revisit parts of the change cycle to fix or embed the problem areas.

- **Re-frame and extend:** In some cases the world will have moved on and certain aspects of the change may need to be augmented or modified to fit the new environment. For example, the original contract to install a new computer system might have specified a particular type of network connection but by the time the system is delivered a new specification has been released. The danger is in simply tacking on a modification at the end. If the variation has any significance, there will always be some benefit in making a quick mental loop through the earlier stages of the Seven Cs model just to confirm that the enhancement is delivered without any problems.

- **Close and exit:** With this the outcome is delivered, contract closed and the primary goal must be to leave the client with a feel-good factor. So long as your client has positive memories about the relationship and the contract then there is a greater chance that you might be invited in the next time the client has a problem.

- **Close and new engagement:** One of the nicest outcomes is the closure of a successful project followed immediately by a further contract. The gains from this situation are many: the client is known, the stakeholders are understood and barring any radical changes in the business or environment, all of the driving forces within the business are understood.

This stage can be difficult because of the commercial and emotional linkage that has developed over the course of a project. After working with the client through a range of highs and lows, there is every chance that the relationship has moved from a formal client-based association to that of friendship. Although this is a positive situation, it is important that you hold onto the basic principle that the change is a temporary process and as such closure must come at some stage. In this case, it is better to ensure that the closure is a positive experience and not one tinged with sadness.

The danger at this stage is that you might decide to use the warmth of the closure as a chance to sell a new set of services to the client. Although this might be appropriate in a few cases, the broad principle must be that taking this action will sour the relationship. If you have not re-engaged the client by this stage, then it is better to walk out as a friend, and then re-enter the door at a later date with a new offering.

> **Back pocket question**
>
> Do you have a plan to exit the relationship in a controlled way?

Exit

All through the life of the change process, the drivers tend to be based around growing the relationship – improving the association so that you develop a high degree of trust and responsiveness with the client. However, as this relationship grows, so the level of dependence grows between the various players. The trouble is that at the end of the day, both you and the client have to let go and break away from the relationship. The onus is on you to ensure that at the point of departure all unnecessary levels of dependence have gone from the relationship:

To have a situation where there is chronic dependence on consultants is an implicit admission of ineptitude in management.

(O'Shea and Madigan, 1997)

When the relationship begins, you are often seen as 'the expert', someone who has all the right answers and will be able to solve the problems. While this can help to ensure that buy-in takes place, the danger is that a dependent relationship is formed – one where the client is sometimes unwilling to let go of your perceived expertise. This is seen in the patient who will only go to see one particular dentist or the preference that you might have for a particular car mechanic. However, a problem can arise when the dentist or mechanic decides to move. You are left high and dry, without anywhere to turn when the next problem surfaces. There is a difficult balance in any client relationship. You must be close enough to develop a trust-based association, but distant enough to allow independence and freedom.

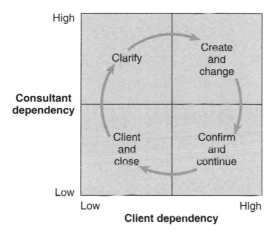

Fig. 12.6   Dependency loop

Although not seen in all consulting projects, a common pattern is shown in Fig. 12.6. The first stage is where you meet the client. There is still a freedom of choice about the relationship, like a couple out on a first date sizing each other up. Once there is an agreement that a relationship will be formed, you will typically have quite a high level of dependency on the client. You will need help to understand the working of the system, access to the right people and confirmation that the initial work seems to be effective. However, once the process goes in the create and change stages, there is a shared dependency – both parties have invested time and reputation in the relationship and cannot afford to see it fail. Once beyond this, you are probably coasting and might well be starting to think about the next project. However, now the client has a strong dependency on you to prove that the outcome is as agreed otherwise it might reflect poorly on him or her. At the final stage, both you and the client should be back at the start of the loop, able to reflect on the relationship in the cold light of day. It is from this rational position that any decision is taken to pursue further options for working together.

Problems can arise where you try to close the relationship while the client is still dependent on you. Change projects often fail because the consultant has gone and the client and the consumer are left high and dry without the real confidence or ability to run with the change. As a result, one of several things can happen:

- The client's organization reverts back to the state that existed before the change.

- The client re-employs the consultant to return and fix some of the problems again.

- The client turns against the consultant and employs a different firm to fix the problems.

Whatever option is followed, the end result is unsatisfactory and one that you should avoid. Dependence is a positive state only when both parties are aware of the condition. If one or both groups is unaware of the reliance, then this can only lead to an unhealthy situation. Your goal is to develop a relationship that is based upon a spirit of mutual interdependence.

> **Back pocket question**
>
> Have I ensured that unnecessary levels of dependence have gone from all sides of the relationship?

Part 4

Seven Cs in action

Chapter 13

The reality

It can be difficult to take a conceptual model and turn it into a practical reality. Questions form in the mind: at what level can I use the model?; what skills do I need to make things happen?; do I tell the client what is happening?; how do I manage that first client meeting? Although there is no right or simple answer for these questions, the following ideas will help to position ways to think about and plan for the client engagement.

3M mapping

When embarking on any assignment, the size of the task can seem daunting. As the range of ideas and tools offered in this book highlights, the large number of possible actions can mean that you are faced with endless choices. One way to deal with the seeming fog is to 'chunk' the engagement into different sizes; to break down the action in two ways, first by stage and then by magnitude. To help this way of thinking, it can help to deconstruct the work into the following chunks:

As the range of ideas and tools offered in this book highlights, the large number of possible actions can mean that you are faced with endless choices.

- **Meta:** a simple but focused definition of the purpose of the stage being addressed. What is the core outcome to be achieved and how does it link with the other stages in the life cycle? For example, your core purpose at the client stage might be to focus solely on the development of an emotional relationship, and to leave the commercial aspects to someone else. Alternatively, your goal might be to use the time as an education process, to bring your client up to strength on the ideas and methodology that will be used.

- **Macro:** At this level, once the purpose is defined you can start to think about what broad actions need to be taken. If your meta-level definition of the clarification stage is to deliver a detailed and robust analysis of the client's IT network, then you will start to define what specific tools need to be employed, what primary tasks have to be created and who will own each element. This is project planning in its simplest form, where some people might develop a comprehensive project plan, but others might only need a basic list of actions.

The approach will depend upon the context of the engagement and skills and knowledge of the consultants.

● **Micro:** Finally, it is important to understand some of the small but important issues that must be covered. These might be simple things like ensuring that the right people are invited to the process reviews, or ensuring that the company name is spelt correctly. The important thing is to understand the client and consumer filters, and be very clear as to what seemingly small things will actually be important to them.

Once the engagement has been broken down into these three areas, then you can consider the total life cycle against a simple stage map in Fig. 13.1. Imagine the consultant who is asked to manage the refurbishment of a company's main office. The board had commissioned the contract on the anticipation that the refurbishment would also increase the company's ability to use more teleworkers. The consultant's role was both to deliver a new office environment within six months and a targeted increase in the number of teleworkers within a year.

In planning the project, the consultant decided from the outset that three of the seven stages would be key to his success: Client, Confirm and Closure. He understood that the client's basic value-added motivation was driven by cost reduction. As such, there had to be clear and demonstrable evidence of the benefits. This was also linked to a clear contract that set out the end-deliverables. At a meta level he would need to ensure that a clear sense of purpose existed between himself and the client in these three stages shown in Fig. 13.1.

	Client	Clarify	Create	Change	Confirm	Continue	Close
Meta	Understand real cost targets				Provide measures to convince city of savings		Desire to manage next stage of the project
Macro	Run client workshop	Run risk analysis Run culture test	Design workshop Run bench-marking workshop	Manage build	Design measures Agree feed-back process	Run after action review	
Micro	Map real decision makers Understand client filters	Agree stakeholders	Find culture champion Identify other market leaders		Assign responsibility	Look for key words in language	Focus on client and key decision makers Take client through value model

Fig. 13.1   Stage map

For the macro actions, the consultant's supposition was that from the outset he needed to get very close to the client. This type of project is one laden with misunderstanding, supposition and ambiguity and as such he wanted to ensure a close and highly interdependent relationship. The initial macro issue was to run a client workshop, where he could pull together the client and consumer representatives to understand their formal and informal issues.

At the micro level, there were a number of core actions that could be identified from the outset. In the Client stage the consultant decided to pay careful attention to the different decision makers within the client unit. At the Create stage, he initiated a number of searches across other industries to identify where similar projects had been successful. Finally, he knew that cost justification of many of the proposals might be difficult, so he wanted to ensure that all project proposals and decisions were built around the value-add model outlined in the Close stage. Fig. 13.1 shows how this idea has been expanded, with different action for different levels of focus in the cycle of change.

This example shows how the framework can be mapped out from the very start of the change. Clearly, it is not practical to specify in advance how all of the Seven Cs tools can be used. The trick is to pick the appropriate models and clearly plan when they will be used and what benefit will be gained from their application. In taking this approach, it will help you to take a more long-term view of the change and give the client confidence that you have the right amount of control over the total life of the project.

> *The trick is to pick the appropriate models and clearly plan when they will be used and what benefit will be gained from their application.*

In mapping out the various actions, the consultant can achieve a number of positive outcomes:

- It allows the opportunity to talk through the total picture with the client. In doing this, it helps to start the journey towards the development of a shared schematic picture of what will happen.

- It helps to take the focus off the task and content and to get the client to understand the transformation process. Too often, commercial and political pressures conspire to force the client, consultant and consumer to go for the quick operational fix and to forgo the long-term view. If the key players can appreciate the process view then it might help to take some of the urgency away from the short-term issues.

- The development of a close working relationship with the client is underpinned by the development of a shared language. The 3M model helps you to develop a language that bridges your process needs with the client's operational goals.

217

Although the 3M framework is clearly just a simple reworking of the project planning process, it does deliver an increased focus on the relationship between the core stages in the assignment and the more important action.

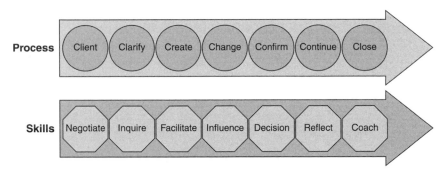

Fig. 13.2   Seven Cs skill set

Skills

In the same way that it is impossible to define the right way to manage a change, it would be foolish to prescribe the right set of skills that a consultant needs. However, it is possible to take each of the seven stages in the framework and suggest what key competencies might be needed to ensure that the process is managed effectively. The seven core competencies in Fig. 13.2 can be expanded:

- **Negotiation** (*Client*): Create a situation where all interested parties are able to reach a mutually satisfying and collaborative agreement.

- **Inquiry** (*Clarify*): Use analytical skills to delve beneath the symptoms and dig out the real problem.

- **Facilitation** (*Create*): Support the client in taking a more imaginative approach.

- **Influencing** (*Change*): Be able to effect change without a formal power base.

- **Decision making** (*Confirm*): Take a reasoned and managed decision without being unduly influenced by any personal or group bias.

- **Reflection** (*Continue*): Help minimize the client's entrenched thought patterns by helping them be more proactive in the management of their own problems.

- **Coaching** (*Close*): Help the client get a clear focus on how they will use the change; what role they want to play in the new world and what their next steps might be.

The objective is not to suggest that these are the only skills to be used within each stage, rather to highlight the most dominant capability that might be called upon to manage that stage effectively. Once understood, you need to ensure that you either have the necessary skill set or have access to the skills via colleagues or other consultants.

One way to understand the skills in a deeper way is by considering them from three perspectives: cognitive, affective and behavioural (Thompson, 1996). A nice metaphor for these three aspects is the head, heart and hands, as described in Chapter 7. The heart is indicative of the passion and feelings that people will have for a subject; the head represents how they might feel logically about the topic; and the hands represent the practical aspect of a situation. It is crucial to consider these three aspects if the Seven Cs are to be applied effectively. This is because:

- Improving how a client 'thinks' will not deliver performance improvement unless they change what they 'do' and 'feel';

- Changing what they 'do' will not be sustainable unless they modify how they 'think' and 'feel';

- Changing how they 'feel' will cause confusion unless they change what they 'do' and 'think'.

While it is easy to improve how you manage the consultancy process, the hard thing is to hold the gain. Unless you are able to apply the Seven Cs on the levels of heart, head and hands, then at some point in the future, revision or frustration is likely to happen. For this reason, each of the seven skill areas has been considered from the three perspectives. Not necessarily to offer the answer, but to encourage you to reflect on your potential in each of the three areas.

> *While it is easy to improve how you manage the consultancy process, the hard thing is to hold the gain.*

Negotiate (client)

- **Head:** In most change situations there is generally a clear line of sight, from thought, to words, then to action. Unless you are able to walk into a situation with a clear intent to negotiate with courage and consideration, then the chances of achieving a fair and collaborative outcome will be minimal. If you think of the Client stage as a battle to generate this month's income, then there is every chance that you will end up in a confrontation. However, if you view it as an opportunity to manage a collaborative exercise, then there is a greater chance that the outcome will be a generative process where the output is greater than the sum of the parts.

- **Heart:** Clearly your emotions will influence the outcome of any client negotiation. Things you have heard about them, previous confrontations, or the business they are in can all act upon the way you feel about them. Although it is impossible to totally subordinate them (and so turn yourself into a robot) you can make yourself more aware of your emotions and choose not to respond to any intrusive thoughts. For example, in many cases you will be in a situation where you do not like the client because of their values or habits. However, you must still be able to negotiate with them in a fair and objective manner. To do this, you must take control of and own the signal that is sent out by the heart. Failure to do this will limit your development as a professional and may well reduce your level of work. At the end of the day, the negotiation must be focused on the problem, not the person.

- **Hands:** The important thing is to behave in a manner that is contextually appropriate. The consultant who adopts an insensitive style when trying to gain a counselling contract with a marriage guidance bureau might have a few problems. Alternatively, the trainer who adopts an overly sensitive and open style when bidding for a contract in the building industry might be seen as too flaky. At the end of the day your behaviour must send a message that you respect both the client and yourself. Failure to do either of these will jeopardize your ability to negotiate a collaborative contract. Even worse, it will act as a dark cloud over the rest of the project. Clearly, negotiation doesn't just happen at the outset of a relationship. It is a process that takes place over the life of your relationship with the client. As such you must develop the capability and sensitivity to recognize when you are in a negotiating situation and be able to take the appropriate actions.

Inquire (clarify)

- **Head:** At the heart of any diagnostic or inquiry process is the ability to separate the process from the content. As the rush of data starts to flow, there can be a tendency to be reactively driven by the content and start to lose sight of the overall methodology. This is not to suggest that you should formally separate context from content, just that you should retain the capability to rise above the situation and understand what is happening at any moment in the clarification stage. So many teams become distracted once their pet subject starts to emanate from the emergent data pile. Unless you are able to both recognize your pet bias and subordinate it during this phase, then an element of corruption might creep into the process, and at worst the diagnostics might be inaccurate and so steer the engagement in the wrong direction.

- **Heart:** There are two key aspects in this stage, the extent to which you are in control of your own emotions and the extent to which you are sensitive to others. There is a real danger that the inquiry process can be severely damaged. Just one insensitive remark or a throwaway comment as you walk in the door can create emotional blockages that can never be overcome. You must be able to tune your emotional sixth sense into the surrounding areas and be sure that any action you take is in alignment with the situation. Second, it can be very difficult to prevent your emotions and flaws corrupting the data gathering and analysis. The best solution is to understand and map your own cultural bias before embarking on any type of clarification project and understand how your emotions might distort the diagnostic process.

- **Hands:** The clarification stage is difficult and potentially damaging. It is where fears become exposed, demons unearthed and false idols displayed. Like David entering the lion's den, you must use all of your stealth and, more importantly, exhibit a behaviour that is non-threatening but assertive. However, take the assertion into aggression and you will push everyone back into the shadow world where the undiscussed becomes even more hidden. Alternatively, by behaving in a soft and flimsy way, you will not truly unearth any of the real problems that face the client or consumer. For an ideal role model consider Colombo, the television detective. This form of inquiry is one that is tenacious and focused but with the sufficient sensitivity to get behind what people are saying.

Facilitate (create)

- **Head:** At this stage, your role is to foster and release the creative spirit that lies within all people and organizations. To this end you must be able to think divergently and help others to open their minds to new ideas and ways of thinking. Most importantly, as a facilitator, you must be able to operate on many levels at any one time. Although you must be aware of the task in hand, you must also be tuned into the process being followed by the group and be aware of any emotional blockages.

- **Heart:** To be able to help others create, you must really understand how others feel. Creativity is about taking risks of a financial, organizational and personal kind. Just think about the ridicule that people often face when they offer radical ideas or solutions. As such you must personally understand and empathize with the pain that other people might be going through when they are trying to build a solution. The key is to understand the extent to which you are personally comfortable with risk. If you are not afraid of taking risks in life, then there is a danger that your free spirit might push people too far in a creative situation. However, if you are risk-averse by nature, then your natural hesitancy might result in the client and consumer failing to originate anything really new.

- **Hands:** Your role here is to support those people who are naturally creative and encourage and protect the more hesitant. Your most valuable weapon in this process is language. You must ensure that anything you say cannot be misconstrued and is not seen as a limiting factor. Avoid making judgements; use 'I' rather than 'we'; use 'could' rather than 'must'; and don't impose your beliefs on the group. Ultimately you must ensure that you say what you mean, and mean what you say.

Influence (change)

- **Head:** Once the change has to be delivered, you will often have to make things happen without any formal power base. Your only tool might be your personal capability to influence other people and change how they think, feel or behave. Long-term sustainable change can only be delivered if people want to change. Before you can influence people to change how they think and behave, you must understand what matters to them. In understanding the other person's needs there is a greater chance that you will be able to effect a fair exchange to secure your goals. So you must see the world as they see it. If you can think as they do, then you will be able to help rather than coerce people to change.

Once the change has to be delivered, you will often have to make things happen without any formal power base.

- **Heart:** The trap that many people fall into when trying to influence others is to feign an emotional state. You will often come across managers who have been on a sensitivity course and who believe that they can make things happen by 'play listening' and saying 'thank-you' to everyone they meet. The successful influencer is one who has authentic feelings and uses them to help make a point with other people.

- **Hands:** The influencing process is centred on bartering. The parent influences the child to do his or her homework by offering to let them off the washing up; the manager convinces her team to do more work late by taking them out for a drink; and the presenter convinces the audience to stay and listen by the promise of a new piece of wisdom. To be effective, you must use appropriate behaviour for each situation. Effective influence is based on three simple steps: understand your schematic view of the world; understand their schematic view of the world; and find a way to bridge the gap through an exchange process. Only by finding this behavioural link with other people will you be able to influence and effect change.

Decision making (confirm)

- **Head:** At the Confirm stage, you will be required to make critical decisions. Has the change been effective, does it need any future work, can the client be billed? Although most individuals will try to take a rational decision, the reality is that most decisions are bounded by a self-imposed framework. This limiting process can be driven by a number of factors. Time and money problems can make it difficult to ensure that all of the necessary information has been gathered; surface and shadow bias will influence people's ability to see any situation from a clear vantage point; people often make decisions based upon heuristic, or rule of thumb, models; finally, decision making by groups can lead to a form of self-delusion where the team loses a sense of reality. You should make sure that you are sensitive to these types of problem. Raise your cognitive awareness of the thinking process and catch the problems before they influence your decision.

- **Heart:** Emotions can affect the decision-making process in two key areas. First, the feeling you have about a topic will influence your decision. No matter how much you try to eliminate personal bias and filtration, some degree of prejudice is likely to creep through. To minimize this you should always try to take key decisions in partnership with another person just as someone to bounce your thoughts off before setting them to paper. The second area where emotions will influence the process is in a group situation. If a team decision is called for, there is every chance that the final outcome will be strongly influenced by the positive or negative feelings that the team members have for each other. If this does occur, then the use of a professional facilitator can help to tease out some of the emotional blockages which affect decision making.

  > *No matter how much you try to eliminate personal bias and filtration, some degree of prejudice is likely to creep through.*

- **Hands:** At this stage, it is important to ensure that decision making is shared as widely as possible. If you are still making decisions in isolation, then the level of dependency is probably too high. If problems are to be raised and corrective action taken, the client and consumer must be involved.

Reflect (continue)

- **Head:** In the Continue stage, your role is often to help the client and consumer reflect on the success of the project and commit to a long-lasting change. However, clients often have an embedded belief that they cannot change and will not be able to survive once you have left. These self-limiting beliefs can be destructive because they act as a rubber band, dragging the client and consumer back to the previous state every time they try to change. Your role is to tackle this cognitive lock-in by challenging and pushing them to new ways of thinking. The goal is to help others to become more proactive in the management of their own problems and empower them to act on their own behalf.

- **Heart:** Clearly, in trying to challenge people you will be in an exposed position. People, teams and organizations will often react in one of two ways when faced with a challenging situation. They might fight back and resist the challenge by offering a counter-assertion. Rather than having to face and deal with your propositions, they decide to prove that you are wrong by force of will, intellect or emotion. The alternative approach is to go into flight, to run away and hide from the issue. So if your proposition is that the project can only be successful if they make certain changes, they will studiously assert that yes they will make the change. But at a deep level they are only fooling themselves. You need to understand and work with both reactions. If you can act as a sponge when their emotions kick in, then you will be able to lead them through the difficult stage and then start to deal with some of the critical issues that will help to ensure continuance of the change.

- **Hands:** Throughout the whole Continue stage, your behaviour must be a subtle blend of confident assertion and sensitive withdrawal. It can be difficult to hand over responsibility for the change to the client and you must ensure that all your behaviours provide the strength and comfort your client needs to take ownership of the transformation.

Coach (close)

- **Head:** At the Close stage, your role is to coach the client through to completion. In moving the client from dependency, you need to carefully manage how they assume responsibility and how your relationship is resolved. In coaching the client through this stage, the primary objectives are to help them get a clear focus on how they will use the change; what role they want to play in the new world; and what their next steps might be. You must help the client to reflect on and learn from the experience rather than simply telling him what has happened. To do this, you might ask the client to think about five questions. What happened at the start of the change; what is the outcome; what happened *en route*; what did they learn from the experience; where do they want to go next?

- **Heart:** Taking the client through this process will call on all your skills. You must empathize with their problems; keep a sense of emotional detachment; provide the necessary care when asked; but still remain emphatically detached if the client tries to entice you back into owning the problem.

- **Hands:** A great deal of the change process will occur at a behavioural level, as the client will look for clues from what you do and say. If your language and behaviour is such that you show a sense of dependence on the client, there is every chance they will reciprocate that style.

By considering each of these seven skill areas, you can start to develop a picture of the competencies that might be used. To do this, consider each of the seven qualities and try to assess your capability, assigning a score out of three in Table 13.1. Although this will be difficult, you should try to force yourself to make an honest appraisal of your competencies. It can help to talk through a colleague's perception of your skill-set, just to give a soft triangulation to the exercise.

Table 13.1 Skills matrix

	Head	Heart	Hands	Score
Negotiate				
Inquire				
Facilitate				
Influence				
Decision				
Reflect				
Coach				
Score				

The first thing to emerge will be the extent to which you need to grow or acquire skills in certain areas. In an ideal situation you might find that you have a high score for all qualities across the seven competencies. But the reality is that to achieve a high score in all the boxes would be very difficult. The score might also indicate if you have a bias for one of the quality factors. It might be that you have the ability to think through an approach but have difficulty in delivering the behaviour. Alternatively, you might have the tacit ability to deliver the appropriate behaviour but can't actually describe the process you follow.

Client understanding

If the client is going to be introduced to the Seven Cs, you need to define how best to present the framework. Remember the filters section from the Client stage of the model? Rather than thinking 'how do I introduce this model to the client?' the question is: 'what will the client see if I show him the framework?' Some people might see it as a lot of jargon dreamed up to increase your fees, or as a valuable tool he might choose to adopt internally. Unless you can understand how the client understands the framework, then overt exposure can be a risk.

Assuming you decide to show the Seven Cs to your client, the next stage is to decide a learning path to take them down. This is where the potential capacity of the framework surfaces. In taking the client through a learning journey, you will effectively be managing a soft change in their cognitive map of the world. As such it will pay to use the Seven Cs as a guiding framework for this process.

Assume that the objective is to encourage the client to accept the Seven Cs as a valid change framework. If this is the desired outcome, then the next stage will be to use the 3M tool to map the change process that you need to manage. So for each of the seven stages, you need to determine what action needs to be taken as part of the change. In particular, you might choose to define a series of diagnostic questions that will help to work through the Seven Cs process. The list below develops a series of potential questions against each stage in the model:

- **Client:** What is the client's current view about the use of change models to aid the transformation project? How can it best be framed in a way that will be acceptable?
- **Clarify:** What are the reasons why he might not use the Seven Cs? Who will influence his views and what are the risks associated with introducing the model?
- **Create:** What are the range of style and methods that can be used to present the idea to the client and what is the best way?
- **Change:** How should the idea be introduced? Is it best to present it at an emotional or practical level? What will he gain by using the framework and how will you react if he doesn't respond well to the idea?
- **Confirm:** How can you understand if he likes the model and when is the best time to check? Do you check if he likes it at a practical or cognitive level?
- **Continue:** How can you ensure that the client will continue to use the model through the life of the change? Is it possible to include language from the model in the various operational processes associated with the change?
- **Close:** When is the best time to ask for feedback on the Seven Cs? How can you find out if the client is interested in using it for other projects?

This example indicates how the Seven Cs can be used for even the simplest type of change. The objective is to help influence how the client pictures the change and in particular to encourage them to use the Seven Cs framework. By mentally working through the framework, it is possible to map out both the questions to raise with the client and how any questions might be managed.

Client meetings

Finally, the point where all of these issues come together is often at the first meeting. It is here that management of the informal, intuitive and emotional factors comes into play. The first point of contact forms the emotional launch pad from which all impressions are formed and judgements made that underpin the psychological contract. Critically, it is here that the psychological theories of primacy and recency come into play. At the end of the first meeting, the two experiences remembered by you and the client are the open and closing events. Any discussion in between is unlikely to be well retained in the client's memory. It is these opening and closing behaviours that help to drive the client's overall impression of you and your capability to deliver.

The onus is on you to ensure that at a minimum, these two phases are tightly stage-managed and that the client is left with positive memories. It might help if you adopt the 'intro–outro' meeting structure as a subtle framework to aid the flow of the first and successive interactions. The intro structure is:

- **Introductions:** Introduce self, include background, previous experience in this industry or market and ask client to position themselves.
- **Need:** Confirm why the meeting has been called and what the drivers are.
- **Time:** Outline how long the meeting should take.
- **Range:** What will be covered and, more importantly, what will be outside the boundary of the discussion.
- **Objective:** What the end objective is for the meeting.

The closing 'outro' structure covers:

- **Overview:** Offer your perception of what has been discussed and agreed. Stress any actions, responsibilities and dates that have been locked in during the session.
- **Understanding:** Check with the client to draw out their understanding of actions agreed.
- **Test:** Confirm that your perceptions align with the initial objective agreed for the meeting.

- **Review:** Discuss what the next steps will be for you, the client and any other people.

- **Outlook:** Close with the outlook for the future, end on a positive affirmation. Particularly, make sure that the client is left with a clear understanding of the positive outcomes that have been achieved and what the next steps are.

The difference between a good and bad opening to a meeting can be likened to the experience of seeing a film. A good film will contain a series of sub-sections that leads the viewer seamlessly and effortlessly through the experience. Although the director and screenwriter will be able to identify each of the components within the story, the viewer will just see the film as a total experience. The success of many films is that people are keen to repeat the experience and so return to see the next instalment. This is precisely the feeling that the client must experience. You must create in your client a desire to meet again so that the ideas and propositions are developed further. However, the converse is a bad film, one where the opening is weak and the ending does not align with the opening gambit or is also weak. Consequently, the viewer is unlikely to have any desire to repeat the experience.

Although in many ways the specific detail of the intro–outro structure might appear too formal for some meetings, the underlying principles are applicable for all types of interaction – the casual conversation on a train, the passing comments as cards are exchanged at a conference or the phone call from someone who reads one of your articles. Although the content and context of the interaction might vary, the core principle is that you must be able and willing to own and stage-manage the interaction process. So even if the exchange is a short one, the impression that you leave will have far more impact on your ability to close the sale than any perceived expertise in a particular field.

Appendix

··

Model deconstruction

The following list sets out all of the key components of the Seven Cs model in the form of a checklist. Although you might not use all of them, it will help you to ensure that some of the more obscure issues are not missed once you climb into the more frantic elements of a project.

Intervention element	Change description	
1) Orientation	Are able to view the problem as the client sees it, not how you see it?	☐
2) Change ladder	Have you removed all the fog from the initial problem by focusing on the area where the change might need to take place?	☐
3) Situation viability	Can the issue be successfully resolved and is the timing right for a change?	☐
4) Desired outcome	Have you tested the clarity of the desired outcome?	☐
5) Decision makers	Do you have a clear picture of the decision makers that can influence the initial stages of the contract development?	☐
6) Ethos	Will the change be coercive or participative in nature?	☐
7) Contract	Is there a contract that sets out a framework for action and offers the measures by which the success or failure of the change process can be measured?	☐
8) Diagnosis	Have you gathered information that will determine the real source of the issue and not just to tackle the symptoms that surround it?	☐
9) Shadow	Is there a clear appreciation of the extent to which unspoken activities and arrangements affect the situation?	☐

Intervention element	Change description	
10) Culture	Do you understand the deep cultural factors that might affect the project?	☐
11) System construction	Is there a clear understanding of the structural make-up of the system and how it is likely to react to any changes that are made to its construction?	☐
12) Stakeholders	Do you have a clear map that indicates who can influence the outcome of the change and to what extent they have the capability and desire to wield their power?	☐
13) Life cycle risk	Have you determined the extent to which known and unknown factors within the change process will affect its potential for success?	☐
14) Feedback	Have you clarified how the client and organization wish to be informed of progress, both in terms of the content and process?	☐
15) Managed creativity	Have you drawn upon the CREATE model to originate and develop potential solutions for the source issue identified in the Clarify stage?	☐
16) Creative blockage	Have all the potential creative blocks been cleared away?	☐
17) Scanning	Have you looked outside your normal domain for solutions?	☐
18) Storyboard	Have you a clear process for deciding on and validating the solution?	☐
19) Resources	Have you mapped the resources to the potential solutions to ensure that the option is viable?	☐
20) Stream owners	Are there clear owners for the solution and do they have the capability and desire to own it?	☐
21) Positics	Have you considered if it is possible to redirect some of the selfish energy and turn negative aspects into positive ones?	☐
22) Methodology	Is there a clear idea as to what methodology will be used to drive the change process?	☐
23) Energy	Is there a clear appreciation of where the change energy will come from and how it will be dissipated across the different stakeholders?	☐

Intervention element	Change description	
24) Engage	Do you know how people will be encouraged to be involved in any transformation process?	❑
25) Entry	Are you clear as to the best level of entry to effect a long-lasting change?	❑
26) System dynamics	How will the system react to any proposed change?	❑
27) Uncertainty	Does the plan have the flexibility to operate in a dynamic and complex world?	❑
28) Resistance	Do you know how people will react to the proposed action?	❑
29) Responsible	Who will own and manage the measurement process?	❑
30) Timing	Have you decided when confirmation and measurement will take place?	❑
31) Design	Are you clear as to the relationship between qualitative and quantitative measures?	❑
32) Depth	Will the measurement be focused on extrinsic issues or will it deal with intrinsic issue such as attitude, motivation and beliefs?	❑
33) Data map	Have the various measurement activities been controlled and managed to ensure that an integrated approach is taken to the Clarify stage?	❑
34) Consulting performance	Do you know if your performance has been up to the standard expected by the client?	❑
35) Costs	Have you a clear view of what impact cost will have on the different measurement processes?	❑
36) Sustainability	Do you have a plan in place to ensure that slippage does not occur once the project has been closed?	❑
37) Language	Have you been able to modify client and consumer language as part of the transformation process?	❑
38) Gravity	Have you ensured that bureaucratic systems will not strangle the transformation?	❑
39) Flow	Do you know what learning has taken place from the experience?	❑
40) Knowledge transfer	Have you ensured that elements of the consultant's competencies will remain in the business?	❑

Intervention element	Change description	
41) Knowledge management	How will any knowledge created as part of the consultancy process be embodied as a tangible asset for the business?	❏
42) Diffusion channels	Is your client capable of diffusing new ideas across the organization?	❏
43) Client's view	Have you encouraged the client to reflect on their view of the world before presenting your view of the outcomes?	❏
44) Outcome review	Have you gauged the success of the programme?	❏
45) Learning	Have you helped the client to consider what has been learned over and above the planned outcomes?	❏
46) Added value	Is there a clear indication of the tangible improvement to the operational or commercial viability of the organization?	❏
47) Build	Have you identified what opportunities exist for further work?	❏
48) Re-engage	Do you have a plan to exit the relationship in a controlled way?	❏
49) Exit	Have you ensured that all unnecessary levels of dependence have gone from all sides of the relationship?	❏

Bibliography

Anon. (1984) 'Mad dogs and expatriates', *The Economist*, 3 March, 67.

Anon. (1996) Obituary of Arthur Rudolph, *New York Times*, 3 January.

Argyris, C. (1992) *On Organizational Learning*. Oxford: Blackwell Business.

Ashford, M. (1998) *Con Trick*. London: Simon and Schuster.

Birch, P. and Clegg, B. (1996) *Imagination Engineering*. London: Pitman Publishing.

de Bono, E. (1992) *Serious Creativity*. London: Harper Collins Business.

Buchanan, D. and Body, D. (1992) *The Expertise of the Change Agent*. London: Prentice Hall.

Carnal, C. (1995) *Managing Change in Organisations*. London: Prentice Hall.

Carter, S. (1999) *Renaissance Management*. London: Kogan Page.

Chambers (1991) *Great Scientific Discoveries*. London: Chambers.

Cooper, K. and Sawaf, A. (1997) *Executive EQ*. USA: Orion Business Books.

Cracknell, D. (1999) *Sunday Business*, 7 February, 1.

Czerniawska, F. (1999) *Management Consultancy in the Twenty-First Century*. London: Macmillan Business.

Egan, G. (1994) *Working the Shadow Side*. San Francisco: Jossey Bass.

Gordon, J. E. (1978) *Structures or Why Things Don't Fall Down*. Harmondsworth: Penguin.

Hersey, P. and Blanchard, K. (1972) *Management of Organizational Behaviour*. Englewood Cliffs: Prentice Hall.

Kanter, R., Stein, B. and Jick, T. (1992) *The Challenge of Organizational Change*. New York: Free Press.

Kotter, J. (1999) in Senge, P. *et al.*, *The Dance of Change*. London: Nicholas Brealey Publishing.

Kotter, J. and Schlesinger, L. (1991) 'Management of Change', *Harvard Business Review*.

Kubr, M. (1976) *Management Consulting*. Geneva: International Labour Office.

Lascelles, D. and Peacock, R. (1996) *Self Assessment for Business Excellence*, McGraw Hill.

Levitt, B. and March, G. (1996) 'Organizational Learning', in Cohen, M. and Sproull, L. (eds) *Organizational Learning*, USA: Sage.

Lissack, M. and Roos, J. (1999) *The Next Common Sense*, London: Nicholas Brealey.

Michalko, M. (1998) *Cracking Creativity*. Berkeley, California: Ten Speed Press.

Michalko, M. (1991) *Thinkertoys*. Berkley, California: Ten Speed Press.

Nagle, T. and Holden, R. (1995) *The Strategy and Tactics of Pricing*. New Jersey: Prentice Hall.

O'Shea, A. and Madigan, C. (1997) *Dangerous Company*, London: Nicholas Brealey.

Randall, J. (1999) 'Survival Can Be a Loss', *Sunday Business*, 31 January.

Rees-Mogg, W. and Davidson, J. (1997) *The Sovereign Individual*. London: Macmillan.

Schein, E. (1994) 'Organizational and managerial culture as a facilitator or inhibitor of organizational learning', MIT Internet paper. Http://learning.mit.edu/res/wp/10004.html

Senge, P. *et al.*, (1999) *The Dance of Change*. London: Nicholas Brealey Publishing.

Senge, P. (1990) *The Fifth Discipline*. London: Century Business.

Stessin, L. (1979) 'Culture Shock and the American businessman overseas', in Smith, E. and Luce, L. (eds) *Towards Internationalism: Reading in Cross Cultural Communication*, Rowely, Massachusetts: Newbury House.

Thompson, N. (1996) *People Skills*. London: Macmillan.

Tichy, N. and Sherman, S. (1993) *Control Your Destiny or Someone Else Will*. USA: Harper Perennial.

Wolfe, T. (1987) *The Bonfire of the Vanities*, London: Picador.

Wren, D. and Greenwood, R. (1998) *Management Innovators*. New York: Oxford University Press.

Index